The
Design
Manual

The Design Manual

160101

DAVID WHITBREAD

UNSW PRESS

For Brigid, Kathleen and Maggie

Some of the material in this book has been previously published by Niche Media Pty Ltd in *Australian MacWorld*, *Australian MacUser* and *MacNews*. David Whitbread would like to thank the editors at Niche for their support over the years: Steven Noble, Richard Foxworthy, Jeremy Templer and Mike Hanlon.

A UNSW Press book

Published by
University of New South Wales Press Ltd
University of New South Wales
UNSW Sydney NSW 2052
AUSTRALIA
www.unswpress.com.au

© David Whitbread 2001
First published 2001

**National Library of Australia
Cataloguing-in-Publication entry:**

Whitbread, David, 1960– .

The design manual.

Includes index.
ISBN 0 86840 658 9.

1. Design — Handbooks, manuals, etc. 2. Desktop publishing — Handbooks, manuals, etc. 3. Computer drawing — Handbooks, manuals, etc. 4. Layout (Printing) — Handbooks, manuals, etc. 5. Web sites — Design — Handbooks, manuals, etc. I. Title.

745.4

Design
David Whitbread

Diagrams
Louise Dews

Index
Michael Harrington

Prepress
Martin Davies,
National Capital Printing

Photographs
Andrew Sikorski,
Art Atelier

See p. 298 for more image credits

Fonts supplied by
FontShop Australia
South Melbourne
www.fontshop.com.au

Paper supplied by
Tomasetti Paper House

Printer BPA

Foreword

There are some 15 000 registered graphic designers in Australia. Professionally trained via tertiary education and industry experience, many produce quality, visually-engaging business solutions which communicate to the hearts and minds of their designated audiences. Their objective: to increase brand equity and market share for their clients. These attractive and powerful visual images also serve to raise consciousness of design within the Australian cultural landscape and beyond.

In order to achieve those business and aesthetic objectives one must go back to the basic principles of graphic design. And this is exactly what *The Design Manual* provides. It is informative and insightful, and to quote what Tom Peters said about another publication, 'a practical reminder of the importance of the subject matter'—the importance of how to make design decisions, and how to get the design job done.

The Design Manual is comprehensive, written in a readable style and supported by extensive tips and step-by-step checklists on how to think, analyse, organise and do. There are plenty of examples to support theories and observations, and to stimulate ideas and strategies.

Who should use this manual? Practitioners and aspiring designers; educators and students; clients and allied professionals. In fact, anyone who is interested in design and would like to learn more.

At a time when rapid change is considered to be the only 'bankable currency', *The Design Manual* is a comprehensive road map that is an essential design companion and I am sure will be a treasured reference with a healthy shelf life. No landfills for this one!

Rita Siow

General Manager,
Australian Graphic Design Association.

Designer Manager, Design Centre
Douglas Mawson Institute of TAFE.

Contents

Preface

The Design Manual was originally commissioned by the Australian Government Publishing Service as a companion volume to their *Style Manual for Authors, Editors and Printers*. As such, it was to do for designers what successive editions of the *Style Manual* have done for editors and writers—and public servants—for over 30 years: to provide guidance and recommendations as a practical reference for preparing publications.

So, as I had written a 'Design' column for a number of years—originally in Niche Media's *MacNews*, which then became *Australian MacUser* and ultimately *Australian MacWorld*—it was agreed that the past columns would become the basis for this publication.

The Design Manual would expand the themes and cover as many areas of a professional graphic designer's tasks as it could. It would focus on the whats, whens and whys of graphic design; rather than the hows, wheres and whos.

So, this book looks at the underlying brief and the assumptions made when someone commissions a design project. Many other publications exist to show you how to use software, for example, or where and who to look to for inspiration—but not many attempt to explain the many techniques available to you for creating a design with impact and a professional edge; when you might use those techniques most effectively; and why they are useful.

In addition, *The Design Manual* looks at graphic design in all media and, as far as possible, discusses the elements, tools and techniques of graphic design as generic. The choice of which medium is most appropriate for which project is also briefly discussed.

As the writing task was nearing its completion, AGPS—which had become AusInfo—reverted the publication rights to the author.

Robin Derricourt of UNSW Press then approached me, expressing interest in publishing the title. We exchanged contracts and the book moved closer to publication, with me as its designer, as well as its author. While this pleased me, it has created its own challenges—not the least being dealing with a finicky author!

It has been a delight to publish *The Design Manual* with the excellent—and patient—staff of UNSW Press, who have been supportive and committed to the success of the project since their first involvement.

As a teacher of graphic design, I have always needed a resource for my students that would go beyond fashion and beyond media choice—so I hope this book has gone some way to providing that.

I also hope *The Design Manual* provides you with the sort of assistance you need—wherever you find yourself in the field of graphic design—and that you will turn back to it to be confident that you have fully considered your project and its design possibilities.

David Whitbread
February 2001

Acknowledgments

Like all books, *The Design Manual* did not write itself. There are so many people who have been influential in my design thinking, learning, doing and communicating over many years, that to list names would be fraught with the very real possibility that people would be left out.

I would like to offer my sincere thanks to the following groups of people who have supported, inspired, challenged and helped me to my present understanding—and ask them to hang in there for the future:

- my wife, Brigid, and daughters, Kathleen and Maggie;
- my parents and the Whitbread, Proudman, Russell, Watson, Gumley and Baker families;
- the principals, my teachers, classes and friends at Melrose High School and Stirling College;
- staff and fellow students at Swinburne Institute of Technology;
- clients of and colleagues in the Design Studio, Editorial Section and Publishing Operations at the Australian Government Publishing Service;
- my teaching colleagues and students at the University of Canberra and the Canberra Institute of Technology;
- attendees at my seminars and workshops;
- my colleagues at Snooks & Co.;
- my colleagues in the ACT Chapter of the Australian Graphic Design Association;
- my editors at Niche Media;
- the editors, production and marketing staff, and management of UNSW Press;
- the production staff and sponsors who have generously supported this publication (listed on the imprint page);
- the many printers, typesetters and prepress specialists; editors and authors; photographers and illustrators; paper reps and Web site developers who have provided their work, skill and patience to an inquisitive designer.

Thank you,
David

Why is this book useful?

Good design enhances the readability and effectiveness of any message, be it a poster advertising the local drama club's latest production, a personal web site exploring your family tree, or a sumptuous coffee-table book. This book is full of tips and ideas to make your design project just that little bit better.

There are so many decisions made in a design piece that it is difficult to know what works and what doesn't. Designers should always ask questions such as 'Which element of this design is successful?', 'Why is the piece weak?', 'Is the type appropriate?', 'Is the illustration poor?', 'How can the layout be improved?' Look at designs of others and analyse what works. Don't copy blindly, but filter the ideas through your own mind and combine your concepts with the best aspects of the work of others. Test and refine, and test and refine again.

The manual will be useful for a variety of people:

- professional graphic designers, editors and desktop publishers
- business people and public servants
- volunteers in community groups
- printers and imagesetters
- students of graphic design and desktop publishing.

Not every section in the manual will be useful for everyone. Nor is the manual aimed at teaching everyone how to print, imageset, use particular software or completely prepare a document to prepress level or to upload it to the Internet. What this book does discuss is how to make design decisions that best use these processes and to recognise their possibilities and limitations.

The part called '**Projects**' describes many of the projects an organisation may be considering.

It provides methods of approaching each project and, in many cases, some ways to streamline the development or production time. There are helpful hints on saving money, too.

The part called '**Production**' starts with design issues such as layout, typography and colour, which affect almost all design projects, and moves on to prepress and printing, and describes types of paper and finishing processes. But if you need a quick guide that takes most of the decisions out of text formatting, the section called 'Document quick fix' is for you. The ideas can be used to create a generic style sheet that will suit many text functions. It effectively summarises the main points for readable text when time is of the essence. There are also suggestions for things you can do to invigorate a boring layout. But these are, as the title of the section implies, simply a 'quick fix' when you are running out of time and the deadline is upon you.

Various check lists and margin notes will help you ensure that you've covered everything possible, and there are references you may wish to consult for greater details or more examples. The section 'Using a designer' refers to standard contracts and practices in Australia, and will help both client and designer understand what to expect in negotiations.

As far as possible, the text avoids reference to specific software programs and hardware platforms, and all terms introduced are currently used in the industry in Australia. Optional terms are explained.

Other features include:

■ MARGIN NOTES
These cover hints, check lists and references. There are occasional quotes from other authors and designers that are pertinent to the discussion in the main text.

■ DOING IT CHEAPER
For the budget-conscious, there are a few tips. Design decisions have a significant impact on the budget, so there are suggestions regarding cheap alternative processes that will keep the design fresh and interesting without costing a fortune.

■ DOING IT FASTER
Efficient delivery of a design job depends on saving time throughout the process, not just in the final stages of production. Printers and production staff are often expected to collapse their already tight production schedule. Techniques for saving time throughout the earlier processes are given here.

■ DOING IT SMARTER
Just as people need to warm up for any sporting event, you can warm up for a design task by honing your skills with a few well-chosen exercises or 'designerobics'. Some of the hints here are exercises with specific outcomes and can stimulate design muscle. Discuss the results with others to see how you are going. Like most worthwhile pursuits, you get better the more you practise. Some of these 'smarter' approaches discuss environmentally considerate ways of preparing work.

■ READ MORE ABOUT IT
References to books are placed near corresponding textual information, rather than in a bibliography at the end of the book. References are usually cited only once.

■ CHECK LISTS
Various check lists act as a summary of design decisions that are explained in greater detail in the main text. The check lists are reminders of all the decisions that should be made regarding a project. Not every project will need every listed item, so pick and choose.

Purpose

What does design do?

'...there is always tension in good design; a tension between opposing forces represented by the creative and the prosaic, for design must work as few other artistic endeavours must work. It must work at many levels, at a practical level and at an imaginary level, with subtlety and obviousness, with clarity and suggestiveness, and with simplicity and complexity all intertwined in time and space.'
Steve Bright in
Hail!Storm

Design is not an optional extra. If something has been presented in a visual form, it has been designed. Thus, everyone who presents information in a chosen form has made design decisions.

You can't say, 'Oh, we haven't got the time or money to design this—let's just get it out there!' because you will still put the material together in some visual form. Without consideration of the design decisions you're making or their effectiveness, you may as well forget the project. A project that doesn't meet its objectives, doesn't communicate to its potential audience and doesn't get seen, doesn't perform. It is a wasted opportunity, wasted time and wasted money. And you probably still have to communicate that message! So take the time now to consider design and its impact on every piece of communication you send and receive.

Good design

Whether design is used effectively (what might be called 'good' design) or ineffectively ('bad' design) is up to you. Effective design is described as the organisation of material which communicates information to a selected person (the 'audience' or 'receiver') using the visual language most appropriate to that person, the information itself, and the information source or author (the 'sender'). When you design, you are attempting to give your project its logical structure and, as a consequence of that, its logical form.

The term 'graphic design' was first used by an American designer, William Addison Dwiggins, in 1922, when he used it to describe his activities as 'bringing order and visual form to printed material'. It is still one of the best definitions, but we would probably be more broad in our media selection and embrace contemporary visual media—television, film and particularly electronic publishing—in addition to 'printed material'.

Design is used as a communication tool to:
- attract attention and arouse interest
- separate the particular message from the many other messages people receive daily
- make your message stronger, more effective and perhaps even memorable
- save money by achieving maximum communication value from whatever resources are available.

Design is not cosmetic. Design will not hide a poorly written text, an out-of-focus photograph, an ill-conceived chart or a jerky animation. The reader must be able to understand the text, the illustrations and the concept.

READ MORE ABOUT IT

Philip B. Meggs, *Type and image: The language of graphic design*, Van Nostrand Reinhold, New York, 1989, ISBN 0 442 25846 1.

Peter Bonnici, *Visual language: The hidden medium of communication*, RotoVision SA, Crans-Pres-Celigny, Switzerland, 1999, ISBN 2 88046 388 2.

Mark Oldach, *Creativity for graphic designers: A real-world guide to idea generation—from defining your message to selecting the best idea for your printed piece*, North Light Books, Cincinnati, 1995, ISBN 0 89134 583 3.

John Newcomb, *The book of graphic problem-solving: How to get visual ideas when you need them*, RR Bowker Co., New York, 1984, ISBN 0 8352 1895 3.

Audiences

Anything that tries to communicate information should be able to be understood. The way material is written, with a logical order and appropriate language, and the way it looks will attract and hold the attention of the desired reader.

Know your reader. Awareness of your readership and all the previous experience a reader brings to the text must have a bearing on the way you design the text.

Since design is the organisation of material to communicate with a selected person, it follows that you should know all you can about that person. Consider the following when preparing a profile of your reader:
- age—and the implied cultural influences and education levels
- life experiences—and family background
- language—words, tone and usage
- visual literacy—comprehension level of symbols and metaphors.

Know *all*.

Massimo Vignelli of Vignelli Associates, speaking at the international design conference, *Sydney Design 99*, reminded his audience of semiotic theory when he indicated that design must be:
- semantically correct
- syntactically consistent
- pragmatically understood by the user

and
- visually powerful
- intellectually elegant
- timeless.

READ MAGAZINES ABOUT IT

Communication Arts
How
Desktop
Publish
Design Graphics
Australian Creative
ITgraphics
Print
Step-by-step Graphics
Computer Publishing
Cre@teOnline
Graphis
Dynamic Graphics
U&lc Online: Upper and Lower Case
Applied Arts
Idea
IdN: International Designers Network
Digital Photography and Design
Australian MacWorld
Marketing and Ebusiness
Professional Marketing
3D World
Eye
AGenDA
Creative Review
Graphics International
Campaign Brief
B&T Weekly
Adbusters
AdNews
Baseline
Emigre
Form
Fuse
P4+
I.D.

Correct assumptions about what will attract and move the audience can ease many production decisions, not the least being finance. The job you conceive of as a full-colour, 'coffee-table' book may be quite wrong for your audience, who may simply need a single-colour pamphlet or a Web site address.

Other decisions such as the final approval of the manuscript or acceptance of a rough design should be made, not on your own aesthetic terms or your personal preferences, but rather by considering the profile of the expected readers.

There may be more audiences than you initially consider. For example, if children are the primary audience, there is usually the secondary audience of parents, teachers, peers and siblings, and perhaps even tertiary audiences of grandparents, aunts and uncles.

Use language your primary audience will understand, but ensure it is appropriate for your relationship to them. There can be an awkward moment when you realise you've used the wrong language even though the vernacular may have been chosen to make an audience feel more comfortable—the audience may feel that this is the wrong way for you to speak to them!

Choose images that will attract the primary audience and use visual language that they will understand. Then modify or allow the text and design to reflect what you know to be the requirements of your secondary and tertiary audiences.

By tailoring information to the user or receiver of that information, the final form the information takes might be different from what you like. But if your assumptions about the audience are accurate and you have an appropriate message and format for them, the material will be well designed.

READ MORE ABOUT IT
Henry Steiner and Ken Haas, *Cross-cultural design: Communicating in the global marketplace*, Thames & Hudson, London, 1995, ISBN 0 8230 0545 3.

Styling

Design is often mistaken for styling. Styling at its worst is a surface or cosmetic treatment—creating form for the sake of form. However, for a designer, an understanding of styling is essential if it is to be used effectively.

Styles and concepts rarely exist in a void—they have value in the associations they trigger:

- their original political context
- their original social context
- their nostalgia value.

To provide the correct triggers, you need to know the audience's life experiences and attitudes.

Styles can stimulate memories, even for those with a 'learned' response to the stimuli, thereby helping to accurately define the target audience. For example, audiences too young to 'remember' can recognise the fashion, music, and architectural and graphic styles of a historical period through exposure to museums, personal recollection by older relatives, print, film and video. But it is often more than just historical association; it can be emotional as well. Typefaces, imagery reproduction techniques and colour palettes all have associations—the response is often intuitive, not necessarily conscious.

Styling is a great tool in that it brings with it these associations which add great dimension to a piece. If you can harness the appropriate associations, you can create powerful designs. Advertisers and filmmakers use styling extensively to unlock an audience's past experiences, so there is a layer on which to build the story. It is a sort of visual shorthand where the viewer fills in detail, meeting the concept and enhancing it intellectually by connecting the combination of triggers that have been supplied.

READ MORE ABOUT IT

Philip B. Meggs, *A history of graphic design*, 3rd edn, John Wiley and Sons, New York, 1998, ISBN 0 471 29198 6.

Richard Hollis, *Graphic design: A concise history*, Thames & Hudson, London, 1994, ISBN 0 500 20270 2.

Laurel Harper, *Graphic radicals/Radical graphics*, Chronicle Books, San Francisco, 1999, ISBN 0 8118 1680 X.

Alan Livingston and Isabella Livingston, *The Thames and Hudson encyclopaedia of graphic design and designers*, Thames & Hudson, London, 1992, ISBN 0 500 20259 1.

Steven Heller and Seymour Chwast, *Graphic style: From Victorian to postmodern*, Thames & Hudson, London, 1988, ISBN 0 500 23525 2.

James Craig and Bruce Barton, *Thirty centuries of graphic design: An illustrated survey*, Watson-Guptill Publications, New York, 1987, ISBN 0 8230 5355 5.

Edward M. Gottschall, *Typographic communications today*, MIT Press, Cambridge, Mass., 1989, ISBN 0 262 07114 2.

Ronald Labuz, *Contemporary graphic design*, Van Nostrand Reinhold, New York, 1991, ISBN 0 442 31887 1.

Donald Albrecht, Ellen Lupton and Steven Skov Holt, *Design culture now*, Laurence King, London, 2000, ISBN 1 85669 210 8.

Real communication

In *Visual Information for Everyday Use*, Harm Zwaga, Theo Boersema and Henriëtte Hoonhout define information as 'data organized in such a way that it can be used by people to serve their goals. The actual organization of the data evokes in the user a meaning. This organization can come into being because the user generates the interrelation between the perceived data, i.e., attaches a meaning to a set of data. The organization can also come into being because somebody else has processed and presented the data in such a way that it evokes in everybody else (ideally) the intended meaning...'

'Communication' is a buzzword, but how much is really being communicated?

Communication happens on different levels: the emotive and the intellectual. Experiences and moods modify it. As a designer and communicator you must try to satisfy all these levels. Will the gut reaction meet the intellectual rigour the reader brings to the message?

In many cases, a client or boss simply wants a design to communicate clearly through a visual medium. Why all the fuss?

The first priority of all graphic design is to get attention. To do that, you must break free of all the competing imagery in the marketplace and target the people most likely to respond to the message with images and design that appeal to them.

Texture, colour, imagery and text are used to intrigue, astound, seduce or provoke that second glance that brings the subject to a reader's attention. The second glance stops the reader from going past your material. Some designers do it with complexity, some with simplicity, some with boldness, some with subtlety—however you do it, do it you must.

In any market there are usually multiple voices, each vying for the attention of prospective purchasers or users of the message. To stand out from the crowd, your 'voice' must be distinct. Against a children's choir, a bass voice will stand out. In a pet shop window's display of white rabbits, a black rabbit will stand out. In a stand of black-and-white brochures, a colour brochure will stand out. This is separation.

To break free of competing imagery, you need to assess the visual form of the competition, i.e. material that surrounds yours or that your reader will be aware of. Then you need to distinguish yours dramatically. If the competition's is multicolour, yours should be black and white. If theirs is illustrative or photographic, yours should be flat colour. If theirs is highly patterned or textured, yours should be flat. If theirs is glossy, yours should be matt. If theirs is homey, yours should be high-tech. This involves research and an understanding of the marketplace into which your communication is going.

So you separate your material, but what else gets attention? Pictures get attention. But not every picture gets equal attention, and in a world with vast numbers of pictures, the impact of 'just a picture' is lessened. In a world where digital manipulation distorts the supposed 'truth' of a photograph, the impact of a picture is lessened even further.

But the impact of a *good* picture is not lessened. If you can find a picture that tells your story with drama, surprise and relevance, you're on a winner. Many pictures do not have these three attributes—so build them in.

Multidimensionality is attractive; layering imagery and text achieves this with implied foreground and background interaction. The juxtaposition of imagery, too, can be surprising or ironic. The incorporation of type into the imagery can mean that both the verbal and visual messages are simultaneously read—and in the era of the sound bite, that's an advantage.

The design of multipicture images has gone beyond the ordinary collage that might have been used previously. You could design a hybrid image that in itself would stop a viewer because of its clever distortion of reality. But is that enough? Not when everyone is doing it. One way to compete with the plethora of hybrid images is to 'separate'. Simplicity and understatement can be attractive in a sea of dynamic imagery; a quiet, plain, minimal statement can succeed.

Some magazines have found that one way of getting attention on the newsstand is to use 'novelty' inks and finishes—fluorescent colours, holograms in laser-etched foils, and metallic inks.

A small, well-chosen area of colour can be very powerful in a layout. Just look at some Chinese *sumi-e*, black ink paintings, where the signature block of the artist is printed in red. That little red block is very powerful as a layout element, even though it takes up a tiny area in relation to the surrounding illustration.

As a layout technique, a favourite for impact is accentu-ated scale relationships. If all around you is big, be small.

When not to design

Making the choice not to design is sometimes as important as knowing how to use design effectively. For example, mass market fiction publishers use cover design to attract attention to a book and to communicate its content by coding it with genre imagery and typography that alerts the appropriate audience. However, graphics can be unwelcome intrusions between the covers.

At what other times do readers resent the imposition of design on communication? In Web sites, slow-loading images are resented when a reference page or an online form is needed. Readers don't want to play with or admire the information, they just want to give or get it and get out. Compulsory forms or paperwork, either on screen or in print, need to be designed for accuracy and speed.

This is not really 'not designing', but knowing when to pull back and let the communication between author and reader happen naturally. When interest is piqued, design. When interest has peaked, don't.

If you have an image of something big like an elephant, reduce it to be the full stop in your enormous headline. Blow up a fingerprint to full-page size to create an interesting graphic, then run tiny type through the spaces.

Another way of looking at this is an old stand-by technique used by photographers and art directors—conceal something that is easily recognised (usually a zoom-in on a detail or texture) or reveal something that is not easily recognised (have you seen those stop-motion photos of a bullet going through an apple or a sugar cube dropped in a cup of coffee?).

Intrigue your audience. Hit them in the eyes with a graphic that is impossible to ignore—and leave your competition back at the starting gate.

But avoid over-design. Actually, 'over-design' is a misnomer—'over-styled' is normally a more accurate description—but 'over-design' is convenient because we recognise the implication that there is too much design intervention between content and audience. What defines 'too much'? When the design begins to be noticed as 'the design' and the content is ignored or hidden, effectively camouflaged, the product has been over-designed. This veneer of 'being designed' is the problem—what should enhance actually detracts or disguises.

So ask yourself if your message will be sought out by your target audience? This is where most design effort goes, and many designs stop there! Once the reader is attracted, is the designer's job done? What about the communication part? Whether the product is entertainment, information or education, designers must spend as much time formatting the text and pictures to keep the reader involved as they did in attracting the reader's attention in the first place. The mass audience is not likely to spend time trying to find the headline, the beginning of the article, the price, the coupon, the caption, the phone number, the dates...

Many of the most effective designs are so simple you hardly notice that they have been designed. The design fits the subject so comfortably, so perfectly, that you would never believe someone laboured over it—and in many cases, you don't even notice the occasional flaw.

READ MORE ABOUT IT
Beryl McAlhone and David Stuart, *A smile in the mind: Witty thinking in graphic design*, Phaidon, London, 1996, ISBN 0 7148 3812 8.
Bob Gill, *Forget all the rules you ever learned about graphic design: Including the ones in this book*, Watson-Guptill Publications, New York, 1981, ISBN 0 8230 1863 6.
Steven Heller and Gail Anderson, *Graphic wit: The art of humor in design*, Watson-Guptill Publications, New York, 1991, ISBN 0 8230 2161 0.
Robin Landa, *Graphic design solutions*, Delmar Publishers, New York, 1996, ISBN 0 8273 6352 4.
Ellen Lupton and J. Abbott Miller, *Design, writing, research: Writing on graphic design*, Kiosk, New York, 1996, ISBN 1 56898 047 7.
Karen D. Fishler, *On edge: Breaking the boundaries of graphic design*, Rockport Publishers, Gloucester, Mass., 1998, ISBN 1 56496 454 X.

Clarity

You've probably read articles and other books on design and typography that encourage clear, legible and readable communication—and you've probably worked on developing a number of techniques that will produce those objectives. But then you see quite the opposite being widely produced, shown to you in design makeover pages and other before-and-after articles, and winning awards. Why? Where does clarity fit, given that the design and typographic 'fashion' appear to be concerned with all but clarity?

To bring the message home effectively, clarity of ideas, logical sequence, relevant visual supporting images and appropriate use of language are essential. But even assuming these have been achieved, a publication can still be ignored.

Clarity of expression and presentation do not necessarily have the power to attract attention. If the message doesn't get attention, the time spent preparing it clearly has been wasted. Clear communication will give people more information in a shorter period of time once you have their attention.

Having attracted a reader's attention, the material should then be presented in such a way that it communicates clearly and maintains the reader's interest. But you must assess when clarity—the unambiguous, fast and accurate communication of ideas—takes over from attention-getting.

The techniques of information architecture are user-focused and based on questions such as: What current knowledge or interest or awareness do readers bring to the text? How are readers likely to want the information?

'The aim of an information design project, and in fact of every design project, is to develop a viable product: a product that compares well with competing products, or serves a specific unique purpose.

This means that a new product should satisfy at reasonable costs not only the needs of the user, but also those of the client/producer, and, when applicable, those of the distributor and retailer. Also the consequences of the introduction of the product for the environment may play a role in the development process. From the point of view of the user this relates to appropriate pricing, easy availability, convenience of use, aesthetic appeal, and safety in disposal.'

Harm Zwaga, Theo Boersema and Henriëtte Hoonhout in their introduction to *Visual Information for Everyday Use*

According to Richard Saul Wurman in *Information Architecture*, there are five ways to organise information, which can be remembered by the acronym LATCH:

L   by location
A   by alphabet
T   by time (many museum shows are organised by timeline)
C   by category (the way department stores are organised)
H   by hierarchy, from the largest to the smallest of something, from the reddest to the lightest red, from the densest to the least dense, and so on.

The main way you organise something is by deciding how you want it to be found.

How are readers likely to search for it? Once they have it, what will they do with it?

The interesting aspect of these questions is that our standard information organisation systems, based on chronology or alphabetical or numerical listings, rarely provide the appropriate 'way in' to the information from a user's perspective. Information analysts try to find the best way to access information for a majority of people. Rather than assuming the knowledge of the educated specialist in that sort of information, information designers use associations or recognised forms and sequences of information retrieval based on their broader audience's experiences.

They also use visual literacy extensively—diagrams, abbreviations, summaries, coding and symbol systems, quick references and cross-referencing systems. Incredibly complex material can often be presented more clearly in a diagram, flow chart or graph or, in many cases, a combination of these.

Flow charts, for example, allow you to ask questions along the way to identify in finer detail the sort of information or way through the information the reader needs. These are used to identify problems and potential solutions in the trouble-shooting sections of manuals for electrical products, for example.

Knowing when and how to use diagrams and other information-organising systems can open the door to real communication.

READ MORE ABOUT IT

Richard Saul Wurman, *Information anxiety: What to do when information doesn't tell you what you need to know*, Pan Books, London, 1989, ISBN 0 330 31097 6.
Richard Saul Wurman, *Follow the yellow brick road: Learning to give, take, and use instructions*, Bantam Books, New York, 1992, ISBN 0 553 07425 3.
Richard Saul Wurman, *Information architecture*, Graphis Press Corporation, Zurich, 1996, ISBN 3 85709 458 3.
Rick Poynor, *Typography now: The next wave*, Internos Books, London, 1991, 'Introduction', ISBN 0 904 866 904.

Words

1.2 seconds. According to some recent sources, that's all the time you have to seduce potential customers with a piece of printed matter. At 1.3 seconds, they've turned the page, zoomed past your billboard, passed the bus, or their attention has been drawn to a competing message.

Let's say we are happy with our ability to grab people's attention with an arresting graphic image, a vibrant colour scheme or a stand-out graphic pattern. That's used a glance. How do we get them to land within the rest of our allotted 1.2 seconds and perhaps choose to stay a while?

Presumably, the attraction has worked because the graphic accurately isolated the audience that is most likely to be interested in our message. We then have to generate interest—and we most often do it with words. But this is still the seduction phase—despite its brevity—and we usually need to use more words to say what readers need to know than it's possible to read in the remaining time.

But think about the mode of attention those potential readers are using. They are still skimming and dipping, like a hummingbird, hovering over our message. They are skimming words, too. The words they need to find are signposts to the greater ideas contained. We use headings as signposts in text. But our readers are not into the text yet—they're still hovering. Marketers understand that words like 'you' and 'new' are good attractors. But for determining ultimate interest (and therefore landing rights), there are certain words in a headline that work harder than others. Our readers should be able to find these and find them fast.

We can use type variation to allow certain words in a headline to be found quickly. They can be:

- larger
- a different colour
- a different typeface
- positioned more prominently
- have more space around them.

Finding words that jump out means we are encouraging cross-reading, i.e. reading out of sequence. Most writers care about their words being presented in the correct order and do not appreciate cross-readings, but cross-reading can communicate faster. If successful, it can encourage more readers to read further into the author's text. The graphic techniques listed above enable readers to keep reading continuously, as is most often desired by authors, but also allow 'attractive' words to jump out and trap them.

Since our language is cluttered with words of less importance, how do we analyse a piece of text in terms of each individual word's ability to attract a person? Let's look at the positioning statement for the Loud festival:

Loud: Australia's first national media festival of youth culture and the arts

The most important word, for advertising recognition purposes, is the name of the festival, *Loud*. The three least important words are *of, and* and *the*. We almost have a tautology with the words *Australia's* and *national*. Why would we want to keep both? What do they each bring to the message? *Australia's* is definitive; *national* implies that the festival is big and encompassing, not just a localised festival that occurs somewhere in Australia. But the fact that posters and advertising are most likely to be placed pretty much exclusively in Australia seems to indicate that both words are less important in the scheme of things. Now, who cares that it's the *first* festival? It could communicate that it's an exciting development and 'new', so it's okay but not clear. Numerical labelling from second onwards usually reminds people of past success.

But really, those first three words in the placement line are not giving people information they need to decide their potential involvement in the festival.

So *media festival* ends up being important: *media* because it defines where the festival is taking place (in media events); *festival* because it defines the product. *Youth culture* is equally important because it defines the audience for participation and involvement. *Arts* is less important because it can be considered a subset of *culture*.

So, in briefly analysing an eleven-word positioning line, we find only four words that are necessary for identification in the skimming process.

An easy way to isolate them is to use well-chosen line-breaks that place these words to dominate:

Loud: Australia's first national
media festival of
youth culture and the arts

There are many other more interesting graphic techniques for allowing those words to dominate. But for those people who have chosen to stop hovering and land on our message, the whole sequence should be able to be reread in context to get the full intent and nuance of the message as the author had intended.

How we read

Rarely, these days, do we sit down with a book, open it to the first page and read through to the last at one sitting. Some new fiction writers who are experimenting with non-linear narrative forms are even challenging this. With the pace of life we are embracing, we snatch moments to read and, if it is a rewarding read, we come back for more snatched moments until we've finished.

More often though, the bulk of text remains unread because our lives, our bookshelves and our magazine racks are too full to make that return visit. Even in our screen-based reading, most remains unread—indeed, with the World Wide Web, it would be impossible to read everything that is available to us.

We flip through publications, scanning for points of interest, spending a bit of time with each one. It is very much related to our embracing of film and, even more specifically, video. Scanning a book is like fast-forwarding to the interesting bit. It is said that children can watch a program in fast-forward with no sound and still give a comprehensive rundown of the content or plot that is very close to the actual. It is termed 'video literacy'—and the traditional, word-based approach to the design of text-based information finds it hard to compete.

In fiction, you find authors like Jackie Collins who understand this video literacy and write short scenes, editing and splicing them in much the same way as a script writer or film editor does. Museum curators and exhibit designers also understand this. The concepts of strolling through different rooms and experiencing the exhibits in different lighting, media and atmosphere is very much like being in a video—you are pacing your own documentary. It is easy to see the appeal of the dynamic, blockbuster exhibit when comparing it with the passive museum experience of yesteryear.

This is not to say there is no room for a diversity of approaches, but the mass audience receives information in a manner that is significantly different from old assumptions. If you are communicating to a broad audience base, you need to recognise the motivations of that broader audience. Presentation technique has a major impact on what readers will choose to spend their time on. Where previously a reader's interest was enough and a page was passive, now page designers, on paper or on screen, are faced with the same challenge as museum curators and film directors—how to involve the modern audience?

Consider why people read what they read. People read fiction mostly as a voluntary activity and are therefore usually motivated because they have selected the material. Their reading is often sustained reading due to the nature of plot and character-based narrative.

The text has to be clear and comfortable to read—the design should almost be 'invisible'. That is, the text design should not disturb the flow of the author's ideas from the page to the motivated reader. If a person is really interested in the subject, it doesn't matter what it looks like.

But with reports, instruction manuals, Web sites, forms, journals, magazines, newspapers and advertising material, readers are often *required* to read the material or *need* to read the material in order to make a purchase or policy decision, or to determine what their next move will be. This is very often not really 'voluntary' reading—readers may be required for work purposes to read something of little personal interest or may feel obliged to read material that holds little appeal. So readers will often resort to scanning the text because sustained reading is difficult when motivation is lacking. Good design is essential to encourage readers to continue. The text must be 'made' interesting, or even entertaining, to motivate readers—because people read best when they are motivated.

With non-fiction or information-based text, few people read from beginning to end. They are more likely to check a contents list and jump to a specific section; flick through, scroll or skim for subjects of interest and graze the information; or check an index or do a word-search to find very specific subject areas.

So how do readers become interested in a subject? Good design can awaken interest and sustain it.

Multiple entry points

By using a series of signposts, a reader can be encouraged to stop at each one. Traditionally, these signposts were called headings and subheadings and it was a poor writer who had to use many of them, but this, too, has changed. It is essential to use many headings—and so many levels now exist that we refer to the lot as a heading hierarchy. All they really do is provide multiple entry points to the information.

We also use pull-quotes. They draw attention to author opinions, as distinct from the signpost headings, which draw attention to subject areas. A pull-quote is a quote suspended within the page, often out of context, but intriguing and provocative enough to encourage the reader to dip further into the text. It need not be a complete quote—it is there to whet the reader's appetite.

Pictures are entry points, too. A reader gets more information more quickly from photographs than from text. Pictures are therefore the most powerful entry points. Furthermore, the size of a picture indicates its relative power, though subject matter also determines this.

This power of the picture has now redefined the power of the caption. Captions were simply labels so you could read the main text and refer to the appropriate picture when necessary.

Captions have now moved beyond simple labelling—they are longer and contain editorial opinion rather than a bald description and together with the photographs they become almost a summary of main points expressed in the text. This is so the casual reader (operating on fast-forward) catches the main points of the text.

Hypertext and film technique

The story behind the story (which in multimedia programs and Web sites is literally on another layer that can be brought forward when selected) also has three print equivalents: boxed text, sidebars, or, in multipage articles and documents, separate double-page spreads of related material. In all cases, a coloured background often distinguishes this text from the main text.

Readers get pushed through the text by the pace in the design of the article and sometimes by very obvious means: arrows, numbers and flowchart-inspired connections. These are all ways of streamlining access to information (or fast-forwarding).

There are also layout techniques that are equivalents of both the cross-fade (an overlap of two images, one fading out as the other fades in) and the split screen (two images viewed concurrently). We have always had juxtaposition, where the brain seeks to connect images that are placed side by side, making sense of the placement. A more recent development, due to the emergence of photographic manipulation software, is layering, the overlapping of text and text, or text and image, or image and image. It is one of the most hotly argued graphic techniques in use.

Layering creates greater involvement with the text and its content by challenging the reader to comprehend the visual interpretation and to understand or make the links that determined the juxtaposition. This, in turn, slows readers down and makes them concentrate on the content.

On the other hand, layering can negate content because the reader will simply avoid the confrontation by turning the page, closing the publication or clicking the next hot link.

Visual processing

When we are reading, we are actually processing a complex set of symbols made up of letters, numbers and punctuation marks which are associated with spoken language. 'Typography' is the technique and art of working with these symbols.

In order to communicate effectively using type, it is essential to understand two most important typographic concepts: legibility and readability.

Legible symbols are those that bear the correct identifying features; their form can be recognised instantly. For example, the triangular form of a capital A enables our recognition of the symbol—if you deviate from a triangular form, you are limiting its legibility and the speed with which a reader will process it.

Readability depends on how easily the arrangement of the symbols can be processed by the reader. We read by recognising the shape of words, not by identifying the individual letterforms that make up words. This explains how we can misread words: the word we misread is often similar in word shape to the word we substituted.

Of the two, readability is more important than legibility. After all, even with doctors' writing, as long as pharmacists prepare the correct dosage of the correct prescription, it doesn't matter whether they can recognise each individual letter in each word. The end justifies the means.

So readability is paramount. Legibility serves readability.

Freshly peppered
Freshly prepared

Visual literacy

A valuable adjunct to our language skills is the plethora of symbols that we use daily, a realm beyond the alphabet and numbers. We use these symbols so regularly that we hardly notice how extensively they operate in our lives.

A symbol is anything that has, over time and with agreed common usage, come to represent something.

When we're driving, for example, we use a whole different language, based on simple geometric shapes and colour. The red octagon means 'stop'; the upside-down white triangle with a red stripe around the edge means 'give way'; the green circle means 'go'; the red circle also means 'stop'; the unbroken yellow or white lines mean 'do not pass'; and the green square with an x means 'green crossing'.

In some cases, like the stop sign, the word 'stop' is also a part of the symbol—but how often do we actually read it? If the word was removed or in another language, the symbol would still be understood.

Colour can also be symbolic. Would you give a wedding invitation a thick black border? What about a blue warning or danger sign? How about a red dot on a cold-water tap?

For multidimensional designs, you can incorporate an army of visual devices, such as symbols, pictograms and dingbats.

In the commercial world, symbols are widely used to identify a particular product or company. They are called logotypes or logos if they have a typographic element, symbols if they are abstract shapes, or pictograms if they are representational.

Many of these symbols also use colour—Coca Cola red; McDonald's yellow arches; Telstra orange; Australia Post red. (By the way, these are logos, because they all represent type in some form, either by whole word or an initial.)

Take a horizontal white rectangle with a red circle in the middle. Please consider.

Then consider the Canadian flag with a pictogram of a maple leaf. Then consider the five coloured rings that interweave: a symbol for the Olympics.

All these symbols are doing is abbreviating information; they are condensing an identity. It's a type of visual shorthand and works most effectively.

Another example of visual shorthand is the star ratings of movies on, say, the SBS *Movie Show* or in newspaper film review columns. Star ratings effectively summarise the film so you can decide whether you want to see it—based entirely on the number of stars.

NRMA, RACQ and RACV accommodation guides also use this visual shorthand to rate accommodation options and to describe the facilities available—whether there is a restaurant or laundry, video hire or swimming pool, and payment options like Bankcard, Visa or MasterCard. The *Good Food Guides* also use this system to advise readers of the relative expense of a meal by using multiple dollar signs. On shelf labels, Liquorland stores use symbols representing different cuisines for appropriate wine selection.

When you walk through an airport anywhere in the world, you will be able to find baggage claim areas, the toilets, post boxes and money changing counters simply by reading the pictograms.

A pictogram is like a simplified drawing of an object. It can be a complex silhouette like Queen Elizabeth's bust on British stamps, or the kangaroo road sign, or a simple representation like the sun and clouds on television weather maps. It can be an indicator of the appropriate cuisine with which to serve particular wines or it can tell you how to wash and iron a piece of clothing. There are also symbols that have developed from pictograms, like zodiac signs for horoscopes and Chinese characters.

This process—from pictorial representation to simplification to the development of a symbol—is how written language came to be developed. It is believed that Cretan pictograms may have influenced the early Phoenician alphabet upon which the Greeks modelled the alphabet we recognise today.

The term 'map reading' also implies a specialised area of visual literacy. Flow charts and instructional diagrams such as 'How to construct your model aeroplane' use similar 'reading' skills. There are conventions in comic book design that we now understand 'intuitively', such as thought balloon and speech balloon stylings.

We can use these reading styles to convert information that is new or foreign into a format that is understandable. The format of a diagram, map or chart, perhaps also incorporating other symbols like a rating system or pictograms, can speed our understanding because it relies on our visual literacy skills.

Using metaphors

A metaphor describes something new in terms of something we already know. An example of a written metaphor is 'The rain's soft fingers caressed the lovers'. Here the text has 'personified' the rain (described it as if it were a person with fingers). The metaphor tells us the rain was not beating down, but was light and even misty.

Metaphors can be tools for effective communication because we 'intuitively' recognise the familiar metaphor and can use or read the new product easily.

You can use metaphors in print design. When a catalogue takes the form of a product encyclopedia—in which products are listed alphabetically and described with diagrams, photographs and text that is akin to that found in an encyclopedia—we intuitively use it like we would an actual encyclopedia. We might even keep it on our reference shelf!

A campaign aimed at teenagers might be written in graphic novel form, and illustrated and formatted in that style, to be more acceptable to its target audience than a more traditional pamphlet might be.

A plant nursery and garden shop might use the metaphor of a naturalist's journal to present its catalogue to its garden club members.

In Web site design, the use of metaphor is more clearly defined and more widely discussed; a gallery, exhibition or trade show can make a good metaphor for a Web site. A gallery includes many elements:

- the general exhibitions that are always there and which draw on the gallery's central collection
- changing special exhibitions
- a lounge where visitors can meet
- behind-the-scenes collections which can be accessed by those with special permission
- the curators' offices, where they provide direct consultation on specialist matters

- special events and performances that bring other art forms into the gallery
- a cafe
- a shop.

These attributes of a gallery translate into a great metaphor for a Web site, with these direct equivalents:

- the Web site's main content describing the organisation's main products and services
- regularly updated, special focus sections describing new products or features
- a registered users' chat line where regular visitors can meet other regular users
- a section that is fire-walled which contains information and documents that only registered users can access
- e-mail links that enable visitors to contact people in the organisation directly and get individual responses to requests
- hyperlinks to other sites that complement the site and broaden the scope of its offerings
- a visitors' resting place that may have light information or games or community bulletin boards
- a place to buy merchandise.

Some excellent cooking CD-ROMs and Web sites use the recipe card index metaphor, even having a tabbed divider card navigation bar across the top of the screen, just like familiar dog-eared recipe cards.

Usability is enhanced through recognition of the metaphor. The best metaphors sit comfortably with and do not intrude upon information. They should enable fast and intuitive access to it.

Why print?

Why do we like flicking through a magazine, receiving a letter or reading a book? And why is it different from the return we receive from a computer screen? In other words, why do we still consume printed matter? More importantly, how can we maximise that return each time?

These days, we are trying to do more with each dollar and focus our efforts on creating more predictable out-comes. More than ever we need to understand what it is that motivates people to pick up a brochure, to fan through a book or to read an advertisement. Then we must harness that and fine-tune our use of those qualities to maximise both our efforts and our resources.

Print need not compete with the computer screen—it can play a different game altogether!

Print is mostly held within our hands, which is a personal involvement greater than just being a visual message received from the familiarity of a computer or television screen. Television viewing studies are already showing that we are more selective about what messages we receive from that medium, using a scanning manner for identification of interesting material, similar to skimming a magazine. The act of reading is personal also, because it is achieved in our heads at our own rate, and we select what we will read and how much attention we will give it.

Further, direct-mail companies know that the value of addressed mail is in its implied personal appeal. Feeling important and unique is part of the value of receiving a letter addressed specifically to us. This sort of personal-isation is becoming more feasible as short-run colour printing becomes faster and more financially viable. Databases are readily accessed through mailing houses and other list sellers.

It means that the whole experience receives greater attention, no matter how jaded we are about computer personalisation. Intellectually we may know that our name has been inserted by a database, and we may recognise that the signature has been digitally scanned and not hand-signed with a ballpoint pen, but we are still intrigued that the message may hold something of interest for us, because someone recognised that the people on that mailing list presumably had some similar characteristics and were thus appropriate targets for the mailing, so the chances are good that there may actually be something here of interest.

Computers may have sound, and whirr, hum and click, but so, too, does print—the rip of an envelope, the flick of pages, the crackle of sheets of paper, the rasp of paper against paper when the letter comes out of the envelope. The pleasurable sounds of interaction with paper allow print to engage a further and unexpected sense.

But by far the most appealing and luxurious pleasure of print belongs to the tactile experience. By skilful paper selection, the sense of touch can be a major interactive feature of print that transcends any tactile experience from a computer—the screen is rarely touched; the mouse and its mat are about as interesting as the tactile experience ever gets.

Largely it is this tactile quality of print that determines its appeal; you can touch it and enjoy the transition of surface textures that the use of textural contrasts can give. From smooth to rough, from slippery to suede, from hard to soft, from ripples to stripes, from linen to hessian, from thick to thin, from flimsy to sturdy, from sandpaper to glass—papers can achieve all these combinations. Some papers even have different temperatures—translucent films and tracing papers are often cooler to the touch than other paper stocks.

With *stationery*, it is also an economical way of introducing additional colour, as stationery systems often require that two pieces be seen together. Making these pieces complement each other in both colour and texture can increase the impact of the system.

For example, the interaction of letterhead and envelope is very important. Letters have involvement too—they must be opened to reveal the contents. There is therefore a tactile response to the opening of the envelope and the aural involvement from the sound of the ripping paper.

Do not underestimate the appeal of sound. Ray Black, an Australian advertising guru, pointed to research indicating that one of the things that milk drinkers like about drinking milk is the sound of milk tumbling into the glass. When

you next see a milk advertisement, listen to the soundtrack—background noise stops to allow your ears to focus
on this pleasant aural experience.

Continuing the opening of our letter, there are envelopes
that have a different colour inside from that on the
outside—why? And why are they used for things like
wedding invitations and special announcements? Because
they have that unexpectedness that can surprise and
subliminally make the receiver feel more special—just what
people want their sales letters to achieve.

Just contrasting the paper of the letterhead with the
envelope also achieves this. Or, as many great designs are
showing, you can print colour on the back of the letterhead:
a pattern, texture, illustration or photograph. This heightens
the pleasure of opening the letter. It becomes a sequence of
colour and textural transitions that lead to the letter inside.
Think of your envelope as a cocoon that gradually reveals its
contents—your message. By using a sequence of paper and
colours in a job, you maximise the effect.

For a *publication*, the cover and the text paper stocks
should contrast, usually in weight with the cover heavier,
but also in texture with the cover either smoother or more
textural. You lose an opportunity to give pleasure to the
reader if the cover and text papers are identical to the touch.

Endpapers have also made a comeback for this reason.
Endpapers used to have a specific task—to hold the book
onto the cover or case of hardbacks. They were glued to the
inside cover and glued down the edge of the title page.

Fake endpapers, a pattern or texture printed on the
inside front and back cover, are sometimes created in
softback brochures and books to give this visual surprise
or delight.

Sometimes a specialty paper insert, like an onionskin (a
thin, semi-translucent white paper) or a tracing paper also
create a pleasant effect—when lifted they can reveal the true
colours of the next page.

Binding techniques such as comb binding or spiral
binding enable multiple paper stocks to be used in this way
without production complications.

You might also incorporate a surprise element like a
pop-up or a cut-out which are both achieved by die cutting.
These interactive playthings can keep attention focused.
They are the print equivalent of an on-screen clickable
animation or hyperlink.

If you introduce some finishing processes like embossing, thermography or lamination (the touchy-feely ones),
you further extend the tactile experience. This will maximise the possibilities of print to engage the audience in a
manner that only print can achieve. It will often cost a bit
more to use these different papers and the alternative
binding and finishing techniques, but you will find they are
that much more effective in communicating the message
and encouraging the reader's interaction with the message.
There is just one decision: Is the additional response worth
the additional expenditure?

Designers are in the business of pleasing readers:
leading their eyes on a trip around a layout, alighting on
images, type and colour; meandering through sensory
delights like texture, pattern and contrast; seducing and
delighting the viewer with a message from the publication
to 'Spend a little time with me'.

Part of the magic of really good graphic design is its
ability to reveal something unexpectedly. Even more now,
this element of surprise or delight should be considered for
printed materials because it helps print to successfully
compete with video and sound products.

The designer is the conjurer who creates surprise
enough to communicate a message to the receiver. In Web
design, there are live graphics and links that achieve this.
In print, there is the turning of pages that achieves the
same thing—revelation.

A further aspect of the power of print is a sentiment so
often forgotten or neglected by busy designers: it can be
treasurable. Print can be an end in itself; a reader may
treasure the printed object as a life-enhancing thing of
beauty. This has the added bonus of an economic impera-
tive—if the printed item is not valued or at least saved,
it may not be displayed; if it is not displayed, it cannot
keep its message in front of viewers for maximum cost-
effectiveness. Yet it also fulfils one of the environmental
imperatives: that objects should be able to be used and
reused, recycled or, at least, reduce the environmental
impact in their production. If a printed object is treasurable,
it will not end up as landfill.

Any colour as long as it's green

Consider some basic practical action you can take to help conserve resources. First, simply ask whether what you're producing should be produced at all and, if so, whether it should be produced in a printed form. Multimedia or screen-based publishing are viable alternatives if your target market has access and will find or seek your message.

If we are realistic, we must acknowledge that much of our printed product very swiftly becomes landfill. How much packaging have you disposed of, or even separated for recycling, this week? How many letterbox drops, community newspapers and catalogues have been glanced at and promptly put in the rubbish bin? How many office memos, newsletters and brochures have gone into the groaning clean office waste bin?

The concept of something being so beautiful, so essential, so special, that you can't bring yourself to part with it, is a challenge to designers and clients. But if that is our new criterion for design justification, just how much would we produce? Perhaps only a small percentage of what is presently gobbling up resources.

READ MORE ABOUT IT

Poppy Evans, *The complete guide to eco-friendly design*, North Light Books, Cincinnati, 1997, ISBN 0 89134 724 0.

Anne Chick, *The graphic designer's greenbook*, Graphis Press, Zurich, 1992, ISBN 3 85709 433 8.

Eco design: Environmentally sound packaging and graphic design, Rockport Publishers, Rockport, Mass., 1995, ISBN 1 56496 083 8.

Lee Chartier and Scott Mason, *Creating great designs on a limited budget*, North Light Books, Cincinnati, 1995, ISBN 0 89134 607 4.

Betsy Newberry and Kate York, *Fresh ideas in limited budget design*, North Light Books, Cincinnati, 1998, ISBN 0 89134 840 9.

Mary Pretzer, *Creative low-budget publication design*, North Light Books, Cincinnati, 1999, ISBN 0 89134 847 6.

Steven Heller and Anne Fink, *Low budget, high quality design*, Watson-Guptill, New York, 1992, ISBN 0 8230 2880 1.

Bryn Millholland Mooth (ed.), *'How' idea file: 50 low budget design solutions*, North Light Books, Cincinnati, 1994, ISBN 0 89134 625 2.

Rockport Publishers, *Graphic design (on a limited budget): Cutting costs creatively for the client*, Rockport Publishers, Rockport, Mass., 1995, ISBN 1 56496 175 3.

Designing with Australian eyes

Occasionally it is worth considering whether graphic design is influenced by Australian eyes—is there a particular way of seeing and representing the world that is distinguishable from how designers in other nations see and represent the world? What does 'Australian-ness' mean in a design context? What features of our design traditions seem to click-in with larger national characteristics?

Photographers and visitors from overseas, and Australians who return from abroad, often marvel at the quality of light, the crispness of the vision and the remarkable natural colours that are so vivid and intense. The colours of our landscape are vibrant, rich hues seen for most of the year in a remarkably clear light.

Ken Done's *Sydney Harbour* 1982

Australian designers and artists like Ken Done, Jenny Kee, Sally Morgan, Reg Mombassa (Mambo), Jimmy Pike (Desert Designs), Brett Whiteley, Maggie Shepherd, Martin Sharp and Linda Jackson use a palette of colours that is so bright and pure that the world takes notice. Even our banknotes designed in 1966 by Gordon Andrews exhibit this confidence with colour. Equally, Australian postage stamps are collected internationally for their beautiful colour illustration and reproduction.

Bright Australian colours are not so different from bright Californian, Jamaican or Tibetan colours, but are often applied with an attitude that distinguishes them. This attitude is a reflection of the Australian sense of humour and casualness. This casual attitude combines with a healthy disrespect for authority and pretension, as represented by national icons like Blinky Bill, Barry Humphries' Dame Edna Everage and Gerry Connolly's Queen, and an ability to laugh in most situations, as evidenced by Wogs Out of Work, Steady Eddy and the perennial 'It's moments like these you need Minties' series. Even the television program *Sex/Life*, the commercial televising of the Sydney Gay and Lesbian Mardi Gras, Andrew Denton's *The Money or the Gun* series and Elle McFeast's specials indicate a certain relaxed attitude to taboo and acceptance of diversity that is refreshing.

These attitudes have fed Australia's great tradition of humorous illustration through the *Bulletin*, Melbourne *Punch*, *Cole's Funny Picture Book* and comic strips such as 'Ginger Meggs' by Bancks and 'Snake' by Sols. There is an equally strong tradition in political cartooning and social commentary, again stemming from the *Bulletin* in the 1890s to the wonderful whimsy of Michael Leunig.

These attitudes may have also translated into our design. The Australian graphic tradition occasionally uses classicism but not in a rigid manner (the avoidance of pretension?) and tends to embrace modern design and dynamic asymmetry (a representation of our casual attitude?). We have even embraced vernacular design (as it represents a realness; maybe a reflection of the national attitude of wanting to see the real 'bloke' beneath the image?).

Of course, icons abound—imagery of the bush; imagery from sports, entertainment and advertising; natural images like the kangaroo and waratah; and, more recently, imagery from the multicultural diversity of the Australian community. But this iconography is no more marked in Australia than in other nations searching for images of self.

As for the use of Indigenous Aboriginal and Torres Strait Islander forms within contemporary Australian design, the best examples come from contemporary Aboriginal artists like Sally Morgan, John Kundereri Moriarty of Balarinji and Jimmy Pike of Desert Designs.

During the middle of the 20th century, there was a push by some white Australian artists to incorporate Aboriginal motifs into a hybrid Australian style. But, while diverting, this was largely unsuccessful because this appropriation is rarely handled with the care and understanding of the sacred connection of the forms with their meaning.

Australians have embraced multicultural cuisines, festivals, arts and pastimes, and perhaps this is what makes Australian design an accurate reflector of a very diversified, multicultural Australia. Australian imagery has become more inclusive. Instead of the white Australian nuclear family in the suburbs or the white Australian bloke on the land that have historically represented Australian society, there has been a shift to more inclusive imagery. A wider variety of ages, races and family types and a more even representation of the sexes—and even a nod towards more inclusive treatment of diverse lifestyle choices, from sexual preferences to religious beliefs—now grace the pages of our magazines and our television screens.

Australian graphic design is mostly contemporary with Western graphic design from North America and Europe. But it tends to be more inclusive, and it doesn't take itself too seriously. But the main identifying feature for foreign eyes remains a confident use of colour.

READ MORE ABOUT IT

(Where there is a series, the most recent publication is cited)

Australian Graphic Design Association (AGDA), *1998 Australian Graphic Design Association national awards*, AGDA, Adelaide, 1998, ISBN 0 9586077 0.

Design Down Under, *Design Down Under 5*, Design Down Under, Terrey Hills, 1999, ISBN 0 9585261 3 3.

Design Down Under, *Discovery 2*, Design Down Under, Terrey Hills, 1998, ISBN 0 958 56210 9.

Ken Cato, *The view from Australia: The work of Australia's leading graphic designers*, Graphic-sha Publishing, Tokyo, 1986, ISBN 4 7661 0403 X.

Steven Cornwell, *Ripe: New design in Australia*, Craftsman House, Sydney, 2000, ISBN 90 5703 422 0.

Armadillo Publishers, *Creative source Australia: The wizards of Oz 14*, Armadillo Publishers, Melbourne, 1998, ISSN 0726 3589.

Robert Imhoff (ed.), *The Australian photographers collection 4*, Society of Advertising Commercial and Magazine Photographers (ACMP), Melbourne, 1998, ISBN 0 646 36010 8.

Melbourne Art Directors Club, *MADC season 98*, Melbourne Art Directors Club, Melbourne, 1998.

Geoffrey Caban, *A fine line: A history of Australian commercial art*, Hale & Iremonger, Sydney, 1983, ISBN 0 86806 012 7.

Roger Butler, *Poster art in Australia: The streets as art galleries—walls sometimes speak*, National Gallery of Australia, Canberra, 1993, ISBN 0 642 13020 5.

Bruce Stannard, *The face on the bar room wall: Australian pub posters 1929–50*, Angus & Robertson, Sydney, 1982, ISBN 0 207 14611 X.

Robert Holden, *Cover Up: The art of magazine covers in Australia*, Hodder & Stoughton, Rydalmere, 1995, ISBN 0 340 62224 5.

Vane Lindesay, *The way we were: Australian popular magazines 1956–1969*, Oxford University Press, Melbourne, 1983, ISBN 0 19 554409 9.

Mimmo Cozzolino and G. Fysh Rutherford, *Symbols of Australia*, rev. edn, Penguin Books, Ringwood, 1987, ISBN 0 14 010275 2.

John Bryden-Brown, *Ads that made Australia: How advertising has shaped our history and lifestyle*, Doubleday, Lane Cove, 1981, ISBN 0 86824 034 6.

Neil Shoebridge, *Great Australian advertising campaigns*, McGraw-Hill Book Company, Sydney, 1992, ISBN 0 07 452871 8.

Peter Luck, *Australian icons: Things that make us what we are*, William Heinemann Australia, Melbourne, 1992, ISBN 0 85561 451 X.

Watermark Press, *Made in Australia: A sourcebook of all things Australian*, William Heinemann Australia, Melbourne, 1986, ISBN 0 85561 067 0.

Vane Lindesay, *The inked-in image: A social and historical survey of Australian comic art*, rev. edn, Hutchinson, Melbourne, 1980, ISBN 0 09 135461 7.

Richard Rae, *Cartoonists of Australia*, View Productions, Marrickville, 1983, ISBN 0 908240 38 4.

John Ryan, *Panel by panel: A history of Australian comics*, Cassell Australia, Stanmore, 1979, ISBN 0 7269 7376 9.

Marcie Muir, *A history of Australian childrens book illustration*, Oxford University Press, Melbourne, 1982, ISBN 0 19 554269 X.

Susan Scobie (compiler), *The Dromkeen book of Australian children's illustrators*, Scholastic Australia, Gosford, 1997, ISBN 1 863 88695 8.

Gordon Andrews, *Gordon Andrews: A designers life*, University of New South Wales Press, Kensington, 1993, ISBN 0 86840 245 1.

Ken Cato, *Design by thinking*, Craftsman House, Sydney, 2000, ISBN 90 5703 641 X.

Ken Cato, *Cato Design*, Thames & Hudson, London, 1995, ISBN 0 500 09248 6.

Ken Done, *Ken Done: Paintings and drawings*, Craftsman House, Sydney, 1986, ISBN 0 9593448 7 X.

Sally Morgan, *The art of Sally Morgan*, Viking/Penguin, Ringwood, 1996, ISBN 0 670 90354 X.

Michael O'Ferrall, *Jimmy Pike—Desert Designs 1981–1995*, Art Gallery of Western Australia, Perth, 1995, ISBN 0 7309 3611 2.

Garry Emery, *Corporate identity: Selected works*, Emery Vincent Design, Melbourne, 1996, ISBN 0 646 28005 8.

Garry Emery, *Idiom: A way of working*, Emery Vincent Design, Melbourne, 1998, ISBN 0 9588188 1 9.

Emery Vincent Design, *Emery Vincent Design*, Image Publishing Group, Mulgrave, Victoria, 1999, ISBN 1 864 700041.

Barrie Tucker, *The design world of Barrie Tucker*, Via International Associates, Tokyo, 1991.

Mambo, *Mambo: Art irritates life*, Mambo Graphics, Sydney, 1994, ISBN 0 646 18798 8.

Andrew Hoyne, *Andrew Hoyne Design: The first five years*, Andrew Hoyne Design, Melbourne, 1996, ISBN 0 646 29694 9.

Storm, *Hail!Storm*, Storm Image Design, Melbourne, 1997, ISBN 0 646 33852 8.

Ian Kidd, *Ian Kidd Design*, Ian Kidd Design, Adelaide, n.d., ISBN 1 86252 333 9.

Inkahoots, *Public x private: Inkahoots 1990–2000*, Inkahoots, Brisbane, 2000, ISBN 0 646 39701 X.

Projects

Publications

Steven Howard in *Corporate Image Management* describes the most important trend as 'moving from a need for content to a desire for context...Today's problem is that there is too much raw information and data available...The need of the immediate future is to package and deliver this content in a meaningful and timely manner.'

'Publication' is a generic term that describes all printed information that an organisation or individual puts out. With all publication design, the aim is to make the information easy and enjoyable for the reader to digest. It should be user friendly.

There is often a great amount of information sadly disguised as boring, difficult-to-understand text—but this can be an authoring problem. A designer's task is to make the best of whatever text is presented and help the reader to find that information easily.

One of the main concerns of the publication designer is headings—the main point of information retrieval for the reader. Attention should also be given to making the contents list clear—no matter how complex or how simple. Equally, indexes require attention, although, as with references and bibliographies, there are fairly standard ways of organising them that have been proven to be successful.

For statistical information, a reader looks to graphs and tables. Both can be dramatically improved by clear typography. A graph shows patterns and contrasts in a quickly identifiable way. A table provides far more specific information that only some readers will use for further study and interpretation.

It helps to have a clear idea of who the target audience for the publication is likely to be, and design text that will enable them to find what they are seeking.

Books, reports and annual reports

The book represents pure typography—the shaping and placement of words to convey the author's intent with a subtle style, clarity and appropriateness.

When designing long documents, such as books and reports, the most important decisions are those which most affect the readability of the document. Choice of typeface size and weight will often determine how wide the text column will need to be and what sort of line spacing is needed. You may need multiple columns on a wide page. You might need to create standard ways of incorporating graphics. You may choose a low-reflective paper to make the book easier to read. You might suggest to the author or editor that more headings are needed through the publication for easier access to information.

Type selection for books tends to favour classic typeface designs, because they have proven their readability and are considered anonymous enough not to drag attention to themselves. Contemporary fonts will sometimes have a graphic detail that distracts.

Books and reports often have one main column of text to a page. They may have a side column for margin notes, like this book.

There is very little you can do to establish a design 'presence' in a book's main text, because, once you have chosen the typeface, you should follow the decisions that will maximise its readability, which is paramount. Where a designer can influence the look of the book is in imagery selection and the decisions made on headings, titles, formatting and page furniture.

Report style with numbered paragraphs

You might assume you should use the numbered paragraph report styling because all the literature you receive is in that form. Be careful of this assumption—people avoid reading material that looks daunting. Even highly educated, articulate and technical audiences find it difficult to keep up with all the reading they are required to do. Anything that is a disincentive minimises effective communication.

Don't let tradition get in the way of communication. Even in scientific reports and technical manuals, the so-called report style that uses numbered paragraphs is appropriate only if the numbered sections, chapters, headings and paragraphs serve a function. This function is usually to do with convenience, accuracy and cost savings in cross-referencing within the document; convenience and cost-effectiveness for complex indexes; and for ease of reference that avoids confusion in meetings ('Please turn to paragraph 9.1 to compare the definitions').

If a document meets any of these provisos, it's best to number the paragraphs and make the numbering clear for fast reference. The numbers might be bold or in a different

CHECK LIST
Attention-getting devices
(in roughly descending order from most to least)
- ☐ Photographs
- ☐ Drawings and illustrations
- ☐ Cartoons
- ☐ Collage and montage
- ☐ Maps, diagrams and flow charts
- ☐ Graphs (line, pie, bar, scatter)
- ☐ Pictograms and symbols
- ☐ Runarounds/contoured illustrations
- ☐ Captions
- ☐ Decorative type treatments
  - – titles and headings
  - – drop initials
- ☐ Colour
  - – splashes
  - – bars and rules
  - – background tints
- ☐ Pull-quotes
- ☐ Side-bars and boxed text
- ☐ Bullets, arrows and other dingbats
- ☐ Reversed headings
- ☐ Texture and pattern
- ☐ Decorative borders
- ☐ Body copy (main text)
- ☐ Space

DOING IT SMARTER
Complex indexes

If a complex index is to be indexed by page number, there can be considerable production down-time while the index is prepared after the page proofs have been finalised. An indexer obviously cannot complete the index until the final pagination is complete.

In the case of a manual or a report that has a critical schedule, it might be more appropriate for the index to be created using paragraph numbers rather than page numbers. The index can then be prepared concurrently with the production process and depends only on final manuscript, which is earlier in the production process than final pagination.

typeface. Usually, blocked paragraphs with space between are used in this styling. For the first line of all headings and paragraphs, there is also usually a tab set that will accommodate the longest number string followed by an em space.

Try to avoid more than three subdivisions within the numbering. Even paragraph 4.12.97 (chapter 4, heading 12, paragraph 97) is getting a little extreme. When you add parts or sections to the front end of this numbering system, it begins to get too unwieldy for clear understanding and defeats its own purpose.

Using that same example, the chapter is simply numbered 4, not 4.0.0. The main heading is numbered 4.12, not 4.12.0. It is also best not to put a full stop after the paragraph number.

Consider the introduction of alphanumeric coding if it will help the reader find the references faster. Alpha coding instead of chapter numbers looks less complex—compare D12.97 with 4.12.97.

Paragraph numbering should be inserted towards the end of the writing stage or even when the final manuscript is approved. If it is done too early, various changes and paragraph insertions and deletions can create numbering hassles later.

For technical and training manuals that are revised and updated regularly—particularly for ring-binder insertion—the numbering should start with each chapter or discrete updateable part of the document, otherwise many pages may need to be reprinted simply to accommodate the paragraph renumbering.

In all cases where there are no cross-references, or where cross-references and the index are by page number, avoid numbered sections, headings and paragraphs. This will make a more inviting and readable document. Chapter numbering is traditional, even though it may serve no useful purpose.

The numbered paragraph form persists in technical documents. This is due to the assumption that many people within those areas expect to see this format. There is a pretentious view that the format identifies a certain type of reader or expert. It is time for change. Even people in those technical areas will read better and faster without the imposition of the numbering system. So break the mould now in documents where numbering is irrelevant.

Certainly, retain paragraph numbering in documents where it enhances the usability of the text, but do not confuse usability with readability.

The problem for readability is that the number interrupts text flow. To partially avoid this imposition on the text, the numbers can be within a wider margin, rather than in the body of the text. Keeping numbers and text appropriately linked is achieved with a hanging indent. The point size of the number can be reduced, as it will have sufficient space around it to stand out. For layout purposes, it is wise to increase the size of the right margin and decrease the size of the left margin, so that the main body of the text appears centred on the page area.

Series

There are three main considerations for series design:

- accommodation of different titles, subtitles and author names on covers, spines and title pages
- colour coding for ease of identification (particularly for staff at an information counter)
- stylistic consistency of illustrations, photograph selection and text treatment.

If you are designing a series of publications, discuss with the author all the likely titles and subtitles in the series so you can accommodate their different lengths. For example, in a series of pamphlets for a veterinary hospital, it's easy to design for the words 'cat' and 'dog' in the title, but 'budgerigar' can create problems. With author names, always design to accommodate both a long name and a short one, such as Eva Cox and Oodgeroo Noonuccal or even a hyphenated surname like Annette Macarthur-Onslow.

If you intend colour-coding the series—i.e. associating a particular colour with a particular title—select a palette of colours for the purpose. Keep this in a file with the series style sheets. You can even have colour coding within colour coding, depending on your hierarchy—a series on animals of the world might divide into domestic and wild animals and then might subdivide into particular species. Choose a colour for each division and a palette of colours that work with that colour for the subdivisions.

DOING IT SMARTER
Parliamentary Papers series
If your document will be tabled in the Australian Parliament, it must be in the B5 portrait format in order to be rebound into the official record of Federal Parliament, known as the Parliamentary Papers. You might produce two versions of a document, one for Parliament and one for general distribution, but this is usually seen as too extravagant and deemed unnecessary.

CHECK LIST
Order of publication
[square brackets indicate option]

The cover
☐   Front cover
  –   title, subtitle, author
  –   publisher's logo, series title
☐   Spine (reads from top to bottom)
  –   title, [subtitle], author
  –   publisher's logo, [series title]
☐   Back cover
  –   blurb and author biography
  –   bar code and ISBN/ISSN
  –   recommended retail price
☐   Dustjacket flaps
  –   blurb or teaser copy (front flap)
  –   author biography and portrait (back flap)
  –   ISBN/ISSN
  –   recommended retail price
☐   Endpaper (or inside front and back covers)
  –   [*Ex libris* block on inside front]

The preliminary pages
☐   Bastard or half title
  –   title
  –   testimonials, reviews, author blurb or teaser copy
  (roman numerals start numbering here but are not printed)
☐   Frontispiece (verso of half-title, i.e. left of title page)
  –   a picture with caption
☐   Title page
  –   title, subtitle, series title and author/s
  –   publisher, place of publication, [date]
  A title page should not be too much of a jolt from the cover but should also
  ease the reader into the text design. An easy way of achieving this is to use
  the title block layout from the cover and add further information in the text
  styling.
☐   Imprint page (verso of title page)
  –   © copyright owner's name, year of first publication
  –   reprint information: number of reprint, date
  –   ISBN (International Standard Book Number: available from the ISBN
      Agency, Thorpe Bibliographic Services, Private Bag 20, Port Melbourne
      Vic 3207)
  –   ISSN (International Standard Series Number: available from the
      Australian ISSN Agency, National Library of Australia, Canberra ACT
      2600); annual reports may have both an ISSN, because they are a
      series, and an ISBN for the individual title
  –   production details such as the names of the editor, designer, production
      manager, printer
  –   sometimes a colophon appears here with the typographical and
      reproduction details, e.g. the paper stock/s used, the typeface/s used,
      the printing process used
  –   cataloguing-in-publication data (CIP available from the National Library
      of Australia, Canberra ACT 2600)

☐ Dedication and/or appropriate quotation (on any page in the preliminary pages)

☐ Foreword (by a guest writer; note 'Foreword' not 'Forward')

☐ Contents at a glance (if the full contents list is very detailed)

☐ Contents list, list of illustrations, list of tables
  (roman numerals start appearing on second contents page)

☐ Preface (author tells why book exists)

☐ Acknowledgments/Appreciation (author's and/or publisher's thanks to contributors or advisers)

☐ How to use this book

☐ Description of activities/objectives

☐ Organisation chart

☐ Mission and vision statements

☐ Financial highlights

☐ Executive summary

☐ Conclusions and recommendations

☐ Chairperson's statement

☐ Introduction (usually by author)

☐ Glossary (sometimes here if short)

☐ List of abbreviations used in the text
  (roman numerals finish here)

The text

☐ Page 1 (arabic numerals start here)
  – parts divide into chapters
  Page 1 is always a right-hand page (recto). It might be a part-title. So if chapters will always start on a recto page, page 3 would be the first chapter title and first page of actual text. If chapters can start on either a verso or recto page, page 2 would be the first chapter title and first page of text. Part-title pages always start on a recto page and often have full-bleed colour to identify them quickly when the reader is flicking through the book.

The endmatter

☐ Financial statements

☐ Supplementary information

☐ Appendixes

☐ References (if not at the end of each chapter)

☐ Illustration sources (if not in acknowledgments or within captions)

☐ Glossary (optional and more traditional placement)

☐ Bibliography (if not throughout the text, as in this book)

☐ Index

☐ Colophon (describes production details—optional placement)

READ MORE ABOUT IT

Rob Carter, *Working with computer type 1: Books, magazines, newsletters*, RotoVision SA, Crans-Pres-Celigny, Switzerland, 1995, ISBN 2 88046 230 4.

Chris Foges (ed.), *Magazine design*, RotoVision SA, Crans-Pres-Celigny, Switzerland, 1999, ISBN 2 88046 450 1.

William Owen, *Modern magazine design*, Rizzoli, New York, 1991, ISBN 0 8478 1385 1.

Nick Renton, *Public relations, newsletters and internet usage for organisations*, Kangaroo Press, East Roseville, 1997, ISBN 0 86417 893 X.

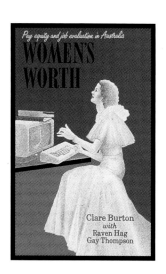

A book cover that uses allusion to a past style to convey something of the book's content.
Client: AGPS Press
Studio: AGPS Design Studio
Designer: David Whitbread
Illustrator: Mandy Orr

Covers

Cover design is like designing a miniature poster. An image needs to attract readers who are browsing in a bookshop, surfing an on-line bookshop or scanning a catalogue. Because of the usually severe reduction of the design used for reproduction in book catalogues, and the lower resolution when they are reduced and published on-screen in a Web site, titles are often larger and tracked wider for greater clarity in reduction. Consider, too, the placement in book racks—titles are usually in the top half of the cover.

Magazine covers must have general appeal and, if they are to compete in a newsagency, clarity from a distance. When considering which models to put on a cover, editors consider not only who will be attracted when a model is used, but who will be alienated. A model who has cross-over appeal, i.e. who appeals to numerous target audiences—young, old, males and females—will have a better drawing power for a general title. Note that it is hard for illustration to compete with photography in the newsagency!

'Teaser copy' is devised to encourage readers to pick up a copy and find a subject of interest to them if the cover picture is not sufficient. In books, the 'teaser' is often the back cover blurb but, increasingly, reviewer's 'sound-bites' are appearing on the front cover and some books have the first paragraph on the front cover to get readers hooked straight away.

Covers can also have 'attitude'—they can make a statement about their subjects or their content or, most importantly, their readers. They attract their target readers by appealing to their visual senses—and most markets are maturing in their visual awareness, so what in the past would have been considered avant garde or experimental is now almost mainstream.

Marketing considerations often affect design decision making in book covers as well. For example, authors may have their name above the title or larger than the title as a marketing requirement, where the author's name is deemed to be the most saleable information on the cover. This might also be a contractual arrangement, where the author's contract states a particular size and position for their name in relation to the title. Mass market paperbacks clearly demonstrate this. Titles and illustrations in many genres take a back seat to author identification.

With genre titles, there is often a visual coding that distinguishes, say, a romance from a thriller. Within genres, there can be sub-genres. The romance genre breaks into hospital romances, time-travel romances, holiday romances, historical romances, and so on.

Consider the differences in each of the following categories: adventure, war, crime, mystery, horror, epic, romance, future, science fiction, science fantasy, historical, classics. Each will have distinguishing characteristics that attract particular readers or, more importantly, purchasers.

Even in annual reports there are the equivalents of 'genres': steady-as-she-goes years, innovative years, traditional-values years, what-we-do reports, focus-on-our-staff reports, merger years...

You can go against the genre styling, of course. Many books that sit in the general reading sections of bookshops and newsagents could easily find a place in a genre section if packaged appropriately, but the publisher has chosen to aim for a general audience rather than a niche audience.

Newsletters, journals and magazines

The typography of newsletters, journals and magazines is complex—and because they need to be recreated each issue, a comprehensive typographic style sheet is necessary. Create templates that establish column width options and include on the master pages the running heads and folios.

In newsletter and newspaper design, consider the impact of folding. It may alter where the first article starts or photographs are placed (say, to avoid folding through the headline or faces). Also consider the impact of Australia Post mailing regulations and the inclusion of a mailing label. Even the weight of the paper stock will have a cost impact at the distribution end—if Australia Post charges extra because the weight of each issue takes it up into the next charge, it can have a significant impact on finances. If the publication will have international subscribers, consider international mailing costs as well.

DOING IT SMARTER
Spine titles
The title on a spine reads from top to bottom. When the book is side bound or saddle stapled, there is consequently no spine dimension on which to print the title. It is recommended that the spine title be printed on the back cover, about 5 mm from the spine, again reading from top to bottom. This enables people to read the title without removing the book fully from the shelf.

CHECK LIST
Newsletters, journals, magazines
[square brackets indicate option]

Cover/front page
□   Masthead/banner
The masthead (called the 'banner' in the United States) is the nameplate of
the publication. It encapsulates the character and content of the document.
It must be distinctive so that it immediately identifies the publication from
others. It often needs to work with the company logo or symbol that will be
alongside or within the title. It is often a different typeface from the rest of
the newsletter and usually the largest piece of type in the publication.

It can run vertically in a side column in newsletters and journals, but
there is a danger in this—it is too easy to avoid reading vertical text. In
magazines and newspapers, it should be positioned in the top quarter of
the front page, to work in newsagent racks.
□   Volume, number
In a monthly, the volume will contain 12 issues; in a quarterly, the volume
will contain 4 issues. The issues start from the month of first issue (so they
do not necessarily coincide with the months of the year—issue 1 need not
be in January, as a volume need not represent a calendar year). These days,
some people prefer to number their issues sequentially, ignoring the
convention of volumes.

Some designers prefer to make the issue number a feature, finding it
makes a stronger masthead. Ensure your design can accommodate two and
three numerals, as issues will quickly reach 10 and could exceed 99 in just
over 8 years for monthlies and in just under 2 years for weeklies!
□   Bar code
□   Date, price
Date and price information is usually linked to the masthead with the issue
numbering or it can be placed with the bar code. It is necessary information
but not important to your reader, so it can be small.
□   Teaser copy
Teaser copy is a listing of a number of feature article topics and can
incorporate page numbers for easy access. Usually, there is a hierarchy of
teasers; the more popular or important topics are closer to the top, in larger
type and in a more attractive colour.
□   Spine (reads from top to bottom)
    –   name of publication, [positioning line]
    –   volume, number, date
    –   publisher's logo
    –   [feature article topics]

The preliminary pages
□   Contents list
Often divided into the departments of the magazine, the contents list may
not be arranged chronologically through the magazine but by level of
importance to the reader, so cover stories and feature articles are often
listed first, followed by special supplements, regular columns and listings.
There will usually be the title, a brief description of the content, the
author's name and the page number. Sometimes there will be an illustration
from the story for recognition purposes. That picture will also have a
caption with the page number, in case people are looking at the pictures
and not reading the list.

- Editorial
  Treat the editorial the same as the text. An editorial is usually an opinion or an introduction of the content, a commentary rather than a presentation of new facts.
- Profiles of contributors
- Letters to the editor
  The text of the letter is usually in the same type as the text of the newsletter, but the salutation ('Dear Editor') and the sign-off can be treated differently. Often salutations are discarded. You will need to design another level of text for the editor to respond to any issues raised in the letter (so the response cannot be confused with the letters). Italics are often used for responses.
- Publisher's information
  - name of publisher and production staff (editor, art director, contributors)
  - mailing address
  - telephone number/s
  - fax number/s
  - e-mail and Web addresses
  - the number of issues a year
  - how to subscribe (including price and any discounts)
  - how to advertise
  - advertising contacts
  - guide for contributors (how to submit articles)
  - copyright information, i.e. ISSN/ISBN

  Americans call the listing of publisher information the 'masthead'; the English call it the 'colophon'; and in Australia it is sometimes referred to as the 'skite box'. It is mostly in very small type. In a newsletter or newspaper, it is often a long thin column on the second page or back page. Often it is on the verso of a contents list and opposite the editorial in a magazine. In a journal, it is mostly on the verso of the title and sometimes on the back page or inside cover.
- Running heads/feet (headers and footers in computer terminology)
  - name of publication
  - date and/or issue number
  - folio (page number)
  - article title on recto pages (in journal)

The text

- Department headings
  There will be department headings that separate distinct subject categories—editorial, letters, recipes, puzzles, news, notes, hints, personnel, and so on. They are usually quite small at the top of the page or column. They sometimes incorporate little illustrations or symbols for visual identification.
- News in brief
  News sections can require different heading levels and typography as they are often set on narrower column measures than feature articles. They may need a dateline: 'Canberra, Monday—The Prime Minister...'
- Pull-quotes
- Boxed text
- Calendar of events
- Listings of suppliers, advertisers

- ☐ Classified advertising
- ☐ Feature article headings
  Feature articles will probably have three levels of heading—the main and two levels of subheading within the article. The main heading for feature articles can be a standard style or vary with each article. Both approaches can work, but the latter is more design-involved, so can slow production. The two headings within are usually, in order, a bold heading about the same size as the text and an italic heading the same size and weight as the text.
- ☐ Author/writer/contributor by-lines
  Sometimes the by-line will just be the author's name. It is usually smaller than the text, often set in capitals, and frequently has a particular layout relationship to the article heading. However, by-lines sometimes include more information about the author (a short 'bio') which needs to be treated as a separate level of information to the text—say, in the secondary typeface or, more usually, in italics. Some magazines and newsletters prefer to feature all their contributors' photos and bios on a page upfront, often following the editorial.
- ☐ Lead paragraphs
  The 'lead' (pronounced 'leed') paragraph is the first paragraph of a story and summarises the content of the story, introducing the subject, its coverage and sometimes the author. It is usually set in a larger size than the text, often to a different width (say, to a double column width). This is a gentle way to ease the reader into the text.
- ☐ Abstract
  In journals, there is often an outline of the content and description of the author's approach to the paper contained in an abstract of 100–200 words that precedes the main text. This is often set in italics in the same size as the text.
- ☐ Body copy (main text)
  This is the most important type decision, as the reader will read more text than any other level of information. It must be easy to read. Spend time deciding on typeface, its size, its width and, most importantly, its leading. Decide whether you will indent paragraphs or space them.
- ☐ Dot points
- ☐ Table styling
- ☐ Diagram style and labelling style
- ☐ Captions
  Captions are sometimes smaller than the text and sometimes in italics. They are mostly positioned underneath the photograph or occasionally in a narrow column to the right of the photograph. There is much flexibility in caption typography. Decorative fonts might be used to continue a design theme into the typography of feature articles.
- ☐ Continuation lines
  There are two styles required here for the lines that direct the reader to the page where the article is continued and to identify, once the reader is on that continuation page, which article is being continued. They can be as simple as 'To p. 5' and 'From p. 1', or they may read 'Continued on page 5' and 'Name of article. From page 1'. Use them sparingly, because there is a considerable reader frustration factor with articles that jump through magazines and, unless they are considerably hooked, people will simply stop reading the article at the jump point.
- ☐ End of article symbol

Custom magazines

There are a number of success stories in custom magazines or client publishing. In-flight magazines such as Qantas's *The Australian Way* and Ansett's *Panorama* are well known and readily recognised custom magazines. NRMA's *The Open Road* started as a newspaper and has moved to a magazine format. The big new area is the magazine published by health insurance companies, community clubs, government organisations, retail stores, shopping malls, and so on.

Corporate magazines like Sanity music store's *Sain Unlimited*, Video Ezy's *Ezy Entertainment* and *Foxtel the Magazine* are popular with their readers for many reasons. They are already purchasers of the product or service and can catch up with the latest offerings; their interests in purchasing or belonging will probably mean that there is a range of related information that further identifies them with that entity so their interests may be linked.

Woolworths/Safeway's *Australian Good Taste* is a good example of a corporation capitalising on its market. The magazine is available only in the store (thus using an existing distribution network and saving external distribution costs). The retailer links with wholesalers and other corporations to cross-promote products. The existing customer profiles provide the readership targets. The magazine also reinforces television advertising.

Not all custom magazines are sold. Many are free to current members or customers. The information becomes a tangible representation of membership—available only to those 'in the know', underlining that corporate 'You are special to us' message.

As another tool in the marketing kit, the custom magazine has some strengths that are hard to ignore. Understanding that it is easier and cheaper to generate a return purchase from an existing buyer than to generate a new lead, the custom magazine is able to keep the organisation's name in the purchaser's mind. Recognising that a purchase decision is usually the result of about nine prior encounters with a product, the magazine has an ability to add to the tally of those encounters. The printed magazine has a longer shelf-life than newspapers, suburban newspapers, letterbox drops and pamphlets—and is likely to be dipped into more times by potentially more people (in doctors' surgeries and waiting rooms around the nation), giving greater value for the investment.

The subject matter covered will most likely have a resonance with the reader, too, since there is already a relationship. As with any other type of magazine, develop a profile of the reader—this will already be on the marketing documentation—customers and potential customers, suppliers and staff.

Often there will be an introduction by the CEO as well as an editorial. The CEO will want to warmly embrace the reader with the image of the caring, responsible organisation. The editor will want to imply editorial freedom from the originating organisation—thereby gaining more credibility as a 'real' magazine and enhancing the image of the product as a magazine, rather than as a brochure or, worse, a catalogue. The perception of distance from the originating organisation is a fine line to walk. There must be sufficient corporate identification and image enhancement to warrant the expenditure.

Of course, the advertising policy will often be quite restrictive. Certainly, competitors do not get a look in. The type of advertising allowed must be decided on and offered to particular businesses or organisations that fit the profile of the magazine's marketplace. This, too, is a fine line to walk—a magazine is expected to have advertising, but a reader wants to be able to find the articles! Advertising also helps defray publishing costs. The magazine publisher may not need to make a profit out of the custom magazine itself, but it might want its production to be as close to cost-neutral as possible. The designer must keep this in mind and work within the publisher's policy.

The editor will probably commission a few feature articles for each issue and have a few regular columns in addition to the expected new product round-up, news pages and product reviews. Designers can use involving devices such as games pages and cartoon strips, and market penetration tracking devices such as competitions.

A custom magazine should fit the corporate image program. It will have, in most cases, a separate identity. It does not have to follow corporate style manuals, grid systems or even typefaces. However, somewhere upfront—either on the cover or the contents page—the organisation needs to be identified using its logo and colours.

It is in the corporate identity's interest that the logo and masthead work in close proximity. This does not mean that the logo must be a component of the masthead. Although this is often done, it is done more in newsletters than in custom magazines.

Sometimes this corporate awareness is achieved simply by having a luxurious amount of the company's own advertising scattered through the magazine. This helps to maintain the image of the magazine's editorial freedom.

Pamphlets and brochures

'Pamphlet' in Australia translates as the traditional form of a two-fold, six-panel pamphlet at 1/3 A4 (210 × 99 mm), generally referred to as 'A4 folded to DL' ('DL being the size of the envelope it fits into: 110 × 220 mm). The 1/3 A4 pamphlet is now so entrenched that if a client asks for a pamphlet and gets another size, a designer has a lot of explaining to do! And reasonably so, since most pamphlet racks and counter boxes are now made for the size and DL envelopes make its mailing cost-effective.

The standard requirements for producing a pamphlet are a front cover that is visually interesting and distinctive and a panel design that continues the style established by the cover.

There are two possible methods of folding—the concertina fold or the gate fold, which give the panels a different order. The panels are considered in relation to one another to ensure they remain interesting as readers progress through the pamphlet.

Because of their ephemeral nature and the speed with which readers process them, the pamphlet should have a series of headings that effectively summarise the content of the pamphlet, including any special offers that might be made. Often, readers will scan only the headings and miss material that is within the body text.

Experimental techniques can be used on ephemeral work like pamphlets where getting attention quickly and cost-effectively is the main requirement. Varying the 1/3 A4 pamphlet size or format in some way will have a greater impact. For example, 1/4 A4 will still fit into pamphlet racks and DL envelopes—it may even suit the information better to have eight panels instead of the 1/3 A4's six panels. Perhaps turn the pamphlet around 90° and open it like a letter. Remember that the title will probably need to be readable in a rack—you can repeat the title sideways if necessary to accommodate this use.

DOING IT CHEAPER
Pamphlet printing

A pamphlet can be cheaper if it can be produced by a quick printer on a pre-cut A4 sheet of paper. This can be done provided there are no bleed areas—where colour extends off the page—and there is a gripper edge of 10 mm along one edge of the sheet on both sides and about 5 mm clearance on all other edges on both sides.

5mm   5mm

10mm

5mm

It can be cheaper still if there is no halftone work (photographs to scan and add in) and it can be printed directly from a good-quality laser print to avoid bromide costs. To improve the resolution, prepare the pamphlet in an enlarged format such as A3 and ask the printer to reduce it to 71%. Remember that, because of this reduction-in-production phase, a 10 point typeface needs to be enlarged to 14 points and tracked slightly looser. Lower resolution output can also be effectively disguised by printing on recycled or textured paper stock.

Concertina fold

Concertina fold vertical

Gate fold

Front

1	2	3

4	5	6

Back

Front

1
2
3

Back

4
5
6

Front

5	6	1

2	3	4

Back

DOING IT SMARTER
Pamphlet covers

The front panel of a pamphlet is often not first seen in its entirety—it will need to be removed from the rack or box. So attract attention to it in the top third of the front cover. Photos can attract attention (but just a bit of sky and cloud, with the main subject obscured by the pamphlet in front, will not cut it these days!). Perhaps put a subject heading at the top of the pamphlet.

Remember, too, that a pamphlet in a letterbox drop or on tables for pick-up will sometimes be seen first from the back. So make the back outer panel attractive, too: let it tell some of the story, or just repeat the front information, perhaps adding the usual address, phone numbers, map and other contact information. In this way, whichever way someone receives the pamphlet, some of the message gets through—even if people never open it further or just glance at it as it lands in the bin.

DOING IT SMARTER
Material to consider for panel 5 in a gate-folded pamphlet

When you open a gate-folded pamphlet, panel 2 is on the left with panel 5 on the right. Opening panel 5 reveals panels 3 and 4. So panel 5 has been seen out of sequence and higher in priority than its number would suggest. As a result, it is often used for material that stands alone:

- Guarantee
- Endorsements
- Order or booking form
- Quote
- Personal invitation (signed)
- Summary of features
- Special offer

If the pamphlet does not need to be read in a rack and is dropped into a letterbox, try a triangular format. Most people will open a triangular format just to see how it works. If you fold an A4 sheet in half to A5 and then trim the top and bottom at 30° angles, you will create an equilateral triangle. There is some paper wastage, but the organisation can preprint bookmarks or coupons on the bits trimmed off, so the paper will not be wasted.

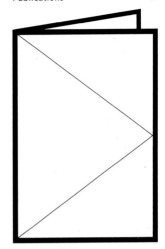

Catalogues

A catalogue can be as simple as a table with columns for each product's name, description and price, photocopied onto an A4 sheet of paper. Or it can be a large brochure in magazine format with editorial content and sumptuous illustrations.

If a catalogue is a complex inventory of a company's products, it can be contained in a binder that is designed to accept regular update sheets. Dividers that identify a particular product range can separate the literature. This sort of catalogue is more often for trade use, rather than for the general public.

The catalogue's colour palette and design can be varied according to the image of the company, its products, and the type of shopper who frequents its stores. It can be understated and stylish, or brash and loud; visually exciting and distracting, or sparse and clean; funky, hip and streetwise, or logical and nerdy.

Catalogues are often seasonal, and seasons are usually associated with particular colour palettes. The spring and summer catalogues will use clear bright colours and lots of white space. In contrast, Christmas catalogues, even in the height of summer, will probably use lots of rich, warm colours and soft-focus photography—filters can give everything a golden, nostalgic glow. The autumn and winter catalogues will usually use warm, dark, rustic colours.

Many catalogues include hints for the customer that involve the products for sale: care and maintenance advice; fashion tips or accessorising options; hints for enhancing business or home life; recipes or activity sheets; guides to collecting complete sets; endorsements by famous users; fictitious stories; and interviews with the makers or with company staff to give that 'personal' touch—effectively a seal of quality.

Most photography in catalogues is shot in a studio. Here, light is controllable, helping the photographer

CHECK LIST
Catalogues
- ☐ Picture of product (photograph or illustration)
- ☐ Product code keyed to picture
- ☐ Description and brand
- ☐ Price, colours, sizes and materials
- ☐ Special deals or original price
- ☐ Product order code
- ☐ Colour-matched swatches
- ☐ Availability
- ☐ Sizing details
- ☐ Supply and shipping options and prices
- ☐ Payment options
- ☐ Order form
- ☐ Location listings and maps
- ☐ Contact information including phone number, postal address, freepost address, fax, e-mail and Web address
- ☐ Legal requirements
- ☐ Editorial content [optional]
- ☐ Hints [optional]
- ☐ Guarantees
- ☐ Product endorsements
- ☐ Special offers
- ☐ Coupons
- ☐ Return policy

capture truer colours and finer details. Sometimes a catalogue will have a full shot of a product, a sequence of detail shots, and a swatch of available colours, each keyed with its name: sand, midnight, jade, charcoal... Each photograph is then labelled or captioned with the product description and purchase information.

If there is more than one product in the photograph, each will be alpha-coded either per page, per double-page spread, or consecutively throughout the catalogue. Using a separate coding table for each double-page spread is preferable because any last-minute changes in product availability will force coding changes only to that one spread, rather than to the whole catalogue.

Some organisations use their inventory codes to resolve ordering issues, but they can often be long sets of numbers and letters that not only can look intrusive when superimposed over the photography, but can be incorrectly copied onto order forms. The coding therefore is often alphabetical rather than numeric, supporting 26 products across a double-page spread. Then the order form will usually ask for a page number and a product code. This means that multiple products will share the same letter code, so to avoid misquoted page numbers (and, truthfully, in how many catalogues can you find the page number that easily anyway?), you can introduce hybrid alphanumeric (A1, A2, B1) or double-letter (AA, AB, BA) codes.

Consider what the organisation is trying to achieve with the catalogue. Is it to get more people through the doors for a 2-week blitz? Is it to get phone orders immediately with credit card payments? Is it to get postal orders? Is it to increase awareness of the product range and build the organisation's reputation so it is thought of whenever someone is in the market for that product?

Each of these motivations has implications for the catalogue's design, so find out what the organisation's motivation is. It's frustrating when a reader decides to buy something from a catalogue, but cannot find complete information or even a telephone inquiries number—only an inconvenient shop address or postal options. The vendor loses the sale.

If the intention is to get people into the store, maybe a coupon that is redeemable only in-store will do it. These coupons can be used by the store to gain some valuable feedback on its customer base and the effectiveness or otherwise of its advertising. The store can count how many coupons are returned from a particular catalogue (a simple code can be placed in the corner of each coupon). If shoppers need to write their names and addresses or even just their postcodes on the coupon before they redeem it, the store can find the boundaries of its catchment area, or whether its offer was more attractive to men or to women. Next time, the store can focus on a particular area where it has found advertising to be effective.

Order forms need to be easy to use. People must be able to fill in the order form quickly and accurately. Codes must be able to fit comfortably in handwriting in the allotted space. Product descriptions need not be too long and should probably follow the code in the original product description in the catalogue, so the prospective buyer doesn't have to search for the description or, worse, make one up from the blurb. If it is likely that a special promotion will be sought by most buyers, then preprint its product code, description and price on the order form. Leave sufficient room for addresses, credit card numbers and signatures.

Menus

If you need to prepare a menu for a dinner for an organisation or for a local restaurant or even for your own restaurant, you might want to consider some typographical decisions that have an impact on the image you are trying to project.

Maintaining a consistent identity is important. So much consideration has gone into the creation of an atmosphere through décor, lighting and entertainment, and the preparation of a selection of dishes and complementary drinks to tempt the palate, it is a shame to break the experience with a poorly conceived menu.

A set of good-quality, long-life menu covers that link with the restaurant logo, décor and table settings and will withstand the rigours of restaurant use are a good investment (and it might be useful to suggest this to the client). The internal pages can then be the only reprinted and discarded pieces with seasonal menu changes, saving both money and the environment.

You need to make design decisions that make the updating of the internal pages fast and accurate. Usually that means avoiding illustrations and relying on type to do the job. Creating a style sheet also speeds the process.

We've all experienced the following frustrations: the prices are too far away from the name of the dish and the dishes are too cramped on the sheet to accurately identify the corresponding price; the descriptions are too small to be comfortably read in the low light of the restaurant; we can't find the drinks list when the waiter has just asked, 'And would you like any drinks with that?'; and there is not enough space between the entries so we associate the price above the dish with it instead of the price below its description.

Consequently, there are four type decisions that need to be made when designing the style sheet for a menu:
- part headings that signal the courses or parts of the meal: entree, main, dessert, side orders, drinks...
- cuisine headings that indicate the type or style of food: pork, seafood, vegetarian, Malay, Szechuan, pasta, cocktails, sparkling wines...
- name of the dish
- description of the dish and its price.

The first and second are signpost headings—they need to jump out quickly to propel diners through the menu to their preferences. You can use more decorative typefaces but keep them in a style that is compatible and reinforces the style of the logo typeface. For country kitchens, perhaps Caslon Antique; for wedding menus, script typefaces (usually kept large—18 points or more—and lower case for ease of legibility); and for French restaurants, maybe art nouveau type.

The name and description of the dish need to be comfortably read and are treated like body text—easy-to-read typefaces. This is where handwriting, though quaint and stylish, can be a hindrance to a good menu. Legibility is important. Classic typefaces are usually good, readable typefaces for this information.

Distinguish the name of the dish from its description by using normal text against italics, or bold text against normal text, or small capitals against lower case. You can use rules to separate the dishes to avoid some reading difficulties. In your style sheet for the dish name, create the rule above the name. It is just as effective to add a set amount of space between entries. This can be as little as 3 points and still work successfully.

Many menus are created like the contents lists in old-fashioned books, with dot leaders from the end of the description, or from the end of the name of the dish, to the price. There are the occasional bizarre designs where 'Rice' is 16 cm of dots from its price! This is not a good look—or good communication. Try to avoid using dot leaders. There is a false sense that the so-called neatness of justified columns means we must accept this foolish spacing. There is no rule that says a menu must fill the full page width, so a narrower text block may resolve the need for dot leaders. In this case, look for the longest dish name and leave a 5 mm space and key-in the price. The resulting line width can become the text block width for the menu.

Prices can be set an em space away from the dish name or a few spaces away. The only problem with this reader-friendly decision is that the price can get lost in the menu and this is a negative for those who are price-conscious. If the prices are all full-dollar prices, do not include the decimal points and zeros. '$10' is better than '$10.00', although psychologically '$9.95' is preferred.

Programs

Regional and suburban theatre groups, community orchestras, amateur dramatic societies, churches and schools present productions that require often complex and fast publishing skills when it comes to preparing the program for the concert, show or event.

There are typographic, layout and production issues to consider. The program should be an adequate souvenir and collector's piece, as well as an official or historic record for the organisation. It should be cheap enough to print within the usually limited budgets and it should add to the whole perception of the event by the community.

Further complications are sometimes required by the performance rights and clauses in professional contracts regarding the size of an author's or actor's name in relation to the size of the title of the production. Thus, to misquote Gilbert and Sullivan, 'The designer's lot is not a happy one, happy one.'

The usual difficulty is coming up with an appropriate typographic treatment for the hierarchy of information that a program contains, creating easily understood and identified listings of production personnel, orchestra and cast, and being a bit theatrical as well!

Type selection and even photo treatments are different, for example, for an *Olde Time Music Hall* and a piece of experimental, improv-based theatre. The florid and eclectic mix of fonts and faces that remind people of Edwardian and Victorian printing styles add an ambience to the entire production for the music hall, where the song-sheet/program is as much a part of the action as the actors. In the same way, decorative borders for each page and possibly even different decorative frames for each photograph—even the use of an oval frame or a *vignette* (fading edges)—help maintain the whole production's illusion of the latter 19th century.

As a contrast, the modern line and detached impersonality of a sans serif typeface like Univers used in an idiosyncratic and perhaps unexpected or risky way helps define the nature of the improv performance. Awkwardly cropped or positioned images, with a bit of overlapping or dramatic interrelationships between the text and the images, also enhance the illusion of the production being a bit daring or unconventional.

Orders of service

Orders of service for weddings and weekly church services have their own design issues. With a wedding service, there is the desire to make a worthy souvenir. Including a list of the bridal party and the words of the readings and songs can make it a pleasant keepsake. Using a different paper that links with the invitations or placecards can tie-in the range of wedding stationery, and incorporating photographs or illustrations can further personalise the order of service.

With a church service, there is often the need to fit a large amount of material but avoid unnecessary additional production costs. Consider the use of columns, narrow margins and different type sizes (larger and lower case for responses and smaller for announcements).

Another issue for orders of service is copyright infringement of song lyrics (and this includes hymns). Respect copyright laws—permission to reproduce must be sought as required (usually the song or hymn book will have instructions as to how to seek this permission on the back of its title page). The citation should be at the foot of the reproduced words with the copyright symbol, ©. Then list the owner of the copyright—it may not necessarily be the author, but a publisher or a company.

Comics and graphic novels

Comics tell a story or communicate information through pictures and text. The sequence of panels shows the progression of time and implies change between each panel: the change of time, completion or continuation of movement, a new location or action, or a change in point of view. In this way, comics work with the reader and expect them to fill in the gaps. Different text techniques like voice balloons, thought balloons and brief location and time descriptors are often incorporated into the illustrations. There can also be linking passages of descriptive text between sequences in the story and introductory text to set the context.

Comics, and the further development of the genre that refers to illustrated strip books as graphic novels, can be used to communicate more effectively to a visually sophisticated audience that is not necessarily reading other forms. The comic can be a more attractive medium than traditional text, particularly for younger audiences. Complex information can be presented most effectively in a comic strip, as assembly and installation instructions for many appliances demonstrate.

The graphic novel is a further development of the comic. Grander in scope, the best graphic novels use a complex mix of text, pictorial and film conventions. This enables them to have more layers of detail and even more engagement of the reader. Often the juxtaposition of different forms of narrative will maintain the reader's interest.

The visual conventions of comics and graphic novels relate strongly to visual literacy as learnt through exposure to film and video. Using film conventions and even appropriating the storyboarding technique used to plan film, information can be presented with dialogue—even sound effects have conventions based on type variation.

Backgrounds and foregrounds can have different characteristics. In Yoram Gross's *Blinky Bill*, photographic backgrounds combine with 3-D models photographed into those backgrounds and 2-D character animation in the foreground. Backgrounds can be drawn with the same qualities as the characters or they can comment on the character's inner life by being drawn in different styles as the mood and atmosphere changes.

Streetwize Comics present educational messages in a more accessible format for their audience.

Clients: Mental Health Services Unit, NSW Department of Health and SA Minister for Youth Affairs
Written and designed by Streetwize Comics

Illustratively, there is no specific style preferred: comic, realistic, semi-abstract, watercolour, oil painting, cut paper, collage, computer rendered, 3-D modelled, photographic, found objects, anything goes...

The interpretation of style here is another visual language, where conventions denote how a particular line is viewed: it could be languid, neurotic, feeble, shrill, depending on its drawn quality. The reader understands these conventions and 'reads' this level of comment or description intuitively.

READ MORE ABOUT IT

Scott McCloud, *Understanding comics: The invisible art*, Tundra Publishing, Northampton, Massachusetts, 1993, ISBN 1 56862 019 5.

Will Eisner, *Comics and sequential art*, expanded edition, Poorhouse Press, Tamarac, Florida, 1990, ISBN 0 9614728 0 2.

Roger Sabin, *Comics, comix and graphic novels*, Phaidon, London, 1996, ISBN 0 7148 3008 9.

Mark Salisbury, *Artists on comic art*, Titan, London, 2000, ISBN 1 84023 186 6.

Stan Lee and John Buscema, *How to draw comics the Marvel way*, Simon & Schuster, New York, 1978, ISBN 0 671 53077 1.

Rod Tokely and Dillon Naylor, *Zap! Splat! Ka-pow!: Make your own comic*, Omnibus Books, Norwood, South Australia, 1999, ISBN 1 86291 397 8.

Grant Morrison and Dave McKean, *Arkham Asylum*, DC Comics, New York, 1989, ISBN 0 930289 56 0.

Jill Bossert, *Children's book illustration: Step-by-step techniques: A unique guide from the masters*, RotoVision SA, Crans-Pres-Celigny, 1998, ISBN 2 88046 335 1.

Proposals

Presentations to clients, curricula vitae, information packs, interim reports and submissions, proposals and tender documents have become a part of corporate life. Keep them simple for speedy, hassle-free production. Often they need to be produced in short order and perform on boardroom tables in a competitive situation.

The designer can help make a competitive submission by attending to the details and being prepared for them. Preprinted material can be incorporated to 'dress up' the presentation. A well-designed piece can showcase the organisation's professionalism. The proposal must look impressive and professional and the receiver should marvel that it could be put together so effectively in such a short period of time—your reputation will be enhanced.

A proposal needs to be packaged competitively—but also be able to be produced quickly. Prepared dividers and folders allow easy updating of the content.
Designers: Louise Dews, David Whitbread

CHECK LIST
Proposal production

Paper selection
- ☐ Front and back covers (maybe with a window to read a title?)
- ☐ Dividers (with generic headings?)
- ☐ Text pages

Sources:
- ☐ Stationery by the piece
- ☐ Giftwrap
- ☐ Preprints
- ☐ Handmade papers
- ☐ Tracing paper/film
- ☐ Acetate/OHP film

Printing method
- ☐ Laser printing
- ☐ Photocopying

Binding
- ☐ Side bound
- ☐ Saddle stitched

with:
- ☐ Staples
- ☐ Wire
- ☐ Rings
- ☐ Plastic comb
- ☐ Ribbon, cotton, twine

Other techniques to consider
- ☐ Colour coding
- ☐ Cutting and folding (windows)

Standard information sheets
- ☐ Description of the organisation
- ☐ Vision/mission statements
- ☐ Organisational structure
- ☐ Curricula vitae of senior team members (with photos?)
- ☐ Profiles of previous successful projects
- ☐ Letters of commendation

Check consistency
- ☐ Spelling
  - – names
  - – titles
- ☐ Figures
  - – calculations
  - – phone numbers
  - – prices

Corporate identity

'At a minimum, the identity system should create something memorable and distinctive about the organisation, something that enables the organisation to stand out from the crowd. In the best executions, a corporate identity system will provide a unique positioning platform for the organisation, something that allows customers and others to develop a feeling of familiarity with the organisation.'

Steven Howard,
Corporate Image Management

The corporate image of any organisation is a complex mix of outsider and insider views of that organisation. The views are determined through encounters and experiences with the organisation. The encounters range through advertising on television to 'Positions Vacant', from letters to reports, from Christmas cards to staff newsletters. The experiences are usually person-to-person dealings, either by letter, phone or in person.

When referring to corporate identity, it is often forgotten that the print or visual identity is really only a part of an organisation's image. But it is probably the easiest part to control.

Many organisations appear to not understand how their visual identity works for them or, in many cases, against them. The print identity affects not only outsiders' views of an organisation but also insiders'. It can help the organisation establish a perception of itself as worthwhile, trustworthy, professional, forward-thinking, up-to-date— alternatively, it can look fly-by-night, cheap, tasteless or muddled.

It can also be an effective, shorthand way of informing people. Once a look that is associated with the organisation has been established, people automatically remember that and the basic information doesn't have to be reiterated.

One of the assumptions many organisations make is that if they use the same symbol on everything they print, it will fulfil the requirements of a visual identity. Money and a great deal of time is spent by management and designers working out a symbol design, and by the time a solution has been agreed, the budget is depleted. The actual 'nuts and bolts' of the identity—arguably the most important part of corporate visual identity is the application—are hurriedly thrown together for a launch and the value of the image is greatly reduced or, worse, totally lost.

To create an effective corporate visual identity, the standards must be applied consistently and creatively

over time. It can be as simple as a corporate typeface
with a standard expression of the name of the organisation
and colour. Provided it is consistently applied, it should
be effective.

READ MORE ABOUT IT

Wally Olins, *Corporate identity: Making business strategy visible through design*,
    Thames & Hudson, London, 1989, ISBN 0 500 01472 8.

V+K Publishing, *The image of a company: Manual for corporate identity*,
    Architecture Design and Technology Press, London, 1990,
    ISBN 1 85454 404 7.

Per Mollerup, *Marks of excellence: The history and taxonomy of trademarks*,
    Phaidon, London, n.d., ISBN 0 7148 3838 1.

Marc English, *Designing identity: Graphic design as a business strategy*,
    Rockport Publishers, Gloucester, Mass., 1998, ISBN 1 56496 388 8.

Steven Howard, *Corporate image management: A marketing discipline for the
    21st century*, Butterworth-Heinemann Asia, Singapore, 1998,
    ISBN 9 810 08085 9.

Peter Steidl and Garry Emery, *Corporate image and identity strategies:
    Designing the corporate future*, Business and Professional Publishing,
    Sydney, 1997, ISBN 1 875680 43 8.

Flett Henderson & Arnold, *How image can make your business more successful*,
    FHA, Melbourne, n.d.

Emily Schrubbe-Potts, *Designing brands: Graphic success through graphic
    distinction*, Rockport Publishers, Gloucester, Mass., 2000,
    ISBN 1 56496 668 2.

Anistatia R. Miller and Jared M. Brown, *What logos do and how they do it*,
    Rockport Publishers, Gloucester, Mass., 1998, ISBN 1 56496 382 9.

Catherine Fishel, *Redesigning identity: Graphic design strategies for success*,
    Rockport Publishers, Gloucester, Mass., 2000, ISBN 1 56496 624 0.

Naomi Klein, *No logo: Taking aim at the brand bullies*, Flamingo, London, 2000,
    ISBN 0 00 255919 6.

A design audit

Regardless of whether the organisation is a one-person
operation such as a small office/home office, a school,
church or community group, a multinational business, or a
government department, the image is projected by a set of
pieces like a giant jigsaw puzzle. Do they fit together, or is it
just a frustrating mess like that bag of old jigsaw bits out in
the garage—maybe two jigsaws mixed together with a few
missing pieces and a few that are broken?

Are your design efforts reinforcing the organisation's
current image in the marketplace? Do they reflect the
changes taking place in the organisation and its desired
image? If not, what can you do to fix the situation?

The image is projected at its most important level by the
staff—in their understanding and consideration of buyers,

CHECK LIST

Brand management

(in roughly chronological order of
product life cycle)

☐ Research and product
   development
☐ Product placement
   – market
   – audience
   – pricing
☐ Positioning statements
☐ Creation of mood boards
   – associated lifestyle
   – attitudes
   – colours and tone
☐ Naming
   – research internationally
     for rights
   – appropriateness of meanings
     in translation
☐ Logo development
☐ Product launch
☐ Marketing, public relations,
   advertising and sales
☐ Research and monitoring
☐ Line extension
   – seasonal extension
☐ Endorsements, sponsorships and
   strategic alliances
☐ Brand guardianship
☐ Long-term strategy

[Based in part on a seminar by
Carlo Pagoda of Primo Angeli Inc.
in Canberra, March 2000]

suppliers and each other. It is evidenced in their telephone manner, their welcoming smile, their demeanour, attitude and ultimately in the job they do. But design, too, at all levels of an organisation, must serve the whole. Image projection occurs through even the smallest and seemingly least important piece of the organisation's identity.

In a worst case scenario, maybe your design efforts are running counter to the organisation's other materials and its stated objectives. A design audit looks at the visual manifestation of the organisation's image through the array of identity materials that represent the organisation to its various markets and enables a designer to identify the successes and failures and to ultimately fine tune the image being presented.

Markets

People sometimes assume their market is only the person who will use the product or the organisation's services. This person may be considered the primary target, but there are many secondary and tertiary markets to be considered. Anyone who has an operational relationship with the organisation is a receiver of its image:

- users of the service or product
- purchasers (who are not necessarily the end users)
- staff, their families and friends
- suppliers
- competitors
- potential employees
- community.

Collection of evidence

A design audit is based on a collection of all the materials produced by the organisation where its identity is in view. There should be a central collection point so that at any moment it can be accessed and assessed.

Assessment

Collecting the material can be a difficult task—but it does not end there! You need to assess whether each of those pieces is adding to the full story about the organisation, or whether it is hindering the message. Then do something about it.

CHECK LIST
Manifestations of corporate identity

Stationery range
- Letterheads
- Continuation sheets (second-page letterhead)
- Memorandum sheets
- Minute papers
- Media releases
- Facsimile cover sheets
- Business cards
- With compliments slips
- Envelopes
- Folders
- Pads and Post-it notes
- E-mail signature blocks

Advertising and marketing materials
- Television commercials
- Radio commercials and recorded messages
- Web site
- Screen-based information systems, such as CD-ROMs
- Newspaper advertisements
  - display ads
  - classified ads
- Magazine advertisements
- Direct-mail packs
- Posters and billboards
- Taxi and bus advertising
- Exhibitions and trade show displays
- Promotional calendars and giftware
- Greeting cards
- Promotional and training videos
- Telephone answering messages
- Product packaging

Publications
- Technical manuals and instructional materials
- Staff manuals and corporate planning documents
- Reports and research documents
- Annual reports and prospectuses
- Proposals
- Newsletters
- Brochures and pamphlets
- Flyers, circulars, inserts and handbills
- Catalogues and price lists
- Product literature and updates
- Guidebooks and programs
- Menus and orders of service

Various internal and external forms
- Screen-based information systems and databases
- Application forms
- Order forms, purchase orders and price lists
- Invoices and statements
- Contracts
- Job records and time sheets
- Cheques and receipts
- Requisition and packaging slips
- Questionnaires and return-mail cards

Signage
- External building signage
- Car park signage
- Directional signage within buildings
- Foyer identification
- Room identification and name plates
- Hours of business
- Vehicles
- Umbrellas and sandwich boards
- Exhibitions, trade shows and displays

Uniforms
- Counter and sales staff
- Office staff and senior staff
- Ushers and serving staff
- Delivery and receiving staff
- Ties and scarves
- T-shirts

Other
- Packaging, bags, mailing labels and wrapping paper
- Product labelling, swing tags and tickets
- Certificates
- Presentation materials
  - overhead projection cels
  - slides and computer presentations
  - handouts
  - charts and diagrams
- Interiors
  - office decor
  - retail stores
  - warehousing facilities
  - counters and booths

Identifiers

Ghostbusters. Now there was an icon. Instant recognition from a combination of classic icons—the red circle with the diagonal red stripe through it which symbolises 'no' from the 'no smoking' icon, and the inclusion of a well-recognised pictogram, a cloud with eyes which is generally agreed to represent a ghost.

Hybrid icons like the symbol for *Ghostbusters* are excellent communicators because they take two readily recognised elements and combine them to make a very clear new icon. The wisest way to create icons is to resist the temptation to re-invent the wheel. It usually helps to design them using the shape tools rather than the line tools. You can progressively simplify a silhouette in order to create an effective icon.

You also need to design an icon, logo or corporate symbol for the future. It must have a quality that will not date or is, at least, updateable. This usually translates into something using 'pure' shapes and 'classic' fonts because they will never date.

Design identifiers by cutting out paper shapes rather than drawing by hand. This forces you to consider shape over line. Alternatively, use a thick black marker and draw your symbol on a recipe card. If the symbol doesn't work because you can't fit all the detail, you know you have too much detail! You need to simplify it until it fits.

Good logos, symbols and icons generally fall into a standard frame (square, circle, triangle, octagon and rectangle), so start by deciding on the desired frame. If you are creating a suite of icons for a program or Web site, you may decide that the frame will symbolise a specific type of feature. For example, the square might represent a graphic, the circle might be a sound bite and the triangle may be an animatic.

Be careful that the triangle does not confuse the reader with a directional implication: when pointing to the right, the triangle symbolises 'forward' movement, and when pointing to the left it symbolises 'backward' movement (from the familiar video interface).

Road signs use subset coding with colour coding as well. For example, round white signs are usually speed-related, rectangular green signs are usually geographical information, and diamond yellow signs show something of the road ahead.

Options for developing corporate marks

- ☐ Symbol
- ☐ Pictogram
- ☐ Silhouette
- ☐ Picture
- ☐ Logotype (full title)
- ☐ Initial/s (one letter or an acronym)
- ☐ Monogram (interlinked initials)
- ☐ Mascot or character
- ☐ Heraldic mark
- ☐ Visual pun

The frame decision should be made before you create the internal detail that identifies the icon's specific role, because designing an icon to fit a square does not mean it will necessarily sit comfortably in a triangle if you later decide to alter the frame.

When you start defining the image inside that will identify specific features, again create the image with shapes rather than lines. Lines tempt you to put too much detail and nuance into the picture—you don't have the luxury of nuance in a 5 mm square graphic that is output on a computer screen! Equally, you can't achieve the detail when you're stitching the logo into a cloth badge or corporate wardrobe. By concentrating on shape, you will find it easier to create a successful icon.

You can certainly use curves, but on a Web-site the graphic will probably be pixelated for the site to maintain its speed of draw, so consider simplifying detail. Fortunately, anti-aliassing (see page 249) can smooth the appearance of curves on screen.

There are few standard icons that use type forms within them: P for parking; i for information; $ for money. In word-processing and page-layout programs, by necessity, some more were created: B for bold, U for underline, *I* for italic. Letterforms imply language dependence and this is why they are normally avoided. Even the $ for money is a culturally specific icon, just as the £ (pound sign), € (euro sign) and ¥ (yen sign) represent other currencies.

But you do not need to worry so much about incorporating letterforms into icons if you know that the person reading the site, program or signage will be using English.

Individualising icons
To further customise icons and make them fit the feel of the site, the style of the interface, or the corporate identity you are designing, you can do some texture mapping and apply colours that link the icons stylistically to the rest of the screen display or stationery. But consider this a separate issue—the icon should work with no texture and no colour. Adding the texture and colour is a decision made on the overall appearance of the interface or range.

Beware the icons becoming lost if they are integrated too well. The user still needs to be able to find them quickly. A soft shadow, for example, is often used to 'lift' the icon off its background.

Symbols

Symbols have an inherent problem—time is needed to establish association of the symbol with the organisation. They are, by definition, abstract. They need to be presented, explained or associated very strongly with a logo initially to enable that 'automatic' association to develop. Symbols nearly always have to be used in tandem with a logotype until recognition is instant. Once that recognition is achieved, the logotype can be dropped from many uses and the symbol can stand alone.

Logotypes/logos

A logotype, as its name implies, incorporates letterforms. Usually it is developed as a format in which the title of the organisation will consistently appear. It can be an initial, an acronym or an abbreviated version of the full title. There is usually a limited range of options developed by the designer for its use with the symbol.

Often the logotype has an 'individualising' feature—this can be spacing, kerning, ligature or swash idiosyncrasy— that will be a unique feature of the identity.

When considering the type characteristics, always look at the words in capitals and in lower case as well. Sometimes, looking at the optional letterforms that you can get in italic letterforms is also advisable. For example, in some type- faces, you can find a great *f, g* or *&* in italics. It is also quite acceptable to mix these letterforms in a logotype, as the mixture can provide that individualising feature.

Often the letterspacing and leading of the typography in a logo will be more extreme than in text setting. Characters might share a letterstroke; there might need to be a dotless i for a descender on the line above to sit comfortably with the line below; optical leading may mean that lines are unevenly leaded. Avoid having text lines too close to the logo or running off it—some designers recommend a particular spatial relationship between logo and surround- ing text and images.

Initials

Some organisations choose to use a single initial or a group of initials that may or may not make an acronym. In these cases, the letterform/s need to be carefully chosen and applied. Usually, initials will also be used with a logotype of the full name of the organisation.

The Australia Post logo
Designed in 1975 by Pieter Huveneers

Monograms

Another technique of creating a logotype is to create a monogram. This is a decorative interweaving or interlinking of the initial letterforms of a person or company name—look at the Volkswagon logo. This technique was very popular in the 19th century and you can see extant uses of it in the monograms for some unions, fire brigades and municipalities.

Mascots/promotional characters

Where would Australian advertising history be without Louie the Fly, Bertie the Aeroplane, Chesty Bond, the Redheads, Leo the Paddle Pop Lion, Zig and Zag, the St George Dragon and the Gobbledok? Corporate characters can provide liveliness to advertising materials, and often hired actors attend promotional events in character which can be more successful than just a logo.

Constable Kenny Koala
Courtesy: Australian Federal Police Museum

Characters often become a way for an organisation to communicate to a junior audience. Junior audiences, of course, have captive secondary audiences like parents, guardians and older siblings that might get the message through the junior members of the household. Constable Kenny Koala of the Australian Federal Police has had comic strips and kids columns in local papers, a television career, personal appearances at schools, fetes and community events, appeared in colouring-in competitions and conveyed many safety messages.

Corporate typefaces

A 'support' typeface that is a clear face for text or forms setting—a face that is easy to read—is often selected to complement the logotype and symbol. For this role, it is usually best to stick to traditional faces, or faces that have been developed from traditional matrices, to avoid dating the identity when a face goes out of fashion.

This face should be used in all stationery: letterheads, business cards, with compliments slips, forms and internal memos. With cascading style sheets in Web documents, it can continue into the Web site, too. It also should be used with its various fonts in all publications: annual reports, staff newsletters, corporate plan documents, reports, product literature, brochures and pamphlets—in fact, any publication that could be considered a corporate document.

Markets for identity

Choose a name for a nightclub such as 'Jitters Night Club'. Prepare three designs using the same wording. The market for each is different, but the product is essentially the same—a good night out on the town with great music, dance floor and bar. You need to differentiate the designs for each nightclub by using appropriate imagery, type, colour and style. The nightclubs are:

□   upstairs at the local football club, next door to its bistro
□   on the thirtieth floor of an exclusive, five-star international hotel in the CBD
□   below street level in the most alternative, counter-cultural area just out of the city centre.

What you produce must immediately communicate to the target audience for each of these venues. What age is the clientele? What price do they expect to pay? What style of dress should they wear? What occasions would be appropriate to celebrate there? What time of night will things really start happening? What style of music are they likely to hear? Design can help to identify all these characteristics by manipulating the choice of type and its layout, the style of illustration (if illustration is needed at all) and the colour palette chosen.

Ask a few people to identify which is which. You'll soon know whether you succeeded.

This is a great exercise if you're developing corporate logotypes, or if you're working on book titles, CD packaging, film titles and show posters.

Some organisations choose more than one 'support' typeface, but this can be an unnecessary complication, and is more difficult to handle with success.

Corporate colour palette

Another significant association in a visual identity is the colour or colours selected to represent an organisation. Starting with the colours used in the symbol and logotype, develop a suite or palette of colours that can be used for different purposes.

Code separate parts of the organisation with colours: stationery from Head Office can use the symbol with a dark-blue stripe; Research and Development can use the symbol with a bottle-green stripe; Marketing can use maroon; Manufacturing can use burnt orange. Annual report sections can then use the colour code to identify responsibility in organisation charts and graphs. The colours can also be used in signage for each of the sections, or on nametags to identify which part of the organisation a staff member represents.

There are colours that are considered trustworthy, colours that attract attention, colours that employees will wear and colours they won't... You may need to create a variation on the print and screen colour palette when it comes to designing uniforms, because some palettes do not translate well into clothing. This is why those print and screen corporate colours are often relegated to ties, T-shirts, pockets, caps, nametags and scarves, rather than suits, shirts, skirts and jackets.

Attitude

An organisation which presents a consistent attitude to its markets is well on the way to establishing an effective corporate image. If the attitude is right, a more visually diverse identity can be presented. There is great flexibility with:

■   attitude
■   a colour palette
■   a standard range of symbol and logotype applications.

An image can be projected in a more interesting way by having some in-built flexibility, so ground rules for the use of symbols, logotypes, typefaces and colours should be laid down, thus giving a set of principles for picture selection and layout that define the attitude the organisation wishes to project.

All this is dealing in intangibles and trying to make them tangible. How do you project excitement and dynamism consistently? How do you plan for it so it doesn't become stale and dated? How does the design maintain its integrity with traditional markets but also encourage new markets to discover it?

You can build an element of fashion awareness into the identity, which enables you to portray fashionable images and use fashionable patterns and colour combinations while maintaining the presence of the corporate palette. Even type treatments that are based on contemporary or fashionable practices can fit if the corporate typeface/s are used in contemporary ways. Leave room for the addition of stand-alone typographic statements so that corporate identification is made in body copy rather than in display text setting.

Always maintain a level of respect for the organisation's investment, but this doesn't mean you can't allow some play with the symbol and logotypes—don't compromise them, but have some fun with them. Can your symbol be cropped? The Qantas kangaroo has been known to party...

Corporate identity manual

Creating a cohesive corporate styling across the corporate identity means maintaining control and effectively managing each manifestation of that identity. To do that, many organisations create an identity manual. It can be as simple as a four-page pamphlet or a job file that contains bits and pieces that enables the identity to be applied appropriately. It can be a bound volume running, in some cases, to hundreds of pages. All identity manuals cover the same material to a greater or lesser extent, depending on the complexity of the identity and the number of likely users or people who will eventually apply the identity.

In the case of multinational corporations that wish to project a cohesive identity in all their marketplaces throughout the world, the answer has been to define all elements of what is often termed a 'monolithic' corporate identity. The idea is to keep it a practical document: if something isn't 'useful', it's not in the manual!

Contents generally fall into three categories, though these are of varying sizes:

- identifiers
- what to do
- what not to do.

There can be varying levels of detail from pernickety to casual, broad-brush description.

Aside from the usual title pages and introductions (preferably from the managing director, CEO, department head, headmaster, priest or president), the first section is usually on corporate identifiers. Corporate identifiers might include a symbol, a logotype, typefaces and colour palette.

The symbol might be provided in both its solid form and an outline form. It will be in black on white and white on black (its 'reverse'), single-colour forms and as full-colour versions. It will be shown in conjunction with type and on different coloured backgrounds.

The logotype might include various renditions of the company name and its divisional identification. There might be an initial format as well as the full name. The divisions might appear under or to the right of the full name in a particular way.

Corporate typefaces include the full font of the typeface used in the logotype. All other corporate text might appear in, say, only two other fonts, so those other fonts and the principal weights would also be included. There might be a description of when to use particular weights, sizes and spacing guides.

The corporate colour palette might be more than just the colours in the symbol and logo. There might be colour coding for corporate divisions. There might be slight variations in the colours when printing in Pantone inks, CMYK inks and in screen colours for Web sites and television advertising.

The section on identifiers gives all the standard specifications for reproduction, and can include details of various suppliers and bromides and digital files for accurate reproduction.

The application section includes specifications for individual pieces of the identity: print and digital applications for stationery, forms, publications, press advertising, packaging, giftware, signage, uniforms, Web sites, television graphics.

In the case of stationery, there are specifications for all type and measurements for accurate positioning. Any grids used are described and specified in detail for accurate drawing but are also usually supplied as templates on disk.

A sort of mini style manual might be included, indicating not only typing guides for positioning text on the letterhead, but also writing guides for different types of letters, memos, minutes, e-mail headers and signature blocks, and Web page content and writing style.

In the case of forms, standards are described in detail and samples shown for signature blocks, section dividers, colour coding, questions and instructional layout.

Press advertising standards include details of the borders and symbol/logotype combinations used in classified advertising and display advertising. Company mottoes or positioning statements are specified in particular typefaces and positioned in various grids.

Publications might include annual reports, technical manuals, newsletters, product literature, or any number of brochures. Full style sheets and grid templates can be included.

Signage can be for buildings (both internal and external), car parks, exhibitions and displays, trade shows, vehicles, equipment and machinery.

Uniforms can be for office staff, ushers, technical staff, work crews. The accessories can be diverse and can include some of the corporate giftware: cuff links, scarves, hard hats, spray jackets, waistcoats, T-shirts, ties and tiepins, caps, brooches, medallions.

For signage, packaging and uniforms, particular materials and fabrics might be specified. Grids for symbol/logo application and spacing in relation to building or box corners can be devised. Suppliers can be noted and combinations of colours and finishes can be specified.

In addition to including what should be done, it is useful to have a section on what should not be done. Often this will feature particular colour combinations that will not work. For example, if a background colour is the same as one of the stripes in the logo, it could cause an incorrect reading of the logo. There are many mistakes that can be made. There might be incorrect proportions used where the logo swamps the symbol. Sometimes, cramming the logo or allowing it to bleed off a page is inadvisable. This section is usually a small but important section as it helps to further define the corporate standards for consistent image control.

Corporate identifiers

Logo for Canberra Couriers
Client: Rod Whitbread

Logo for Proudman Building
Contractors
Clients: Sean and Brenda Proudman

Symbol for the Australian Amateur
Music Theatre Awards
Client: Coralie Wood

Logo for Tuggeranong Veterinary
Hospital
Clients: Kym and Malcolm McKnown

Logo for Maison de Parfum, a
perfume retail store
Client: Nina Gayne

Pictogram for the Canberra Area
Theatre (CAT) Awards
Clients: Kate Peters, Coralie Wood

Logo for a hairdressing salon
Client: John Martone

Symbol for Priority One Consulting
Clients: Karen McKenzie, Sue Bennet

Logo for a CD and concert
Client: Colin Hoorweg, Muzair Productions

All identities on this page designed by the author

Stationery programs

Bearcage Productions stationery (*above*) includes video labels and covers.
Studio: Swell Design Group

Priority One Consulting (*left*) uses a full-colour sticker for the logo to be hand-applied to envelopes, business cards and letterhead.
Clients: Karen McKenzie, Sue Bennet
Designer: David Whitbread

Stationery

A4 is the standard sheet for laser printers and photocopiers. But, of course, pieces of stationery can be any size, provided they do what is needed of them. You can feed all sorts of odd-shaped papers through a typewriter (triangular, square, parallelograms, even circles), but there are fewer options with laser printers—and with filing systems at the receiver's end—all accommodating the assumed A4 sheet. Optional sizes, though, can provide interesting format options for information and, consequently, can help a message stand out from its competitors.

Many stationery items will be based on the letterhead design which is usually printed on an A4 sheet.

Letterheads

A letterhead is normally A4 folded to 1/3 A4 and posted in a DL envelope. But an alternative is to fold the long side of an A4 letter in half to A5 and then fold the long side of that in half again to A6. This fits another standard envelope, the C6 envelope.

A letterhead is a preprinted sheet that contains all the contact information that the receiver might need, presented in an appropriate way to establish and maintain the corporate image. This will often include the symbol and logo printed in corporate colours. All the information and corporate identification will appear in the margins surrounding the text area.

These days, the back of the letterhead is often considered an appropriate place for some corporate identification or imagery as well. It can distinguish the organisation if there is an impressive look to the letterhead as it comes out of an envelope.

The main text area for the overprinted letter usually starts about one-third of the way down the page with a generous left margin of about 30 mm or more (for filing purposes at the receiver's end and for the sender's records) and a narrow right margin. Often the address of the receiver, the date of the letter and the salutation have specific alignments that are determined to complement the letterhead design.

Positioning is often defined in a typing guide sheet in the corporate style manual, or even in a digital template that is provided, so that anyone about to prepare a letter can meet the standards. A small rule or even a dot at one of the

CHECK LIST

Letterhead

- ☐ A4
- ☐ Organisation/business name
- ☐ Corporate symbols/logos
- ☐ Postal address
- ☐ Location address
- ☐ Phone number/s
- ☐ Central fax number
- ☐ Central e-mail address
- ☐ Web site address
- ☐ Positioning statement/slogan
- ☐ Other locations
- ☐ Senior staff/board/partners
- ☐ Affiliates
- ☐ ACN (Australian Company Number)
- ☐ ABN (Australian Business Number)

CHECK LIST

Invoice or 'Tax invoice'

As letterhead but with:
- ☐ ABN (Australian Business Number, required for GST claims)

Depending on your business, it may also feature:
- ☐ Product code and description
- ☐ Quantity
- ☐ Price (inclusive of GST)
- ☐ Total
- ☐ Any legal requirements

fold points makes folding to one-third for the DL envelope easier for staff.

Continuation sheets

When a letter spills over into an extra page, the organisation may choose to have a continuation sheet printed with the logo. Usually this has simply the corporate logo positioned appropriately, often smaller than the letterhead and in a similar position to the letterhead, and rarely with any textual information preprinted. The typing guide sheet for a continuation sheet will probably advise a letter identification line to start the second page, which includes the date of the letter, maybe the initials of the sender, and the page number expressed simply as '2' or '2 of 3' as preferred.

Fax sheets

A fax sheet, which is the first page of a facsimile transmission, tells the receiver who the fax comes from and how long it is. It can serve as an introductory sheet or the actual message may start on it. It is preprinted in black only on white paper as it needs to consider the output at the receivers' machines. Receivers will not necessarily be able to receive fine detail, so the design is often more solid than the letterhead—the text and symbol/logo are larger for clarity when bitmapped by the receiver's printer. Sometimes designers will use sans serif type for the fax because it is clearer than a serif type in transmission.

Sometimes the sheet is preprinted with the assumption that someone will quickly fill-in the required information by hand. But it is more likely that the organisation would prefer a generic fax sheet blank for installation onto all computers for staff to fill in on-screen and print out when needed.

Memoranda sheets and minute papers

Memos and minute papers do not need full organisational contact information like letterheads because they are mostly internal documents, but they will usually have corporate identification and a standardised look to their presentation.

The memo is headed by a standard set of four references: the names of the receiver and the sender, the subject of the memo, and the date.

The minute paper has the place and date of the meeting it documents and the title of the group that met. It lists those who attended and who apologised for not attending

CHECK LIST

Fax sheet

- ☐ A4
- ☐ Organisation/business name
- ☐ Corporate symbols/logos
- ☐ From (person)
- ☐ Fax number (sender)
- ☐ To (person)
- ☐ Fax number (receiver)
- ☐ Re (subject)
- ☐ Number of pages in transmission
- ☐ Message [area]
- ☐ Postal address
- ☐ Location address
- ☐ Phone number/s
- ☐ Central fax number
- ☐ Central e-mail address
- ☐ Web site address
- ☐ Positioning statement/slogan
- ☐ Other locations
- ☐ Senior staff/board/partners
- ☐ ACN (Australian Company Number)
- ☐ ABN (Australian Business Number)

CHECK LIST

Minute paper

- ☐ A4
- ☐ Organisation/business name
- ☐ Corporate symbols/logos
- ☐ Minute *or* Minute paper
- ☐ Date, time and place of meeting
- ☐ Present (list of people in attendance)
- ☐ Apologies (list of people unable to attend)
- ☐ cc (list of people who will receive copies of the minutes)
- ☐ Text (area)

Memorandum

- ☐ A4
- ☐ Organisation/business name
- ☐ Corporate symbols/logos
- ☐ To (person)
- ☐ From (person)
- ☐ Re (subject)
- ☐ Date
- ☐ Memorandum *or* Memo
- ☐ Text (area)

CHECK LIST
Media release

- ☐ A4
- ☐ Organisation/business name
- ☐ Corporate symbols/logos
- ☐ Media release *or* Media brief *or* For media only *or* For immediate release
- ☐ From (person)
- ☐ Name, phone number, e-mail address (for further inquiries)
- ☐ Release date (and limitations, if any)
- ☐ Headline (area)
- ☐ Text (area)
- ☐ Number of pages ('1 of 3')
- ☐ Postal address
- ☐ Location address
- ☐ Phone number/s
- ☐ Central fax number
- ☐ Central e-mail address
- ☐ Web site address
- ☐ Positioning statement/slogan
- ☐ Other locations
- ☐ Senior staff/board/partners
- ☐ ACN (Australian Company Number)

and the people who will receive copies of the minutes. The minutes follow the agenda of the meeting. Sometimes it concludes with a reference to the next meeting's date, time and place.

The cost of a preprint and colours can be avoided because they are internal documents. By providing staff with on-screen generic memo and minute blanks, they can generate the document and print it out as needed. For colour identification of memoranda and minutes, and to help staff find them in their in-trays, consider overprinting them on continuation sheets rather than on letterheads.

Media releases

'Media release' is preferred to 'Press release' in order to encompass television, radio and on-line media, as well as the traditional 'press', which were specifically the print media, i.e. newspapers and magazines.

A media release is very similar in feel to a letterhead and includes much the same corporate information, but it is often designed in a more lively or dynamic manner. A media release needs to stand out when received. It often has coloured bands at the top or in the margins that distinguish it from a letterhead. It often needs to work in a corporate folder or a specially designed media kit.

It must have a clear space for identification of the sender (usually the person to whom the media can direct further inquiries) and contact phone number/s or e-mail address. It also defines when the news can be released: 'For immediate release' or 'For release on [date]' or 'Under embargo until [date]'.

Its text has an appropriate headline and the details. It should still have a clear blank text area for scanning of the release to be effective. The media need to be encouraged to use it, so make it easy for them.

Business cards

A business card can be one of the most effective advertising investments a person can make—it is an advertisement that people carry around in their pockets that reminds them of both the individual and the organisation. A business card can also be one of the biggest design headaches because, like small press ads, there is only a small area and usually too much information to fit into it. But there is a lot happening in business card design so be creative and consider your options.

The standard size for a business card is changing from 50 × 90 mm to 55 × 85 mm, because wallets are now designed for Bankcards and other credit cards. People often keep their cards in their wallet to distribute—and the recipient often puts the card into a wallet. Make sure the ones you design fit.

This size variation has helped the design to be more flexible—there are greater possibilities, the most popular of which is simply turning the card from a horizontal to a vertical format. This often suits the information levels.

Some companies have realised the potential of the business card as a greater advertising tool. Some cards are printed on the back—restaurants might have a map showing their location; organisations might have a mission statement, corporate philosophy, guarantee or motto; some advertise new products; some service companies outline their areas of expertise; some are miniature advertising booklets; and some offer discounts. With all this extra information, some have a folded card.

Be careful how small the type gets on the business card—people need to read it easily. Consider tracking the type a little wider when it gets down to those small sizes.

Single-colour or two-colour business cards are one of the standard pieces of a corporate identity project but you will often see full-colour designs. This is partly because of the impact of computers, partly because limited-run full-colour is more readily available, and partly because competition in the marketplace is causing people to use approaches that stand out from the competition.

Coloured paper stocks, varnish or laminate, photographs, heat-raised lettering and multicoloured logos all get more attention and the recipient is more likely to keep the card—an ad in someone's pocket is a constant reminder.

With compliments slips

Designed for a short personal message, the with compliments slip contains the same amount of information as the letterhead plus a salutation line. It leaves an area for a short handwritten message to be added—this is a personal response sheet.

CHECK LIST
Business card
- [ ] 55 × 85 mm *or* 50 × 90 mm
- [ ] Organisation/business name
- [ ] Corporate symbols/logos
- [ ] Personal name
- [ ] Position
- [ ] Personal phone number
- [ ] Personal e-mail address
- [ ] Postal address
- [ ] Location address
- [ ] Phone number/s
- [ ] Central fax number
- [ ] Central e-mail address
- [ ] Web site address
- [ ] Positioning statement/slogan
- [ ] Other locations
- [ ] Senior staff/board/partners
- [ ] ACN (Australian Company Number)
- [ ] ABN (Australian Business Number)

CHECK LIST
With compliments slip
- [ ] 1/3 A4 or A6
- [ ] Organisation/business name
- [ ] Corporate symbols/logos
- [ ] With compliments *or* With the compliments of...(name and/or position) *or* With our compliments *or* Compliments
- [ ] Postal address
- [ ] Location address
- [ ] Phone number/s
- [ ] Central fax number
- [ ] E-mail address
- [ ] Web site address
- [ ] Positioning statement/slogan
- [ ] Other locations
- [ ] Senior staff/board/partners

1/3   1/3   1/3

Image area	Address area	Stamp area

15 mm

Envelope
- DL *or* C6
- Organisation/business name
- Corporate symbols/logos
- Postal address
- Postage Paid Australia
- Positioning statement/slogan
- Teaser copy

Media kits
- Folder
- Media releases
- Photographs for reproduction
- Background briefings or information sheets on:
  - organisation
  - products
  - personnel
- Contact information
- Gimmick (as a memory trigger)
- Pad and pen

Folder dies
Ask your printer what folder dies are available and if you can have a blank to design the surfaces for. Using a standard die will save money. Select a sturdy paper stock that folds without cracking and choose a stock colour that fits the corporate palette (if it's well chosen, this can save you printing an extra colour).

Envelopes

All the information Australia Post requires is a return address and a stamp or the Postage Paid Australia type where the stamp would go, but usually organisations include the name of the organisation, the symbol/logotype and some form of graphic that fits the corporate stationery range. Information is provided for identification or to encourage opening, so it can include teaser copy and imagery.

Labels, stickers and seals

Stickers can be an inexpensive method of getting corporate identification onto many pieces of stationery with little outlay. They can be used as seals on certificates and envelopes. Instead of printing the logo in colour on each piece of stationery, the one logo sticker can be printed and hand applied to business cards, letterheads and envelopes. This is appropriate for smaller businesses and organisations, but can be frustrating for an organisation that uses much stationery.

Folders and media kits

Folders with corporate identification are handy for presentations to clients, for in-house training session materials and for public distribution at trade shows. There should be appropriate corporate identification, room for a business card to be inserted inside, and they should comfortably accommodate a number of A4 sheets without them spilling out. So the size is usually A4+ (305 × 220 mm).

The number of pockets and whether they will be along the short or long side of the folder needs to be considered. One pocket may need diagonal cuts for business cards.

For a media launch, there may be a suite of materials including badges, corporate gifts, stickers, and a pad and printed information sheets. Information sheets can be overprinted on media releases, minute paper or continuation sheets, run-on copies of advertisements, memoranda or letterhead to maintain corporate identification without too much additional expense.

READ MORE ABOUT IT

Chris Foges (ed.), *Letterheads and business cards*, RotoVision SA, Crans-Pres-Celigny, Switzerland, 1999, ISBN 2 88946 390 4.

Rob Carter, *Working with computer type 2: Logotypes, stationery systems, visual identity*, RotoVision SA, Crans-Pres-Celigny, Switzerland, 1996, ISBN 2 88046 231 2.

Forms

A form might be a simple name and address registration with a few tick boxes in a pamphlet or return card, or a more detailed order form, or even a questionnaire that runs to booklet size. It can also be a response vehicle at the end of a Web site. On-screen forms have similar design issues to paper-based forms.

Once a form has been drafted, and the information it contains analysed and logically grouped, the task of designing it for ease of use begins. Users don't want to spend a great amount of time with forms, so it is best to sacrifice graphic interest to utilitarian aims. Keep it simple.

By sketching a plan for the form, you can work with modules of particular sets of information. You can create a logical flow to the form that presents the information in a sequence that suits. You can also work on the tonal arrangement of instructions, headings and fill-in boxes to create a form that is welcoming.

There are at least two users of a form: the person who fills in the information and the person who needs to read that entered information and transfer it to some other media. Both need to be able to find information quickly and accurately. It is useful to print the form in a colour different from the pen colour likely to be used by the person filling it in. Blue, black and red are the most usual ink colours that people use to fill in forms.

If a form is filled in on-screen, the ground provided for the user to type in information should be sufficient for most users to be able to read what they've entered. Usually more information can be entered than the ground will show, but there is a frustration factor if the complete entry can't be reread.

Sometimes you need to separate distinct parts of the form from others as some parts will be filled in by all respondents and some parts by only a few. You need to identify these clearly so respondents can move logically through the form.

Use numbers, coding, arrows and directions to other sections as necessary. Directional information should be clear. Rules, bands and bars of tone and colour can help this segmentation into the logical sections of information needed. Colour coding can also be effective here if the budget allows. Sans serif headings reversed out of solid black rules can separate sections.

A pattern of stripes can distinguish one question from another by changing background tone for each second question. This will stripe the form but also make the divisions clear. It also saves using dot leaders.

Instructions need to be obvious and easy to digest. Set a style for this level of information—it should be easily distinguished from the body of the form. Further instructions can be given in a narrow column or side bar. Typographic styling for them should be distinct from other stylings. This effectively codes the instructions as such.

To ascertain whether your design works, test the form with a few different people to see whether they fill it out accurately. If not, analyse why the mistakes were made and determine how you can fix them. Poorly conceived and prepared forms can collect inaccurate and ultimately unusable information.

Give specific directions for information that might be filled in by people from different countries—particularly in Internet forms. Specifying 'DD/MM/YY' (Australian preference) or 'MM/DD/YY' (US preference) helps dates. Use 'given name' (rather than 'Christian name' or 'first name') and 'family name' (rather than 'surname')—this is more multiculturally aware and respectful. Title options should include 'Mr/Ms/Mrs/Miss' and might include 'Prof./Dr/Rev.' depending on the likely respondents to the questions.

Using appropriate icons can also speed communication. The icons must be clear and unambiguous. For example, a paper clip icon can indicate that the user needs to attach something to the form.

For readability, lower-case type is recommended. We read it faster and more accurately than text set in all capitals. Do not slow down the user of the form by putting instructions and important information in capitals. Rather, distinguish that information typographically, using the type variations available to you, altering typeface, font and size.

For continuous reading, serif typefaces are recommended. But in a form there is not usually much continuous reading. So sans serif is recommended for its greater legibility (the clarity and speed with which you can recognise the letter shapes). Sans serif type is also easier to read at small sizes because of its constant stroke thickness —and you often need to fit a form into a limited area.

READ MORE ABOUT IT

David Sless, *Name and address please: A guide for form designers*, Proceedings of seminar conducted by Communication Research Institute of Australia, Canberra, 1987.

Harm J.G. Zwaga, Theo Boersema and Henriëtte C.M. Hoonhout (eds), *Visual information for everyday use: Design and research perspectives*, Taylor & Francis, London, 1999, ISBN 0 7484 0670 0.

Response area

It is important that the user of the form knows where to write the information. How many times have you got to the bottom of the form, only to realise that all your answers were written on the line above the identified piece of information instead of the line underneath? To avoid this sort of confusion, it can help to have white boxes for the user to fill in. To help them stand out, a light shade of grey or, preferably, another colour should be used in the background of the form. If printing a second colour, do not use anything heavier than 20%. If your form is printed in only one colour, do not go heavier than 10%—the dots start to distort the letterforms and inhibit legibility.

Onscreen forms have variable text area where the respondent can key-in their answer which scrolls across and down to accommodate the extra length.

Other response modes are tick boxes, check boxes or radio buttons (which can also be white on a tinted background and are filled by hand or when clicked); and sliding scales with numbers that the user circles (strongly agree/strongly disagree, and so on).

Numbers in scales should be tabbed with an even amount of space between each. An explanation of the grading system should be clearly indicated in an instruction preceding the scales.

It is not necessary to have little nicks or little boxes for each letter in address lines—like those that are sometimes provided for credit card numbers. A clear, white area of sufficient size for the information is appropriate.

Alignment and the appropriate clustering of information is important in forms so connections are clear to the user. Consistency in the way questions are asked is important within the same form or from the same organisation. If users are likely to be filling in more than one form, it can be frustrating to have inconsistent methods of asking for name, address and birth date. Internal consistency makes forms faster to fill in accurately.

DOING IT SMARTER

Tick box options

Respondents are most likely to tick boxes—even if asked to cross them! Tick boxes might follow the word they apply to in a one-line entry:

YES ☐   NO ☐   UNDECIDED ☐

They might be aligned at the left following the answer code number:

13 ☐   YES
14 ☐   NO
15 ☐   UNDECIDED

DOING IT SMARTER

Response boxes

The minimum width recommended for handwritten responses allows 5 mm for each written character. For these standard requests, the recommended width is:

☐	Given names	40 mm each
☐	Family name	50 mm
☐	Address	140 mm
☐	Business address	210 mm
☐	Postcode	20 mm
☐	Phone numbers	50 mm
☐	Fax number	50 mm
☐	E-mail address	100 mm
☐	Web URL	80 mm
☐	Credit card number	80 mm
☐	Expiry date	20 mm
☐	Date	30 mm
☐	Signature	70 mm wide and 20 mm deep

For all other blocks a depth of 7 mm should be sufficient.

Forms production

Black is the easiest colour to read for text. But other colours are acceptable, provided you use the deepest hues: chocolate brown, flag blue, maroon, royal purple and bottle green. This enables you to use a range of tints, particularly if you choose to print black and a second colour. You then have all the tints of black and the other colour and the option of printing black over the second colour, reversing the second colour through black, and reversing through black and its tints and through the second colour and its tints.

Limit the use of a second colour to tinting the background and/or colouring bars to separate sections. It is best not to use it for large amounts of text—better to use it as a coding device for levels of information and as a way of making the form look more interesting.

The paper should be matt, rather than gloss—ballpoints, pencils and markers all write better on matt paper.

The users' needs should determine all your decisions.

FIND OUT MORE ABOUT IT
The Communication Research Institute of Australia (CRIA) in Canberra has provided advice on forms and communication clarity to many corporate and government clients. They can be contacted on the Web at www.communication.org.au.

Instructions for completion

Print clearly. Illegible, unclear or incomplete application forms *Note* may delay processing.   All e

Applicant's details

Name   Prev

SURNAME   TO

GIVEN NAMES   New

Designation   TO

Date

Section/Branch

Date

Are you a permanent officer?

[ ] YES   [ ] NO

New location details

Address of dwelling/land purchased   Soli

NA

Section of a form showing instruction zone and fill-in zone
Designer: Louise Dews

Signage

Wayfinding systems are signposted using a combination of symbols and text. In areas where there will be users who speak many languages, signs need to be non-language-dependent. At airports, hospitals, stadiums and car parks—and to a lesser extent, theatres and universities—people rely on pictograms, numbering, symbol systems and colour codings with multilingual maps or computer information kiosks.

Clarity and speed of communication are paramount. Imagine how visitors or users will move in the spaces and what information they will want at any particular point. Understand their mental state—whether they will be nervous, late, relaxed, or urgently seeking assistance.

Signage should also enhance the spaces it adorns. In corporate identification, it needs to be consistent with other manifestations of the identity. The logo may need to be rejigged into a three-dimensional form. In foyers of head offices and particularly in retail outlets and trade shows, 3-D logos are a part of the fit-out.

There are different levels of production for signage, as the nature of the signage environment dictates. Permanent displays use different materials and finishes from changing displays. Low-traffic areas use different surfaces from high-traffic areas. There are public safety issues as well as public convenience to be considered.

Internal signage

Wall, floor and ceiling signage has architectural impact and implications for lighting, cleaning, wear-and-tear and sightlines. Booths and counters, corridors and doors, lift wells and stairwells all have labelling requirements that need to be in keeping with the corporate identity. They will probably use one of the corporate typefaces and possibly incorporate the identifiers and colour scheme.

Floors might have logos or directional information woven into carpets, detailed in marquetry or tiled into mosaic. Walls may be adorned with neon tubing, sculpted reliefs, tapestries, painted murals or lighting effects. Ceilings may have backlit signs, neon directional lighting in colour codes, wrought iron type...even windows may have information stuck to them or sandblasted and sculpted into their glass. In all surfaces, objects and frames can be

READ MORE ABOUT IT

Cheryl Dangel Cullen, *Large graphics: Design innovation for oversized spaces*, Rockport Publishers, Gloucester, Mass., 2000, ISBN 1 56496 692 5.

James Grayson Trulove, *This way: Signage design for public spaces*, Rockport Publishers, Gloucester, Mass., 2000, ISBN 1 56496 752 2.

Sign gallery: From the editors of 'Signs of the Times' magazine, ST Publications, Cincinnati, 1997, ISBN 0 944094 23 6.

Joan G. Salb, *Retail image and graphic identity*, Retail Reporting Corporation, New York, 1995, ISBN 0 934590 62 1.

Akiko Busch, *'Print' casebooks 10: The best in environmental graphics*, RC Publications, Rockville, 1994, ISBN 0 915734 90 7.

embedded or attached for display, information purposes or even storage.

When selecting materials for signage, remember the impact of lighting and shadows, reflections, people obscuring the view and extreme viewing angles on the clarity of the sign.

For particular events or promotions, banners, flags, free-standing units and projection techniques can be used to create an effective but quickly demountable display.

External signage

External signage has two roles: identification on the sides of buildings and at street level, and directional signage in car parks, on walkways and on fences. It can be simply painting a logo onto the building or its front door but, at the other end of the scale, it can become a major sculptural and architectural feat.

The main considerations, beyond clarity and efficiency in communication, are materials that will weather and how the signage will enhance the image of the organisation. The materials must also be able to be cleaned efficiently and perhaps consideration should be given to discouraging vandalism and defacement. Materials will shrink and enlarge in different weather conditions and temperatures so sign companies know the amount of stress a material can handle and how to accommodate these changes in the design of external signage.

The image issue has implications for lighting systems and the shadows they throw, as well as the shadows thrown throughout the day by sunlight as it moves across the signage—and its seasonal variation.

Clarity from a distance is an issue and each approach to the building needs to be considered. Look closely at highway signage; you will find that the typography features lower-case letters, widely spaced or loosely tracked. This enables our eyes to identify the letterforms by their shape from a distance and read the sign earlier.

Equally, the needs of each person arriving on site need to be considered. For example, the height of signage in the car park will be lower for a driver than the height for signage on walkways for pedestrians.

External signage also includes flags and banners that might be used for a limited time.

Vehicles

Buses, trucks, vans, trains, aeroplanes, pantechnicons, tractors, helicopters, cars, carts, horse-drawn coaches, trams, motorbikes, bicycles and even rickshaws are all vehicles which are used by various organisations to carry corporate livery.

For some businesses, a magnetic-backed printed logo on the car door is sufficient. For others, a fully detailed, total surface design is worthwhile to make a moving corporate statement.

From taxi and bus advertising to total surface design of the vehicles, an organisation wants its statement to be simple and memorable as it whizzes by its audience. Some logos that will be seen predominantly on moving vehicles should be given readability tests at speed to see if they can be accurately identified.

Creatively combining the corporate palette and identifiers, you should create impact for the vehicle that will enhance the corporate image. Consider the appropriateness of coloured reflectors within the design for night impact.

Although slogans, Web URLs and positioning statements might be appropriate, phone numbers are less so. Unless a phone number is particularly memorable, it should probably be left off a vehicle. (And you should probably leave the cute, backward type on vehicle fronts for reading in rear-view mirrors to ambulances.)

Exhibitions, trade shows and conferences

There are three distinct levels of signage at exhibits: the titling and entry area of the exhibition which might have its own logo; the signage that is seen from a distance that moves people through the exhibition and identifies the thematic areas of interest; and the detailed captioning of displays. In this way, the signposting is used as a technique of guiding visitors by placement and attraction, so they anticipate what's next and do not create bottlenecks, clogging the exhibition.

Exhibition designers must take into account this movement pattern of visitors through the area. There will be fast points where people are moving to the next significant area of the exhibit. There will be slow points where people will congregate, reading and viewing specific displays of interest. These need to have larger floor areas for congregation.

Giles Velarde in *Designing Exhibitions* has these reminders, among others, for exhibition designers:

Do remember people's eyesight varies.
Remember:
- bifocals
- short-sighted people
- short people
- tall people
- disabled people
- people who want to touch things

Do remember people have noses and ears as well as eyes.

Do remember people have needs:
- to sit down
- to quench their thirst
- to go to the toilet
- to hang up their coats
- to protect their valuables

Disney theme parks have developed people movement to an art form. Each surface even in queuing areas is considered a part of the whole experience and supports the theme, making queuing almost a pleasure!

At trade fairs, work out the approaches most visitors will make to the organisation's stand and design for those sightlines. Unfortunately, you have no control of the displays around you but you can make some assumptions of people movement through the show.

Exhibits and trade show stands—and even conferences—are often themed or have thematic events. The development of the theme is often achieved through a combination of artefacts and graphics. Using stage design techniques—including costume design for attendants—environments are recreated as time capsules for the visitor to experience. The theme experience heightens the involvement of the audience with the exhibit. A creative combination of authentic material and recreated material will often help to control costs. Use modern reproduction methods on fabrics, banners and posters to quickly create screens and dividers for the space. The more thorough the references to the theme, the more effective the whole event will be.

Lighting of 3-D graphics can be controlled to a much greater extent indoors, and you can also mostly control the angles from which material is seen, though you cannot entirely control how visitors will propel themselves through the space. You can, however, design spaces in your movement plan where you can conceal lighting, hide projectors and install computer units.

Also be aware of reflections from other exhibits and realise that visitors will obscure parts of the exhibit as well.

READ MORE ABOUT IT

Giles Velarde, *Designing exhibitions*, Design Council, London, 1988, ISBN 0 85072 223 3.

Ken Cato and Leigh Cato (eds), *Graphics in the third dimension*, Graphic-Sha Publishing, Tokyo, 1992, ISBN 4 7661 0678 4.

Conway Lloyd Morgan, *Expo: Trade fair stand design*, RotoVision SA, Crans-Pres-Celigny, Switzerland, 1997, ISBN 2 88046 263 0.

Rob Carter, John De Mao and Sandy Wheeler, *Working with type 5: Exhibitions*, RotoVision SA, Crans-Pres-Celigny, Switzerland, 2000, ISBN 2 88046 437 4.

Gail Deibler Finke, *Festival graphics*, Madison Square Press, New York, 1999, ISBN 0 942604 60 0.

Edward K. Carpenter, *'Print' casebooks 10: The best in exhibition design*, RC Publications, Rockville, MD, 1994, ISBN 0 915734 91 5.

Screen-based media

If it's on screen, it must move. It should use colour and sound. If it's on the Web, not only must it move, be colourful and be heard, but it should also be interactive and have hypertext layers and links.

All the usual rules of attracting an audience and keeping their attention apply to screen-based media.

Television and film graphics have trained your audience; their moving image literacy is at a high level of sophistication and visual comprehension. They also receive and process moving images and sound very fast, making the connections between scenes quickly and even having the ability to 'read' a video on fast-forward or rewind.

Watching television and film is instructive to the screen-based media designer, particularly when layering type and images for titling or credit sequences.

A film title designer needs to consider what will happen to the film title when it transfers to video, as it inevitably will. The film screen is wider than a television screen so the edges will be lost or the film will be distorted and squeezed or it will be reduced even further and bands of black added top and bottom. Nuance is lost in colour and detail when the lower resolution of the video and television screen is trying to recreate the film experience. A good designer recognises these limitations and sees them, rather, as challenges.

In-house, promotional and instructional videos, whether used for training or corporate communications, are competing with mainstream media for space in the audience member's head. It must be worthwhile watching or production money will be thrown away.

The speed with which the program moves needs to consider viewers' and users' attention span and reading ability. If there are sequenced text screens, for example, ensure you have left enough time for people to read the text. It is preferable to give them the controls for changing the screens in multimedia and Web sites. In television graphics, you need to test the timings with a few viewers.

DOING IT SMARTER
Inclusivity
Representation reflects the cultural diversity of the marketplace so be inclusive of different ages, body shapes, sexes, races, sexual preferences and lifestyles. Many government and commercial ads— and programs for that matter—now recognise and celebrate a broader definition of families, and are more inclusive in their representation of people of different races and beliefs. Although stereotypes still exist, we are fortunately embracing more dimensional and complex characters in mainstream media. If they feel they are included, viewers can relate better to the imagery.

READ MORE ABOUT IT
Steve Curran, *Motion graphics: Graphic design for broadcast and film*, Rockport Publishers, Gloucester, Mass., 2000, ISBN 1 56496 646 1.

Web site animation

The blinking eye, GIF-animated
sequence from Swell Design Group's
self-promotional Web site.
Studio: Swell Design Group

Multimedia

People in training or educational industries that are considering multimedia as part of a flexible delivery package, or in the information kiosk business, or in the technologically assisted sales area need to consider the full variety of media available. Some modes achieve more than others—something need not be described if it can be shown or heard. Some have drawbacks—often showing or hearing is more expensive to develop than describing in writing.

To effectively use multimedia techniques, assess which media are most appropriate for which roles and deploy them to their greatest effect. Many of these basic considerations apply equally to Web site design and multimedia project design.

In both, avoid the overuse of media. Too many media going at once—even too many media options on one page—can be confusing and distracting for the reader. Consider the appropriate placement of media within the project and build the reader's experience through the project's structure.

Whereas in a Web site you scroll, in a multimedia production you click on navigation tools and jump to continuations and other parts of the product in hypertext screens. In multimedia products, most screens are produced at a 640×480 pixels and black the rest of the screen.

Audio

There are three sorts of sound you might consider: speech or dialogue, music and sound effects. Sound editing and design is a specialised discipline where an audience is often unaware of the layering of the sound they are hearing.

To make sounds in a home sound more natural, an empty house is recorded to mix over the dialogue track in a studio. In that way, you'll hear kids in the park down the street, cars going by, a radio in the house next door, doors slamming and sprinklers going in the neighbourhood, and the usual house settling sounds like a fridge or air-conditioning system whirring. If an audience doesn't hear these ambient sounds, something will feel strange and unreal about the domestic scene you're presenting.

Sound can be used in more psychological ways by layering music tracks and sound effects with the dialogue.

DOING IT SMARTER
Interactive tests
In instructional multimedia design, you may be writing or preparing interactive tests or creating lists of choices. For example, you may ask questions on what your readers have just learnt, so they can be sure they can move on to the next section. There are three standard ways of coding the responses:
- true/false
- alphabetic options: a, b, c, d
- numeric options: 1, 2, 3.

Create feedback for each selection for correct, partly correct and incorrect answers. The feedback could be linked back to the section that discusses that topic in the preceding training material.

When a character screams, you might layer an elephant trumpeting underneath the scream to heighten the effect.

A sound file can distract a reader from a text block. You know it's true—how can you concentrate on a book with the *Grease* megamix going? Spoken or sung words can distract readers from the text. However, instrumental or wordless music and sound effects are unlikely to have the same level of distraction.

Get professional advice about the levels at which you record and play your sound files. You do not want distortion, crackling or 'white noise' like tape hiss to draw your listener's attention from the content of the product.

Avoid looped sounds where a sound file is continuously repeated. If you loop something, give the reader the option of turning it off, and provide a volume control.

Video

Video footage timing is expressed in an eight-digit code, thus: 00:00:00:00 where the first two digits are hours, the second two are minutes, the third two are seconds, and the fourth two are the number of the frame. In film there are 24 frames per second but in video there are 30 frames per second.

The moving image with sound is one of the most powerful tools available because it involves more than one of the five senses. The moving image is also something that makes multimedia 'not a book'. You are not using multimedia to its full effect if there is no movement.

Your options for video are documentary footage which is perceived as 'real', live action as distinct from animation, re-creation or dramatisation that is 'staged', and demonstrations that are either simulated 'live' action or animated.

Beware that 'gritty' realism used in police shows, which really owes more to home video than cinematography. There is a place for both but we are likely to see more of the less competent or accidental video for a while. Professional filmmakers can make a difference to how a product or organisation is perceived.

Talking heads are one of the sad clichés of multimedia—a dead giveaway that the boss wants to be seen in cyberspace. Sound files in most cases are more effective than the talking head—unless it does something funny or unusual!

Staging through dramatisations can be very expensive—just look at feature film costs—whereas documentary footage is often cheaper. You may even find a clip available through a video or film stock library that saves you shooting the footage yourself. To save wasted footage, you should script your video before shooting it.

Television directors also know what to avoid: fine patterns in clothing such as neckties and jackets can create moiré patterns on screen where the patterns appear to move, and venetian blinds in backgrounds should be avoided for the same reason. White in costumes and backgrounds flares with lighting.

Graphics

There are many types of graphics to consider in multi-media: photographs, illustrations, charts, diagrams, maps, graphs, icons, symbols and navigation tools. Many of the most powerful graphics will also exhibit a unifying feature that enables the screens within the document to look like they belong together.

A custom colour palette deploys colour in a similar way throughout a project—maybe coding particular levels of information with text or background colours; or even just producing illustrations, photographs and diagrams in a limited spectrum of colours, which can be as simple as just black, white and grey!

There is often a level of stylisation imposed on a document to achieve a unified effect. The stylisation may be in the technique used for the drawn graphics—hard, loose, soft. In the same way, there might be a particular treatment applied to photographs following scanning, even though they may have come from different photographers or photo libraries. This could be a feathering of their edges or a particular border treatment; it could be cropping in a similar way—maybe consistently zooming in on details or always tilting the horizon at lurching angles. These techniques can build the graphic 'attitude' of a document.

READ MORE ABOUT IT

Nicholas V. Iuppa, *Designing interactive digital media*, Focal Press, Butterworth-Heinemann, Boston, 1998, ISBN 0 240 80287 X.

Roy McKelvey, *Hypergraphics*, RotoVision SA, Crans-Pres-Celigny, Switzerland, 1998, ISBN 2 88046 313 0.

Bob Cotton and Richard Oliver, *Understanding hypermedia 2.000: Multimedia origins, internet futures*, Phaidon, London, 1997, ISBN 0 7148 36575.

Lisa Lopuck, *Designing multimedia: A visual guide to multimedia and online graphic design*, Peachpit Press, Berkeley, 1996, ISBN 0 201 88398 8.

Susan Fowler, *GUI design handbook*, McGraw-Hill, New York, 1998, ISBN 0 07 059274 8.

Apple Computer, *Human interface guidelines: The Apple desktop interface*, Addison-Wesley, Reading, Massachusetts, 1987, ISBN 0 201 17753 6.

Ron Goldberg, *Multimedia producer's bible*, IDG Books Worldwide, Foster City, California 1996, ISBN 0 7645 3002 X.

Andrew Bonime and Ken C. Pohlmann, *Writing for new media: The essential guide to writing for interactive media, CD-ROMs and the web*, John Wiley & Sons, New York, 1998, ISBN 0 471 17030 5.

Peter Fenrich, *Practical guidelines for creating instructional multimedia applications*, Dryden Press, Harcourt Brace College Publishers, Orlando, 1997, ISBN 0 03 009264 7.

Bob Cotton and Richard Oliver, *The cyberspace lexicon: An illustrated dictionary of terms from multimedia to virtual reality*, Phaidon, London, 1994, ISBN 0 7148 2826 2.

Lisa Baggerman, *Design for interaction: User friendly graphics*, Rockport Publishers, Gloucester, Mass., 2000, ISBN 1 56496 652 6.

Storyboarding

A storyboard is a series of frames showing changes in the imagery seen on-screen, with a script beneath that describes the action and any special effects in greater detail and includes all dialogue and references to sound effects and music. You can superimpose text, graphics or animation as required. These graphics, too, can move.

A storyboard should accurately describe the imagery you intend the audience to see; the storyboard is given to a director or production company to shoot. Storyboards are now also being created in multimedia and Web site design companies to show what the program or site will look like before going into the final costly production phase. Location finders, set decorators, costumiers, composers, editors and casting agents also use storyboards to guide their part of the process and to estimate costs.

To sell your idea to a client, the storyboard may be turned into an animatic—where the storyboard frames are filmed in real time and a soundtrack added—to give an impression of the final piece of film. Comic books use similar techniques to tell a story, but comic artists have a variable frame size and page layout issues, which you do not have with a film, television or computer screen. Create the images of your storyboard through illustration, rough sketching, photocopying, collage or any combination of these.

The techniques of sequential imagery are relatively simple—we look at one picture, look at the next and note the differences. The differences through a series of images compound and we understand the movement that is being implied in the sequence. With most sequential imagery, you need a set of three frames to define movement accurately: the beginning, middle and end of the movement. In this way an object can enter, travel through and leave the sequence quite clearly.

Objects can move forwards or backwards, towards or away from us; move to the left or right, up or down; move behind or in front of other objects; or they can turn or spin. The action can be fast or slow depending on how many frames it takes to accomplish the movement. You use cuts in the action to move the sequence on, to enhance the atmosphere and to increase the pace.

Animation

Inanimate objects and drawings have the appearance of coming to life with animation techniques. As well as its traditional uses in cartoons, television and movie screen advertising, and special effects, animation is used to create moving logos, icons and advertising for Web sites and multimedia interfaces. Many special effects are now achieved with a combination of live action and animation.

2-D animation

The more traditional form of animation, 2-D animation is based on a series of 2-D pictures that are drawn as a set of *key frames*, with the necessary multiple drawings of the movement between them called *in-betweening*. In-betweening is mostly generated by computer, once the key frames have been identified and rendered.

With film animation there are 24 fps (frames per second), but computer animation uses the video frame convention of 30 fps.

Animated GIFs

Animated GIFs are the computer equivalent of the flip book, where a sequence of slightly different still images is viewed in time and appears to move. So a set of GIF files are timed to appear in a sequence that effectively animates their subject. To speed the processing of GIFs, you might animate just a small portion of your image. Despite the jerkiness of the movement and its clumsiness in comparison to what we have come to expect from television and film animation, animated GIFs have become the standard for Web site animation. Although it takes time to load each GIF, it is still the fastest way to take advantage of one of screen-based media's greatest opportunities—to incorporate movement in otherwise static information.

Once loaded, the animated GIF sequence can be looped, creating a continuous repeating sequence. But give the viewer the opportunity to stop the looping; it is a visual distraction that very quickly aggravates.

TELEVISION SCREEN

3

4

MOVIE SCREEN

1

2

Movement

Zoom in or out

Split screen

Pan up or down

Film techniques in storyboard form

Storyboard frames are traditionally 90 × 120 mm landscape (in ratio 3:4) for a television screen; 90 × 180 mm (in ratio 1:2) for a movie screen; and similar for 9:16 plasma television screens. A text block beneath the frame contains the accompanying dialogue or voiceover (VO) and describes the soundtrack (music and effects). It also describes any action, details or visual effects that are not clearly visible from the frame.

Movement within the frame is shown by arrows. For example, in a chase sequence, a character may run through a particular scene and appear twice or more in the same storyboard frame to save redrawing the background. The arrow between the two drawings will indicate where the person has moved within the frame.

A *close-up* (CU) is shown by drawing the character or object larger in the frame. A *zoom in or out* is shown by drawing a miniature frame in the same dimensions as the outer frame and connecting the corners with fine lines. In the text block below the frame you define whether the zoom is a 'ZOOM IN' or a 'ZOOM OUT'.

Panning is where a stationary camera turns or tilts from right to left, left to right, up or down. It is shown in a storyboard by stretching the frame in the direction of the pan. In the text block beneath you define the direction of the pan, e.g. 'PAN L–R' or 'PAN DOWN'.

Tracking is where the camera physically moves to follow the action. It can be drawn the same way as panning with the instruction to 'TRACK'.

A *cross-fade* is a technique of dissolving one image into another. As one scene fades out, the next scene is faded in over it. It is indicated in a storyboard by a cross connecting the two frames.

Morphing is a special effect where one character or object turns into another by animation. In a storyboard it can be shown as before-and-after frames with a cross-fade connecting them. The text block below would simply state the character/object was morphing.

A *split screen* is where two or more moving images are sharing the same screen. It might be the classic split down the middle showing two people across the world talking to each other on the phone or it could be a bird's-eye view of the action with a close-up of a race. You just show the split screen as it would appear in the frame.

When *layering* or sandwiching film with film or film and graphics, you create the resulting image in the storyboard frame and explain below.

Special effects (FX) can be shown in the frame and explained in the text block below it. 'SFX' indicates 'sound effects'.

Pan L–R or R–L

Cross-fade

3-D animation

3-D animation describes that in which characters or subjects and the space in which they move are first modelled. This has been achieved with puppets, plasticine (*claymation*) and paper cut-outs in cartoons and training films but, in many cases, this now involves creating a wireframe skeleton in a 3-D computer-modelling program, which is then rendered with techniques such as texture mapping. The shape can also be given transparency, reflection or refraction attributes. Lighting is then played on the shape, often with multiple light sources of differing intensities. Then the movement of the object or character and the movement of the point of view and light sources are specified. Most computer games and special effects for movies are created in this way.

Animating logos and other 2-D graphics

There are some basic moves that will animate even a two-dimensional form. It can simply enter and exit a frame; it can grow or shrink; it can spin and stop. You can close in on a very fine detail in an extreme zoom, and pull out to the full logo in frame. You might tilt the horizon rather than the logo to imply movement. Simply condensing the logo can have the appearance of falling forwards or backwards if condensed from top to bottom, or turning sideways if condensed from left to right.

But with digital publishing applications such as Web sites and multimedia, you must consider three-dimensional form, time and movement within space, and combine them with sound effects and music to use the media effectively. You could be titling television and video programs, even in-house or training videos; or preparing interactive graphics for Web sites, games software and multimedia packages; or creating a corporate signature for film, television and Internet advertising; or creating a virtual reality space.

Sometimes you will be working with graphic materials such as symbols and logos that work in two dimensions— and still need to work in their two-dimensional forms— that also must work in these new contexts. You might also be working with something that is well established in print materials and you do not always have the luxury of designing for the new forms.

Basic 2-D movement strategies

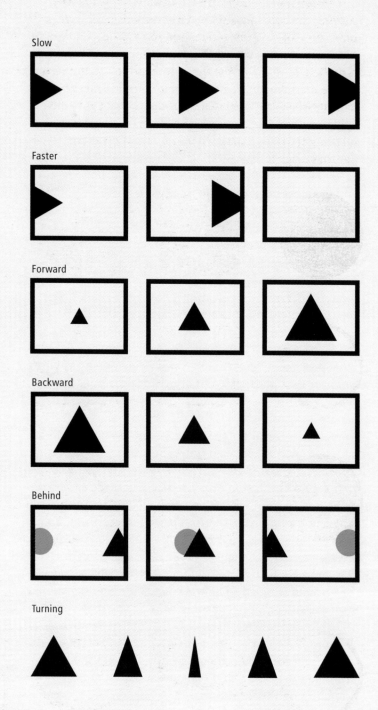

One of the easiest ways to approach animation of a two-dimensional form is to give it a third dimension. Then, moving in space around the three-dimensional form, you have more options for interesting moves. Adding the third dimension can be simply imagining the form is cut out of a slab. Better than this, though, is to look at a triangle and see a cone or half cone; or look at a circle and see a sphere; or look at two concentric circles and see a car tyre or even a sphere with a crater; or look at a line and see a piece of wire lurching through space or a thin plane like we imagine Saturn's rings to be!

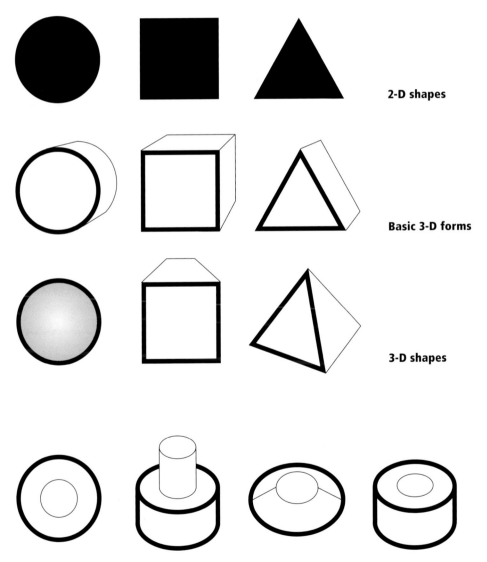

2-D shapes

Basic 3-D forms

3-D shapes

A 2-D design (left) with three representations of alternative 3-D forms based on it

Once the third dimension is added, you can explode it into its components. You can then assemble them or move them around until they are all in the right position to read the logo—like setting up an unruly family for a Christmas portrait for grandma. This assembly might be read accurately from one viewpoint but look quite odd from other views. It could be an optical illusion that obscures the logo (say, starting from behind the logo and moving to the front). You might move through as if it's transparent.

Also, since you now have the third dimension, your light source can become dynamic—that is, the light source or multiple light sources can move about your shape, casting shadows that enable its dimensionality to be seen. Similarly, as your viewpoint changes, the shadows alter.

Light intensity also alters colour perception, so your light source intensity may vary in order to play different colour effects across your 3-D form. As a simple example, you will probably recognise the clichéd logo bathed in the warmth of a sunset that deepens into evening with occasional flashes from passing shooting stars!

You might also texture-map each piece. Like gift wrapping, texture mapping applies a veneer to a three-dimensional rendering. It might be applying wood grain or a chrome finish. With chrome, glass and other reflective finishes, you can distort your backgrounds in your logo. You can then project this shape in perspective from a given viewpoint. Simply altering the viewpoint progressively sets up an animated sequence. You can approach it in a zoom in or move away from it in a zoom out; you can maintain a set distance from it but slowly move around it in a pan; you can follow it as it moves through space in a tracking shot. If you take a low viewpoint, your logo will look monumental, or you could fly over it for a bird's-eye view.

It can fade in or fade out. It can cross-fade where as it fades out another image fades in. It can morph as a smooth transition into something else or from something else. You might ripple or melt the logo or wave it like a flag. Any number of distortion filters can produce interesting effects.

READ MORE ABOUT IT

Kit Laybourne, *The animation book: A complete guide to animated film-making—from flip-books to sound cartoons to 3-D animation*, Three Rivers Press, New York, 1998, ISBN 0 517 88602 2.

Martin Lambie-Nairn, *Brand identity for television: With knobs on*, Phaidon, London, 1997, ISBN 0 7148 3447 5.

Web sites

A Web site, like all graphic design, should be user-focused. Through talking with people most likely to be interested in the product and imagining how the expected user will respond to the design, you develop a user-focus: Is it going to scare them off? Is it using language that is comfortable and understandable for them? Does it have a logical flow for someone with their level of knowledge about the product or information? Once they are interested, is there an ease—or speed—of movement through the information? Is there a consistent application of layout, colour usage and informational hierarchy throughout the site?

Frustration factors in Web sites abound. It may be slow to load because it is graphics-heavy. It might have annoying details like looped animations or sounds or flashing buttons. It might be content-listed in an organisation-based hierarchy rather than a user-based hierarchy. Or it might just have too many levels to navigate successfully. Maybe its links are not flexible enough and visitors cannot get where they wish to go next without many backward steps.

Try to give the reader only three clicks to the information they need. This has site-plan implications—how do you create a hierarchy that enables you to explain the increasing complexity of the information but still retain only four levels of site? Three clicks beyond the home page is the fourth level.

Scrolling to the right can be cool. Scrolling down is ubiquitous. But scrolling both ways on the one page is incredibly frustrating. Plan it better.

Screen sizes are measured in pixels and the standard Web screen is recommended to be 480×640 pixels. However, while this may be the screen area, it is not all usable area so users could be thankful for a smaller screen area on the site. A screen area of 600×310 pixels will work with no scrolling in both the major browsers, Netscape Navigator and Microsoft's Internet Explorer. Navigational icons should appear at both the top and the bottom of each page if vertical scrolling is necessary.

Keep the site fast, both in the site loading time and the time it takes to navigate. Spare the scrolling in early pages! If you have large image or sound files, tell viewers how large and give them the option to load them or not. At this point, avoid the big multimedia experience in a Web site

In *Hypergraphics*, Roy McKelvey discusses well-designed sites: 'Well-designed web sites have several things in common. First, they have a clear understanding of their audience. They are designed to provide specific information to users in an efficient and appropriate manner. Second, they focus on using web technologies not for their own sake, but for their power to improve the site's message and services. Well-designed sites are simple in conception and consistent in their organization and interaction. Third, they are designed to accommodate change and growth. Web sites are, almost by definition, evolutionary documents.'

According to Jakob Nielsen in *Designing Web Usability: The Practice of Simplicity*, the four criteria that are the foundation of good Web design, based on things users most want, are:

H   high-quality content
O   often updated
M   minimal download time
E   ease of use.

If you can provide these four elements, users will be happy and you will have a good site. But it is not enough to simply give users what they want. You need to go beyond the four basics to have a truly stellar site. To move from HOME design to a HOME RUN design, add the three extras:

R   relevant to users' needs
U   unique to the on-line medium
N   net-centric corporate culture.

Jeffrey Veen, in *Hot Wired Style*, describes the two extremes of Web document structure: 'On the one hand, some sites are a vast sea of information, organized rigidly with a strong sense of hierarchy: they're all about function. Others are a pure expression of artistry, with sparse information presented through a strong aesthetic sense: these are all about form.

'Think of the two extremes as the library and the gallery.

'The library has a vast collection of information available in numerous formats. It isn't concerned with the display of the information, just the method of organization. It expects that you know what kind of info you want, so its main goal is a clear, organized system to help you find what you want as quickly as possible. It doesn't necessarily put the best books closest to the front door; it doesn't open their pages to give you a peek.

'Conversely, the gallery offers a controlled presentation of its artwork. It is a carefully orchestrated space designed to give every visitor the same, meticulously curated aesthetic experience...

'Being clear on where your project fits on the library–gallery continuum is the first step toward successfully navigating the maze of compromises and tough questions that working on the Web will demand of you. The goal is to balance pure information with an aesthetic that not only complements the message but also becomes a part of the voice.'

because the file sizes are simply too large and few users will be bothered. Be happy with something considerably less than broadcast-quality video and sound; jerky animation and odd pixel dithering will be with us for a while.

Use live graphics and hot text links that jump the reader to another part of the site. This can avoid opening layer upon layer.

When creating the structure for the contents, think about what the target audience might want to know, not about how it is most convenient to get the information from sections of the organisation or how you can re-jig last year's annual report and product brochures.

Do not lead off with a profile of the managing director if that is not the most important piece of information readers need to know. Too many times, a Web site reflects internal organisational structures and politics, rather than catering for most external visitors' needs. Having a home page for each section of the organisation is not necessarily the most appropriate solution for the site visitor.

Almost certainly, the most important information will not fit an alphabetical or even a chronological hierarchy. Sections can be identified by different colours. Choose a palette of colours that look consistent in intensity when seen together on the home page. The colour can be a live graphic that transports the reader to the next section with a click. The colour is then repeated at the head of that page. Colour coding can mean the next visit to the site will be faster.

Keep navigational icons intuitive. This will enable quick responses and propel your reader through the site. Make the entry sequence and home or core page/s both attractive and fast to load. A reader's decision to stick with the site can be made by this attraction alone. Does the site look worth entering? Put the best contents forward and imply how easy it is to get to them. This is the reception desk— make it welcoming and appropriate.

Use corporate identification—colours and logos should be used that relate the site to all other manifestations of the corporate identity in the marketplace, from printed communications such as letterheads, brochures or annual reports to the television identity. Consistency of image is important.

Sometimes people confuse consistent with inflexible or, worse, boring. Consistency of application means that the target market receives non-conflicting messages. With a cutting-edge print and television identity, a boring text-only first-generation Web site with a logo and the ubiquitous grey background is not the way to go. Equally, with a restrained, subtle and distinctive print identity and refined product brochures, a Web site that is a visual fireworks display with wild type and blinking graphics will not be very appropriate.

Avoid blinking or flashing graphics and looped animations and sounds, or at least make them stoppable. Flashing and movement set up a distraction that constantly drags readers' eyes to that point of the page and away from other important information. It can certainly highlight that single aspect to which you're drawing attention—but so effectively that you won't communicate anything else without creating a frustration factor. People will have to be determined to ignore or read through the distraction. Similarly, continuous sound can become a frustration factor.

Backgrounds can also create confusion if they begin to impose themselves onto the text. Readability can suffer. Text and background colours need to be separated by a tonal contrast (dark against light). Any variation in the background must maintain the tonal level of the background otherwise it starts to interfere with the legibility of the letterforms in the foreground. If the background has an image or a pattern, ensure it is subtle and 'ghosted' sufficiently for the text to be read unhindered.

Use e-mail links and links to other sites as a service to readers. But try not to lose readers to other sites too early. Internal links are more important upfront to get readers further into the site. Hot-linked icons and images are a fast way of propelling readers through a Web site or multimedia program.

Computer users are accustomed to visual representation of concepts through icons—thanks mostly to the Macintosh interface that was pioneered at Xerox and is now the basis of Windows. The system of icons created to navigate programs, from selecting programs from the desktop, to selecting tools from toolboxes and selecting text attributes from rulers and menus, have currency and relevance to readers of screen-based material. Because the Web and multimedia are read on computer screens, it is safe to assume readers are familiar with screen-based icon systems. Do not lose this familiarity by creating a series

DOING IT SMARTER
Sound loops
Sound files can play once and stop, play a defined number of times and stop, or be looped to play continuously. If you wish the Web site you're designing to have a distinguishing sound, create a background sound that is on an infinite loop. For sanity's sake, keep it to a low volume. Better still, with all sound files, give the viewer the control to change the volume or stop the sound altogether.

DOING IT SMARTER
Logos on background colours
When you want logos and other graphics to sit comfortably on the background of the site page, apply the transparent option to the background area of the logo or image GIF to blend it into the site background. Alternatively, if the background is a flat colour, simply make sure the GIF background has that exact hexadecimal colour description of the site background.

DOING IT SMARTER
Site testing
Test the site in at least the two
leading browsers, Netscape
Navigator and Microsoft's Internet
Explorer, before loading it. Observe
how the pages look as each browser
converts the HTML tags, and check
how quickly the various files load.
Get someone who is unfamiliar with
the site to surf it with you, and make
any changes to improve or streamline
the site. Check it in both browsers
again, not just the current versions
but also the last two versions of
those browsers. Most surfers do not
upgrade their browsers on every
release.

of new symbols for them to learn. Rather, use that familiarity to create hybrid symbols that individualise your document but retain the readability and instant recognition that classic icons have.

All decisions should be made by asking: What will readers do now? What will they want to know? What will keep them interested?

READ MORE ABOUT IT

David Siegel, *Creating killer web sites: The art of third-generation site design*, 2nd edn, Hayden Books, Indianapolis, 1997, ISBN 1 56830 433 1.

Jeffrey Veen, *Hot Wired style: Principles for building smart web sites*, Wired Books, San Francisco, 1997, ISBN 1 888869 09 7.

Jakob Nielsen, *Designing web usability: The practice of simplicity*, New Riders Publishing, Indianapolis, 2000, ISBN 1 56205 810 X.

David Siegel, *Secrets of successful web sites: Project management on the world wide web*, Hayden Books, Indianapolis, 1997, ISBN 1 56830 382 3.

Vincent Flanders and Michael Willis, *Web pages that suck: Learn good design by looking at bad design*, Sybex, Alameda, California, 1996, ISBN 0 7821 2187 X.

Roger Black with Sean Elder, *Web sites that work*, Adobe Press, San Jose, California, 1997, ISBN 1 5680 346 7.

Robin Williams and John Tollett, *The non-designer's web book*, Peachpit Press, Berkeley, 1998, ISBN 0 201 68859 X.

Roger Pring, *www.type: Effective typographic design for the world wide web*, Weidenfeld and Nicolson, London, 1999, ISBN 0 297 82539 9.

Anne T. McKenna, *Digital portfolio: 26 design portfolios unzipped*, Rockport Publishers, Gloucester, Mass., 2000, ISBN 1 56496 467 1.

B. Martin Pederson (ed.), *Graphis: New media*, Graphis Press, Zurich, 1996, ISBN 1 888001 06 2.

Molly Holzschlag, *Web by design: The complete guide*, Sybex, Alameda, California, ISBN 0 7821 2201 9.

Jennifer Niederst, *Web design in a nutshell*, O'Reilly, Sebastopol, California, 1999, ISBN 1 56592 515 7.

Laurie McCanna, *Creating great web graphics*, 2nd edn, MIS Press, New York, 1997, ISBN 1 55828 550 4.

Ken Coupland (ed.), *WebWorks: Navigation*, Rockport Publishers, Rockport, Mass., 2000, ISBN 1 56496 662 3.

Marc Phillips, *Behind Australia's most successful websites*, Bookman, Melbourne, 1997, ISBN 1 86395 280 2.

Andy Shafran, *Creating your own web pages*, 2nd edn, Que Corporation, Indianapolis, 1997, ISBN 0 7897 1232 6.

Paul McFedries, *The complete idiot's guide to creating an HTML web page*, Que Corporation, Indianapolis, 1996, ISBN 0 7897 0722 5.

Geekgirl [Rosie Cross], *The friendly grrls guide to getting on the internet*, Geekgirl, Sydney, 1997, ISBN 0 646 277793 6.

CHECK LIST
Web site or e-zine

Entry sequence
- ☐ Splash screen or front door (keep it fast)
- ☐ Animated sequence to open (keep it fast)
- ☐ Entry tunnel (keep it interesting, interactive and fast)
- ☐ Counter to track hits

The principle behind the splash page/entry sequence is that it introduces the site while the rest of the site is being opened and gives an instant response to the user. Therefore, the most important factor is speed of response. Keep it graphically interesting, but condense the files as far as they can go and then some. This is an opportunity to reveal a part of the corporate identity but not necessarily the whole—hold back something for the home page!

Consider having a set of interchangeable splash pages that will give a different look to the site over a few visits.

Possible lures for entry
- ☐ Free stuff
- ☐ Gimmicks
- ☐ News
- ☐ Deals
- ☐ Games
- ☐ Club membership
- ☐ Questionnaire

Home page or core page/s with internal links
- ☐ Contents list
- ☐ Site map (hyperlinked?)
- ☐ Pictures
- ☐ Pull-quotes
- ☐ New features
- ☐ Start of content
- ☐ Legal statements as required
- ☐ Last update

Some of the most effective home pages have attractive graphic banners, but realise that it is still just a person looking at a screen— size is not so important but corporate identification is. The home page is like a contents list and visitors want everything active. They do not want to have to click into a secondary contents list because the graphics or the dot points or the words were not links.

Content of the site with internal and external links (local and remote)
- ☐ About us
- ☐ News and regular updating
- ☐ Help
- ☐ Frequently asked questions (FAQ)
- ☐ Catalogue
- ☐ Advertisements
- ☐ Firewalls for registered user access only
- ☐ Security system for e-commerce, confidentiality and privacy

Graphic interface
- ☐ Banners
- ☐ Consistent colour palette, text
- ☐ Links or hyperlinks

- ☐ Clickable image links
- ☐ Image maps and text option
- ☐ Images with text alternatives
- ☐ 360° sewn images
- ☐ Warnings for large file sizes (audio/video/image)
- ☐ Optional downloading of large images
- ☐ Interlaced images (a low-resolution image loads first and is gradually upgraded to higher resolution)
- ☐ Preloading image files
- ☐ Tables
- ☐ Logos
- ☐ Backgrounds
- ☐ Video clips
- ☐ Audio clips or sound bites
- ☐ Games
- ☐ Animation
- ☐ Controls for play, stop and volume
- ☐ Virtual reality experience
- ☐ Rollovers

Text colours
- ☐ Body text
- ☐ Links
- ☐ Visited links
- ☐ Pull-quotes
- ☐ Headings

Navigational aids
- ☐ Page header
- ☐ Scroll bars
- ☐ Buttons
- ☐ Icons
- ☐ Frames
- ☐ Search capability for the site
- ☐ Links to content further down the same page (saves scrolling)
- ☐ Page footer (include last update, copyright information and other legal status, contact details and navigational links)

Exit sequence
- ☐ Response form
- ☐ Order form
- ☐ Chat line, forum or guest book
- ☐ E-mail feedback link or mailto commands

Graphical user interface (GUI)

Up until recently, with the advent of multimedia and Web design, the design of a graphical user interface (called GUI—'gooey') was a fairly rare thing to encounter. Now with many people creating the interface for Web documents and the user's guides for multimedia productions, this previously specialised area is becoming more mainstream.

So how do you approach the design of a successful interface? As far as possible, keep the interface intuitive. If the icons and screen layout maintain a certain familiarity or ease-and-speed-of-recognition factor, the interface should be successful. As in many design projects, good use of visual metaphors will enable the user to employ previously learned modes of information retrieval.

To work out how a design can be recognised intuitively, we need to consider the number of interfaces we encounter daily. There is your microwave, but most microwaves use a word-based, rather than an icon-based, interface. Word-based interface is fine but has limitations—it is more time-consuming and is language-dependent, but it is faster to load.

Consider the road user interface—signs, lights, road markings and services; and the car's internal interface— petrol gauge, speedometer and dashboard system. These systems give us red warnings, flashing lights for attracting attention, various sirens, the red octagon stop symbol, the give-way triangle, the broken lines for crossing if you need to pass, the green, amber and red circles that indicate go, caution and stop respectively, and the gauges that fill or empty (which are akin to the file transmission gauges that fill when the file is complete). The system is rich in icons.

On a similar tack, mapping is rich in symbolism that may be appropriate to consider as a part of the interface design primer: the symbols for farms, historical sites and industrial areas; information counters or booths; highways, surfaced and unsurfaced roads; and others.

What about much older interface systems? There are the systems used for star signs in horoscopes (not the illustrations, or pictograms, but the streamlined versions of them that create almost abstract symbols), the Christian cross (which can also symbolise death due to its use in cemeteries) and fish, the male and female signs (not the little man and woman pictograms used to label public toilets, but the circles with, respectively, a diagonal arrow and a downward cross).

Intuitive user interfaces often use metaphor as an effective 'vehicle of exploration', according to David Siegel in *Creating Killer Web Sites*. His examples of metaphors include: 'galleries, comic strips, television channels, TV remote controls, magazines, tabloids, store environments, museums, postcard racks, amusement parks, going inside things (computers, human body, buildings, ant farm, and so on), safaris, cities, and cupboards.'

Horoscope symbols

On Netscape the symbol for returning to the home page is the classic five-sided house made from a square and a triangle. The letterbox pictogram is used in e-mail systems. These are virtually instinctive symbols. If you asked a child to create a symbol for home or letterbox, those simple shapes are probably close to what they would create. Somewhere inside our heads we respond to these shapes as having these meanings. This is good interface design.

Other signs that seem to be instinctively understood are the heart for love, the ear, speaker or music note for sound, the eye for vision or picture, the old-fashioned movie projector or camera—or even the clapper boards with the black and white diagonals—for moving image. These are handy for multimedia selection...

Then there is the sound system. Like a microwave, it relies for some information on words. But the important element here is the symbol (or icon) language used in the cassette deck and CD deck buttons. The forward triangle, rewind triangle, fast-forward double triangle, stop square and pause double lines constitute one of the most influential symbol systems recently developed. You will also have noticed how we use them instinctively in multimedia productions. Although the symbols started with cassette tape players, they have moved through CD players, video players and into multimedia, Web documents and information kiosks.

Another daily interface we encounter is the computer screen, which features windows, icons, rulers, menus and tool boxes. The symbols that have been developed to speed our use of this interface are quite well refined now and, due to the fact that readers of screen-based information are sitting at a computer, it is a safe assumption that the interface can incorporate some conventions from computer interface design.

Do not stray too far from symbols that work in an effort to create a new interface. If a reader must learn the new system before using the product you design, you will lose a number of potential users. As Jeffrey Veen asks in *Hot Wired Style* (p. 83), 'What would television be like if every show had a different remote control?' It is commonsense to use a familiar navigation system in your interface design.

You might create a version of an existing symbol that stylistically fits your design. Use a colour palette that fits the site backgrounds and images, and a texture or illustration style that sits comfortably with the display type and site metaphor. But be careful not to obscure the clarity of the navigation system with style for the sake of style.

The best icon systems use an interface that weds recognisable pictorial, symbolic, sound and moving elements in a layout that streamlines selection process. Users don't want to have to dart all over the screen with the mouse or scroll up and down the page to find the options. The nature of the system you develop should have ease of use at its core with minimal explanation needed for the interface. That way, the reader can concentrate on the content and message, rather than how they will extract the message.

Using HTML

If you are designing text for the Internet, you have probably come up against the limitations of the Hypertext Markup Language for text layout. Although many of the limitations for what is called display text (headlines, feature titles, section headers) are being circumvented by using text-based GIF image files, the majority of text content still needs to work within the HTML boundaries.

For typists who learnt their skills BW (Before Wang—we could call this pre-history), this is not a problem, because the limitations of HTML resemble the limitations of the old golf-ball typewriter. So how did you create readable—even quite pleasant-to-look-at—documents a few technologies ago? And what use is that for HTML applications?

There isn't any reliable typeface selection capability because, even with cascading style sheets, you are dependent on the user's font collection. The default type on the reader's screen is the font they will see, regardless of the font in which you create your document. Times Roman, Helvetica, Courier...it doesn't really matter given that you don't have the controls. Don't lament it, move on. Be at peace with the Web and go placidly amid its noise and haste; no doubt cyberspace is developing as it should.

Type attributes

The HTML type attributes appear greatly limited but they are adequate. You have the option of bolding, italicising or underlining text; you have a number of heading sizes; and you can capitalise. You can create lists and use indent levels. Given those attributes, you have more than enough flexibility to create readable text documents.

David Siegel, in *Creating Killer Web Sites*, describes his restaurant model for Web sites: 'I use a restaurant metaphor when thinking about sites. You hear about a restaurant from an advertisement or friend, or discover it while passing by. You check out the daily specials chalked on a board out front and smell the aroma in the doorway.

'Once through the door, you make a quick stay-or-bail decision. In a popular restaurant, you might have to wait for a table. If you stay, someone shows you to a table and hands you the menu. You make your selection.

'When the food arrives, you have no urge to rearrange the various items on the plate. The food and presentation are the creations of the chef. You sample the various items, skipping among them, mixing flavors and textures.

'When you are finished, you have dessert, ask for the bill, and pay. You leave a tip, pick up the card next to the cashier, and maybe exchange a few pleasant words with the owner. Later, when you are hungry again, you return or you don't, based on the quality of that first experience.'

File types

The file types you are most likely to encounter in Web site and multimedia design are:

Text, page and site description files
HTML   Hypertext Markup Language
SGML   Standard Generic Markup Language
DSSSL   Document Semantic Style Specification Language
XML   Extensible Markup Language (subset of SGML)
CSS   Cascading Style Sheets (subset of HTML)
EPS   Adobe's Encapsulated PostScript
PDF   Adobe's Portable Document Format
SVG   Scalable Vector Graphics

Image files
PICT   Picture
TIFF   Tagged Image File Format
GIF   Graphical Interchange Format   ('giff' not 'jiff')
JPEG   Joint Photographic Experts Group   ('jay-peg')
PNG   Portable Network Graphics   ('ping')
Wavelets

Video and animation files
QTV   Apple's QuickTime Video
AVI   Audio Video Interleave
M-JPEG   Motion JPEG (from the Joint Photographic Experts Group)
                                                     ('em-jay-peg')
MPEG   Moving Picture Experts Group   ('em-peg')
MNG   Multiple-image Network Graphics (PNG animation)
                                                     ('ming')

Audio files
MIDI   Musical Instrument Digital Interface   ('middy')
RealAudio
QTV   QuickTime Video can carry audio layer only
AIFF   Audio Interchange File Format
WAV   Waveform Audio File Format
SND   Sound
MP3   MPEG audio layer

Three-dimensional site description files
VRML   Virtual Reality Modelling Language
QTVR   Quick Time Virtual Reality (seamless 360° pix)

Site transfer—how computers 'talk' to each other
FTP   File Transfer Protocol
HTTP   Hypertext Transfer Protocol

Stress within text is normally created using italics because they do not interrupt the line. Italics can make a sentence read differently—compare 'It was *really* excellent' with 'It was really *excellent*' and even 'It *was* really excellent'. The only limitation of italics in Web site design is their low screen resolution, which often makes them a little confusing to read for any length of time. A single word or phrase is mostly fine. Extensive use of italics and the <I> tag is not recommended for Web documents.

If you are signalling the hypertext (linked text behind the textual reference), colour variation and underlining are used for the link. Readers will assume they can jump to another part of the document by clicking on this piece of information. This is the only excuse for underlining—which limits readability by striking through and confusing the pattern recognition of the descending characters of the letterforms. Colour variation by itself should be enough to signal the link.

Underlining also interrupts the flow of the text and signals the reader to read what is underlined out of context. That is, the underlines are seen before the paragraph is read, so the reader often reads the type that is underlined first and then returns to the beginning of the paragraph. This means the reference is then out of context, but this speed of scanning is what hypertext is all about, so underlines are used. But as far as possible, avoid the <U> tag.

Bold type is usually reserved for headings and, in HTML, bold is used for all heading levels, so avoid using paragraphs of bold text. Changing a word to bold mid-sentence is the same as underlining it—do it only if you want it to stand out for some reason.

Given that you do not have luxuries like leading and other linespacing attributes unless you're using CSS, size variation in headings is fine. But once you start using more than about three sizes in a hierarchy, the reader will be confused. Within the three sizes, introduce variations like full capitalisation or italics. This will immediately give you nine possible heading levels—more than enough.

Most Internet documents ignore the possibility of capitalising headings. Just changing the size of a heading is often not sufficient to create a successful hierarchy of information. Some of the smaller bold headings are too small for comfortable reading on screen anyway, so by using full capitals, you can double the heading possibilities.

Jeffrey Veen in *Hot Wired Style* likens designing for the Web to playing with Lego: 'Every piece of Lego fits with every other piece, just as every HTML document can be viewed on any computer in the world. However, you can't make 45-degree angles in Lego, and the chunky projects that result from building with Lego parts show that. Same too with HTML. In its purest form, HTML cannot control the simplest of graphic layout techniques; there is no face or font size selection, no margin control, and very little ability for placing objects in relation to one another. So the Web's visual building blocks don't make designing easy.'

Netiquette?
Type in all capitals is considered to be 'shouting' in e-mail and Web sites. Although it may be considered good etiquette to avoid all capitals in digital publishing, avoiding capitals is more accurately—and valuably—aiding readability.

Remember one point about the use of capitals—capitals slow down reading so use them only for short headings— one- or two-word headings are fine. For the same reason, never type a paragraph in full capitals.

Horizontal rules are used for separation. Use the <HR> tag sparingly and avoid decorative and animated rules. Do not use the horizontal rule as an underline to a heading, otherwise it separates the heading from the text that logically follows it. Rather, use it as a cut-off line for a section. As far as possible, avoid using horizontal rules— they just increase the scrolling the reader has to do.

Don't get carried away with lists within lists, menus within menus, wheels within wheels... Avoid large and animated bullets. Two levels of indent are usually enough so fight the temptation to indent recklessly.

Cascading style sheets (CSS)

The principles on which CSS is based are greater typo- graphic and page layout control, more akin to the production of style sheets for a print document. The style sheet is loaded first and contains all the typeface and font attributes and layout requirements of the document including spacing and colour specifications. These become the 'rules' for application when the document requires a particular tag.

However, you are reliant on the font set that is installed on the user's machine. This is one of the most significant limitations of CSS. If users don't have the font you have defined, a font will be substituted from their font set.

There are two methods of applying the cascading style sheet. You can create the style sheet (which might be named '.../stylesheet.css') as a separate document that all the other text documents in the site are linked to. In this way, any change that is required need only be made to the style sheet and it will automatically flow through the rest of the site. The second way of applying the style sheet is to import it at the beginning of each text file. This allows more than one style sheet for a particular document.

The style sheet will then 'cascade' into any elements until the style is overridden by another style, such as an *inline style* (where a style is defined at the application point).

As far as layout issues are concerned, measurements on screen can be defined in the style sheet by number of pixels, points and picas, ems and x-heights (variable measures that depend on typeface selection), millimetres and centimetres, and inches. Each element on screen is considered to be in a box and you position the boxes by defining margins, *padding* (the equivalent of runaround), borders and other display attributes.

Advertising

Jim Alexander in *How to Create and Evaluate Advertising that Sells*, defines advertising as 'professional salesmanship multiplied by media'.

The eight greatest lies you'll ever be told, according to Jim Aitchison in his book, *Cutting Edge Advertising*, are:

1   You must have a unique selling proposition.
2   You must offer a rational benefit.
3   Humour doesn't sell.
4   You must have a memorable slogan.
5   You must have a logo in the ad.
6   You must show the product in the ad.
7   Every ad in a campaign must look the same.
8   Creative ads don't sell.

The one creative truth is:
Every ad must have an idea in it.

'Advertising' covers reserved space in a publication or air time on radio, movie screen, television or Web site that is paid for. Unpaid time or space is generated by 'publicity' and is called 'news', 'free listings', 'community service announcements' or 'sponsorship'.

Advertising has a lead time (pronounced 'leed'); there is a production schedule to accommodate. In the case of newspapers, a week or preferably two is required to book space, and a few days before publication for provision of artwork or electronic file lodgment; in the case of newsletters and magazines, two months is usual.

Advertising agencies will often employ market researchers; a creative team of writers, art directors, film directors and production staff; account management people; and strategists. This service comes at a price, so many people decide to do it all themselves. Although this can save money, it can limit success. Effective advertising more than pays for itself—it generates brand awareness and sales that increase profit. If it is not doing this, it is not working.

However, another problem here is that a single ad placement will not necessarily generate that profit. An organisation needs to create enough awareness and keep the product in the mind of their consumers by advertising regularly. It has been found that consumers need to encounter a product a number of times before they are confident enough to purchase.

Advertising needs to convey information about the benefits of a product or service to the users and purchasers of that product or service. It also needs to provide differentiation from competitors—other sellers or service providers.

An advertisement can give information that leads to a purchase decision but the deciding factor is rarely from a logical progression of analysis of the data presented—it is nearly always influenced by an emotional response to the product, service or the company offering it. So organisations establish credibility and recall through what is called *brand advertising*. An organisation can create distinction in the marketplace by associating its brand with particular traits that consumers will find attractive. Organisations establish attitude through their advertising, or associate with a particular mood or create an atmosphere around their product range.

There will also be different audiences that an advertiser needs to attract. So the advertisements might have different messages that emphasise different product attributes for those different audiences. In that way, the purchasing information needed can be targeted and placed in appropriate media.

If there is the likelihood that advertising to one audience might alienate another, there is a choice to be made. Often, advertisements that are not aimed at certain people are ignored or filtered anyway, so this alienation may not manifest itself.

Media selection is based on that media's 'reach', which is why ratings and circulation figures are gathered. If a magazine knows the majority of its readers are young professional women, advertisers can be confident that their message will get to the right audience by advertising in that magazine.

Sometimes an organisation will use advertising not so much to attract consumers but to appeal to their staff. This level of *image advertising* can help staff see their organisation in a favourable light and develop pride in it. Image advertising can also help when an organisation has some public challenges to face, like the Arnott's biscuit recall in 1998. If a strong image is established and the crisis is managed well, an organisation can come back stronger than before.

READ MORE ABOUT IT

David Ogilvy, *Ogilvy on advertising*, Pan Books, London, 1983, ISBN 0 330 26985 2.

John Machado, *Creating desire*, Sympress, Kuala Lumpur, 1996, ISBN 983 99149 0 1.

Jim Aitchison, *Cutting edge advertising: How to create the world's best print for brands in the 21st century*, Prentice-Hall, Singapore, 1999, ISBN 0 13 012897 X.

Max Sutherland and Alice K. Sylvester, *Advertising and the mind of the consumer: What works, what doesn't, and why*, 2nd edn, Allen & Unwin, Sydney, 2000, ISBN 1 86508 231 7.

The Designers and Art Directors Association of the United Kingdom, *The copy book: How 32 of the world's best advertising writers write their advertising*, RotoVision SA, Crans-Pres-Celigny, Switzerland, 1995, ISBN 2 88046 258 4.

According to Gallup & Robinson and Readex, two US research organisations, the six principles of creating print ads that work are:
1 Be specific in promoting the benefit for the consumer.
2 Make the product the big benefit.
3 Keep your advertisement simple.
4 Use large spaces to emphasise the benefit.
5 Personalise the benefit.
6 Don't obscure the benefit—being catchy and cute don't always work.
[as described by John Machado in *Creating Desire*]

Roy Grace, a US creative director, has a check list for creative ideas:
1 Is it the kind of idea that's never ever been done before by anyone else in the product category?
2 Is it an idea you can do many variations on, enabling it to last many years?
3 Is it not only informative but entertaining as well? Does the message move you?
4 Does it make people think? Are people actually involved in the selling premise so they participate in the ad?
5 Do you like it—not because it's correct, or clever, or powerful—but genuinely like it? Because if you do, the chances are your audience will like the product.
[also cited by John Machado in *Creating Desire*]

Advertisements
Might include:
- ☐ Free offer
- ☐ Announcement
- ☐ Trial or sample
- ☐ Story
- ☐ Gift
- ☐ Coupon
- ☐ Comparison
- ☐ Innovation
- ☐ New feature
- ☐ Example
- ☐ Directions
- ☐ Price
- ☐ Australian made
- ☐ Imported
- ☐ Endorsements
- ☐ Case study
- ☐ Client list
- ☐ Product list
- ☐ Sponsorship
- ☐ Location/map
- ☐ Logo
- ☐ Slogan
- ☐ Jingle
- ☐ Contact information
  - – phone
  - – fax
  - – mobile
  - – URL

Event posters
- ☐ Presenters of event
- ☐ Name of event
- ☐ Positioning statement/advertising line
- ☐ Date/s
- ☐ Time/s
- ☐ Venue/s
- ☐ Cost/s (not always given)
- ☐ Ticketing information (often just phone number of booking agency)
- ☐ Featured items or performers
- ☐ Legal and copyright requirements as necessary
- ☐ Logos of event sponsors

Herschell Gordon Lewis, *On the art of writing copy*, 2nd edn, Amacom, New York, 2000, ISBN 0 8144 7031 9.

Bob Pritchard, *Marketing success stories*, Milner Books, Burra Creek, NSW, 1997, ISBN 1 86351 201 2.

Ian Oshlack, *Advertising without agencies: A guide to successful advertising for small business*, The Business Library, Information Australia, Melbourne, n.d., ISBN 1 86350 093 6.

Superbrands Pty Ltd, *Superbrands: An insight into 65 of Australia's superbrands*, vol. 1, Superbrands, Sydney, 1997, ISBN 0 646 32253 2.

Superbrands Pty Ltd, *Superbrands: An insight into more than 80 of Australia's superbrands*, vol. 2, Superbrands, Sydney, 1999, ISBN 0 9577000 0 8.

Torin Douglas, *The complete guide to advertising*, Macmillan, London, 1984, ISBN 0 333 38639 6.

Jim Alexander, *How to create and evaluate advertising that sells*, Newspaper Advertising Bureau of Australia, n.d.

Posters

The usual mistake people make with posters is information overload. A poster will be most effective with a dominant image and with a minimal text area, often in a strip down the right-hand side or across the bottom. Posters herald the existence of something and inspire, interest or engage the viewer.

Remember where the poster will be seen. If it will be on a hoarding, design it so it looks good in multiples and creates a pattern at its joins. If it will be in store, it should contrast with the store's walls and roof colours to stand out. If it will be in the window at the local shops or on the community noticeboard at the shopping centre, it should be A4 or smaller and in full colour to contrast with the photocopied and handwritten signs. These are all separation techniques—your poster needs to stand out from others.

People need to know what the event is, and when and where it is. They are the determinants of interest and need to be the most obvious. Include the organisation's symbol, school badge or church logo. Although relevant, because people want to know who they are supporting, the symbol can be small because it's not as important as getting people interested in the product or event. Concentrate on the benefits to the viewer of purchasing or attending.

Do something with additional text that gives the information clearly but doesn't clutter the poster. Usually it can be very small in a block or a column. The poster needs to attract attention (and mostly the image and colour are what will achieve this), so minimise the text area to maximise the image area.

List sponsors and include any other necessary information—a map of where to find the outlet or event, times of opening and closing, ticket prices, and a phone number to contact for further information. These can be quite small, because you've gained people's attention by now.

Postcards

There are a number of reasons that make the postcard or mini-poster an attractive marketing and advertising form—it's personal, collectable, and cheap to produce and distribute. It's also easy to update and keep fashionable. An organisation's image won't become stale if it is reinvented regularly and with creativity.

People seem to respond well to postcards. They are small enough to keep, as distinct from posters, which are often too intrusive on our personal environments.

A sequence of mailings can be produced at the same time for little extra cost if it is a series of postcards. Greater interest can be added to the mailing sequence if there is a teaser mailing, where the full intent becomes clear after a few have been received. Postcards are great inclusions with letter mailings, too. They become miniature full-colour posters to retain even if the letter goes into the bin.

Some organisations are creating such a great series of images that they can repackage them into a gift set, enabling even greater marketing opportunities and cost-recovery if sold.

There are two sides to this particular story. The front is, of course, the main event—it is best to have a single message and an arresting image. But the back is the opportunity to enhance it, with details and credits, to continue the visual message using graphic style that supports the front and perhaps creating a dynamism of its own.

There is a cute option here. You might make the stamp area, which is often just defined by a rectangle (25 × 20 mm), an opportunity for a company logo or a new graphic, illustration or copy-line. You can continue the character of a hand-drawn graphic with hand-drawn lines for the address instead of the ordinary fine ruled ones or just a blank area.

You may choose to have details about a product on the left-hand side or leave it blank to encourage someone to use the card, thereby communicating with two people, the

DOING IT SMARTER
Sponsorship
Remember that when someone donates to an organisation, it is customary to give them recognition or advertising in return, either by mentioning them as a sponsor in all materials or giving them a credit line on the piece they are sponsoring. Ask them for a bromide or digital file of their logo so you can reproduce it professionally.

Credit lines can read:
- ☐ X is proud to support Y
- ☐ Proudly sponsored by X
- ☐ Generously donated by X
- ☐ Y appreciates the support of X.

sender and the receiver. If the information fills the back, there will be only one receiver.

Sympathetic typography that reflects the typographic treatment on the front keeps the card operating effectively. There should be some level of front–back interaction—the message can start on the front with the punchline or an ironic twist on the back.

Flyers, information sheets and handbills

With flyers and handbills, consider the distribution method. Many are handed out to people at shopping centres or in foyers at trade shows, conferences or theatres; many are home-delivered as a letterbox drop; some are stuffed under windscreen wipers in carparks, or pinned on work bulletin boards and community noticeboards at shopping centres, or inserted into magazines or newsletters.

Consider how they will be received. People feel frustration and inconvenience with these particular forms of communication, but they can deliver information appropriately. Much of the print run is wasted, but assuming that is known by the organisation, they can generate more value from their outlay.

A simple idea is to print on both sides of the sheet, since a two-sided flyer increases the communication value of the piece. How many times have you thrown out stuff from your letterbox without opening it up to see what was advertised inside the folded one-sided flyer? Flyers and handbills can be considered mini-posters—with the bonus option of giving extra information on the back, such as duplicates of advertisements that are running in magazines or newspapers. Some magazines offer this as a service to their advertisers anyway. When the reprint is received, the local copy shop or printer can print extra information on the back which might localise the ad for a particular region, introduce local staff, or include a special deal or coupons.

Small-space press ads

These are time-consuming, little, and they usually have to include *War and Peace*! Small-space ads are getting smaller, too. With the rising cost of advertising space in newspapers, magazines and the *Yellow Pages*, and the diminishing marketing dollar, many organisations have reduced the physical size of their advertising.

DOING IT CHEAPER
Piggyback marketing
Two parties can creatively join forces to jointly market each other. You can see this when Disney releases a film and McDonalds or KFC have the movie tie-in merchandise available in-store, thereby marketing the film and the fast food for the same advertising outlay.

At a suburban level, if there's a regular letterbox drop by a local store or organisation, another organisation could piggyback its message. Sometimes one organisation might give another a mention in their ad or let them use the back of their flyer in return for sharing the costs or a sponsorship line.

If competitors are booking long, skinny, one-column ads, you should book a wide, squat, three-column ad. If all the ads around yours are white with black type, be the one that is black with white type.

People often buy or reserve space in a publication, write the copy to fill an A4 sheet and then give it to a designer or typesetter and say, 'Make it fit!' Ugh! There are a few techniques that can minimise your grief if this is your task. Delete all repeat references in the copy. Often the name of the organisation, shop, product or company is repeated several times. It is better to display the name once only, but make it bigger—to encourage recognition of it or the logo.

Readers who skim the publication and are not interested in your client's reasons for advertising could still notice the client's logo—there is still a recognition advantage. Getting that logo large in a small-space ad is difficult, so don't repeat information unless there is good reason.

Consider the material carefully and give helpful suggestions about what might be deleted and why—clients will usually respond positively. Does the copy include a postal and a street address when a phone number alone would do? Would just a street address be sufficient? 'Woden Plaza' may be quite sufficient, rather than 'Shop 158, Woden Plaza'. Other deletions could include unnecessary punctuation—'29 February 2004' could become '29 Feb 2004', saving quite a few letters. Dates can be expressed numerically also, e.g. '29/02/04' or '29/2/04' (or 29.2.04) but note that in the United States this would become '02/29/04'. By saving spaces you can save lines and dramatically reduce the area devoted to copy.

In a small-space ad, you need to retain legibility. Both printing and on-screen reproduction can result in a less than perfect reproduction of your ad. Also remember that you can fit more lower-case letters than capitals in a line— and lower case is easier to read anyway!

Sans serif typefaces that are slightly horizontally scaled will reproduce best. They reduce well and are quite readable at small sizes—even at 4 point! Look at the telephone book and classified ad sections to see how well they can be set. One tip here is to set the tracking looser for a small-space ad. Small type will read better if it is tracked wider.

Avoid slab serifs like Rockwell which, although they reproduce well enough, have serifs that take extra room on the line so it will set wide. Serif types like Times Roman get too fine and spindly in small-space ads, causing the type to break (where the fine lines do not reproduce at all) or fill in (where the small white spaces within letters like *a*, *g* and *e* can't hold out against the tide of ink). Serif types also don't reverse well. When you use bold type, you increase the area you need—so use it sparingly but effectively.

Include an image or some space even in a small ad, as a picture or symbol can attract attention. This is a good reason for reducing the area devoted to copy. Even if there is no image, a little breathing space in an ad is a positive thing. Try to discourage your client from filling it with more product information.

Use a border, but don't cramp the type. Leave some breathing space between the type and the border, even in the smallest ad.

READ MORE ABOUT IT
Cheryl Dangel Cullen, *Small graphics: Design innovation for limited spaces*, Rockport Publishers, Gloucester, Mass., 2000, ISBN 1 56496 693 3.

Classified ads

Establishing a corporate presence in the classified pages can attract people to ads with very little effort on their part, as they will want to find what the organisation is offering, such as a job, tenders, public notices, or items for sale. An organisation does not want to pay an exorbitant amount of money for this identification, so it must not take up much room in the area of the ad. The options come down to:

- borders
- banners
- attitude.

An effective way to stand out in the classifieds is with large type, because everything is small, or space (but this is expensive blank area and likely to be difficult to justify, particularly to a committee who will see it as wasteful). Bold or reversed type also stands out in that sea of grey. Unusual angles and curves in a border stand out because so many people use every square millimetre in their allocated or purchased ad area. Handwriting always provides a noticeable contrast.

Magazine and display ads

Magazine advertising can be very seductive with its colour, comfortable size, or full-page bleeds. Consequently, text-heavy advertising can be very successful in this format.

If advertising is read like the articles, that's okay, and is probably preferable. This is where ads in lifestyle magazines feature products with recipes in the ad. Advertisers can even create the effect of a feature article by buying a set of pages.

In magazines, there are options of one-column, half-page and full-page ads, double-page spreads, and multipage advertising features. In newspapers, column widths are bought by the centimetre, and half pages, full pages and double-page spreads. In both magazines and newspapers a premium is paid for guaranteed placement, which most agree is worth it if it guarantees a right-hand page or a specific section or, in magazines, the back cover and inside front and back covers.

The back cover of a magazine can be expensive. A very cute trick that some advertisers have used well is to buy the back cover, the inside back cover and the last page. They've turned the magazine upside-down and effectively created their own magazine. Busy newsagents will sometimes even put it out separately on the shelf. When you open it, their advertising continues on the inside spread and then the whole magazine goes upside-down. Magazines will sometimes use that technique themselves for a special feature or supplement.

The price for magazine advertising is usually justified on readership statistics (who buys, who reads, in what localities, and what percentage of the marketplace they deliver), the amount of time a magazine is kept and the number of people likely to see each copy. In doctor's surgeries and waiting rooms, on coffee tables at home and in aeroplanes, a magazine ad has a greater 'reach' than, say, a newspaper ad. Newspapers are immediate, but thrown away at the end of each day. Magazines are often kept until the next issue arrives and sometimes they are used much longer or collected.

Coupons or competitions in an ad generate leads (pronounced 'leeds') that enable an organisation to gauge the effectiveness of the ad and give a database so they can direct-market to likely prospects. Ads that feature a full-page or double-spread image and are text-sparse can be a great rest place in busy magazines and newspapers. Type doesn't need to be large in magazines, so a single line of well-chosen text below can hold the attention after the attraction of the graphic.

Tom Patty, in *Design for Response* by Leslie Sherr and David Katz, says that in order to figure out the means of persuasion in each particular case, one must:

1   understand the elements of persuasion (including the physiology of persuasion)
2   determine the purchase process for the given product or service
3   determine the persuasion task for each stage in the purchase process
4   determine the credibility of the brand or speaker
5   determine the personality of the brand or speaker
6   develop a fully integrated persuasion plan.

Some advertisers have created some interesting sets of ads by buying the same space on two or more consecutive right-hand pages. This allows them to ask a question on the first page and answer it on the second.

READ MORE ABOUT IT

Dave Saunders, *20th century advertising*, Carlton Books, London, 1999, ISBN 1 85868 520 6.

Bryan Holme, *Advertising: Reflections of a century*, William Heinemann, London, 1982.

Allyn Salomon, *Advertising photography*, Thames & Hudson, London, 1982, ISBN 0 500 54081 0.

Direct-mail advertising

In direct mail, more information is good and more involvement is good. Short words and sentences are quick and easy to read and therefore reach more people. The design should be kept lively and feature many headings and self-contained text units. Format variation will keep the mailer interesting.

This is one-to-one selling so it needs to be written in a conversational and even intimate tone. The message should be individualised so the recipient can feel a relationship developing with the advertiser through the material. Customising is made that much easier with high-quality digital printing technology.

The mailer needs to entertain and involve the target. Some involvement tricks are taste tests, samples, free gifts, CDs, videos, boxes, assembling things, scratchies, and folding, licking and sticking stamps onto reply coupons. The more relevant and involving these gimmicks—even to sophisticated markets—the more effect will be created.

A series of mailings is sometimes used to build interest. There can be a teaser mailer that simply says something interesting will be arriving in the mail box in two days time.

Direct marketing is sometimes referred to as Customer Relationship Marketing (CRM) and often involves direct mail as well as other techniques like telemarketing and email marketing.

CHECK LIST
Direct mail

Envelope
- ☐ 'Teaser' copy that encourages the receiver to enthusiastically open the letter
- ☐ Stamp
- ☐ Personalised

Letter
- ☐ Personalised
- ☐ Text that highlights benefits to customer
- ☐ Headline at top of text
- ☐ Letterhead with company name, logo, address, phone numbers
- ☐ Signature
- ☐ PS
- ☐ Special offer or time limit

Brochure
- ☐ Text that highlights benefits to consumer
- ☐ Picture/s of product/s
- ☐ Endorsement/s, awards
- ☐ Product description: size, colour range, price
- ☐ Order form with freepost envelope or card
- ☐ Optional purchase methods
- ☐ Company name, logo, address, phone numbers
- ☐ Guarantee
- ☐ 'Involving' devices like stickers, scratchies, pop-ups

Leslie Sherr and David Katz in *Design for Response* wrote: 'Designs should reflect the visions, tastes and aspirations of the target audience. This not only ensures that the recipient pays attention to the mailer, but also, when multiple components are part of the package, that the reader's attention is transferred from one element to the next. Tactile additions, such as perforations or unusual materials, create interesting shifts that invite the recipient to explore every piece mailed.'

READ MORE ABOUT IT

Vin Jenkins, *Direct mail advertising in Australia: A handbook in 6 volumes*, Australia Post, Melbourne, 1984, ISBN 0 642 89539 2 (set).

Malcolm Auld, *Direct marketing made easy*, Harper Business, Sydney, 1997, ISBN 0 7322 5676 3.

Leslie H. Sherr and David J. Katz, *Design for response: Creative direct marketing that works*, Rockport Publishers, Gloucester, Mass., 1999, ISBN 1 56496 380 2.

Sheree Clark and Wendy Lyons, *Creative direct mail design: The guide and showcase*, Rockport Publishers, Gloucester, Mass., 1995, ISBN 1 56496 143 5.

Ian Kennedy and Bryce Courtenay, *The power of one-to-one*, Margaret Gee Publishing, Sydney, 1995.

Production

Layout

'Each time a page is turned, a curtain rises to reveal a fresh scene.'
Jim Aitchison in
Cutting Edge Advertising

A layout is really a piece of abstract art. You're fiddling with basic shapes in different tones and trying to get them to sit comfortably, logically and interestingly together in order to tell a story and impart information clearly. As with any abstract composition, the aim is to lead the viewer's eye around the piece, and entertain it with repetition (pattern and texture), contrast (scale, tone and colour), and direction (created through the interaction of shapes and lines).

If you can reduce text and photos, headlines and subtitles, pull-quotes, captions and logos (these are all called 'elements') to their basic shapes, and the tone or colour that those shapes have, it is easier to create an effective layout. The interaction of the basic shapes and tones is what creates the 'layout'.

But page design is not an accident determined by how the text is given to you, what photographs or illustrations the author has supplied or considered appropriate, and how you then put it together in an abstract composition. The 'accident' needs to be arranged to lead a reader through it, so a good designer relates pieces of the puzzle to one another until the connections are visually communicated as well as being textually discussed.

Errors of alignment can occur when the designer has not read and understood the text, e.g. pictures might be scaled to sizes that distort their logical relationship and confuse the reader. If elements are grouped together without a logical relationship, the reader will seek to relate them to one another and possibly distort the message that was intended. Ensure that you group elements in a page design appropriately. While accidental cross-readings can be fashionable, intriguing and diverting, they tend to limit communication clarity.

In layout, you make choices about the positioning of the elements (imagery, text and space) of the design. The variables are then brought into play.

Images can be square-cut, free-form or soft-edged. Text can be *display text* such as titles and featured type; *body copy*, which is the bulk of the textual content; or short text bursts such as headings, captions and pull-quotes. Space can be placed in bands, e.g. margins around the perimeter of the page, gutters that run between columns, or text drops where an invisible line runs across the layout from which text is hung. Space can also be free-form.

You make decisions at each step of the way about specific placement and details such as colour, weight and size. But it can be a bit hit and miss. The quick way to make these sorts of decisions—to work every time—is to look underneath it all, behind the actual to the implied. There is an invisible layout structure that enables some layouts to succeed better than others.

Many people are too concerned with getting the obvious correct, concentrating on text details such as punctuation, the positioning of picture credits and colour balance in images. But these do not of themselves create a good layout. The details need to be correct but not at the expense of the success of the piece—after all, if people don't notice the piece, they don't get the opportunity to admire the detail!

The relationship between certain elements should be maintained throughout a layout. For example, you should treat and place captions in the same way throughout and keep spacing around headings constant. This consistency will help readers to decode the message without distraction. Hanging your text from a chosen line—like washing—also achieves this. It is better that the relationships between elements (that you have decided will best suit the reader's requirements) are maintained, than that the columns fall to the same depth, for example.

DOING IT SMARTER
Design file
Keep a file of interesting design approaches and techniques that you have photocopied from advertisements, magazines and books. Refer to the file when you know you need to achieve a particular result but have either run out of time or momentarily lost your inspiration.

DOING IT CHEAPER
Don't bleed
When ink prints off the side of a sheet of paper it is said to 'bleed'. This means the sheet of paper that is printed needs to be bigger to accommodate the image that continues off the page, and the space around that image that is necessary for the printer to get the page through the printing press. This produces waste and means you have to purchase a larger and therefore more expensive sheet than you need.

Create a design that fits comfortably inside the border with 10 mm of blank space—that is, no ink—on the same edge on both sides of the sheet of paper. This is called the gripper edge. On the other three edges, 5 mm clearance is sufficient.

The subtle distortions of the text blocks in this layout reiterate the shapes of the illustrations, creating a relationship between the text and images that brings unity and logic to the composition.
Client: University of Virginia
Publication: *Art from the Land: Dialogues with the Kluge–Ruhe Collection of Austrlaian Aboriginal Art* edited by Howard Morphy and Margo Smith Boles
Designer: Maureen MacKenzie-Taylor
Studio: Msquared Research Assisted Design

And don't forget the underlying layer—the layout is the abstract composition that is the aesthetic basis of your design. There are potential distractions in this 'invisible' layer, too.

To demonstrate the implications of even simple decisions, take a blank A4 sheet of paper and type a line of text in the centre of the page. This line of text creates a number of implied or invisible lines and shapes within the page:

- An invisible line runs through the text horizontally and continues from the beginning of the text to the left-hand edge of the page and similarly from the end of the text to the right-hand edge of the page, dividing the page into two segments.
- Those two segments are two implied rectangles.
- At the beginning of the text is an implied vertical line connecting the first letter of the text to the top and bottom edges of the page.
- Similarly, at the end of the text there is another implied vertical, which connects the top and bottom edges of the page through the last letter.
- These verticals further divide the page area into invisible shapes—you now have six rectangles implied.

Part of the reason that these verticals and horizontals are so strong is that the edges of the page create vertical and horizontal stress or at least conform to it; in a different shape, the implications may be different. There is an even more subtle tension that can be a further complication to exploit in your layout—the diagonals connecting the beginning and end points of the text line to the two corners closest to them.

So the placement of one line of text can create this amount of clutter! Can you see why playing about with many elements becomes so difficult?

One way to ease the resulting angst is to limit the numbers of implied lines and shapes, by using the same ones many times, instead of creating new ones at each introduction of a new element. This strengthens the layout.

The secret formula to successful layout—particularly in poster and cover design—is to limit the number of vertical and horizontal divisions of the space. Let the same line do a few jobs. It could:

One vertical division can perform many roles

- be the edge of the title block
- be a picture's border

- be where the author's name runs from
- point to the publisher's logo at the foot of the page.

The last point here also introduces the concept of implied direction. Lines can be said to direct us or 'move' to the right and down, due to our understanding of standard eye flow.

Eye flow

It may seem obvious, but we sometimes forget that we read from top to bottom and from left to right. Therefore, at whatever point we enter a layout, we automatically continue to the right and down. It is a contrary movement to go 'backwards', either reading up from the bottom to the top or backwards from the right to the left. This is why captions are expected to be at the bottom or the right of photographs or illustrations.

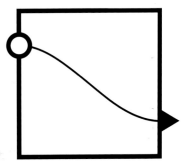

That is not to say that our eyes are not tempted back to those other areas of the layout. But be careful to avoid too many 'backward' moves in a layout.

In double-page spreads, it is understood that the eye travels in a parabolic arc from the top right-hand corner (where the eye follows the double page as revealed by the turning action), across to the far left and back to the exit point at the bottom right. It is suggested, then, that there should be something on the left-hand page that drags your eye fully across the spread. In many magazine feature stories, the left-hand page is a full-page illustration and the title, and the start of the story is on the right-hand page. This follows the standard understanding of hierarchy—the large picture has the most attraction value and, from there, eye flow leads into the headline. It also explains the marketing wisdom that insists that advertisers pay the premium for right-hand page advertising space in magazines and newspapers, because the reader's attention may never get to the left page!

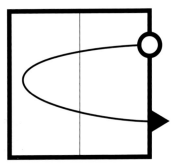

Parabolic curve of entry/exit for double-page spread

READ MORE ABOUT IT

Colin Wheildon, *Type and layout: How typography and design can get your message across—or get in the way*, Strathmoor Press, Berkeley, 1995, ISBN 0 9624891 5 8.

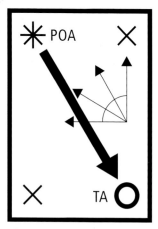

The Gutenberg diagram
Based on the diagram devised by
Edmund Arnold, a US typographer,
who described the basic eye flow
(shown by the solid arrow) as the
Axis of Orientation. The entry point
is coded as the Primary Optical Area
and the exit point as the Terminal
Anchor. Arnold identified two fallow
corners with crosses as being dead
spots in a layout. Fine arrows in an
arc represent the angles within the
page that are considered to be
backward movements that the
eye avoids.

Backwards movement

How often do you read backwards? That is, how often do
your eyes travel against the assumed eye flow from top left
to bottom right? All the time. As layout designers, harness-
ing eye flow and understanding how each layout decision
you make will affect it is actually what layout 'is', the
positioning of elements within a space for impact and
effective communication in order.

Understanding that backwards movement is natural but
contrary to the standard flow enables you to use it more
effectively. It is recommended that you limit the amount of
backwards movement required in a layout, because too
much will confuse readers and they'll leave the layout
without finishing it, missing the communication your client
expects them to receive.

On a printout of a layout, draw a line of the journey the
reader's eye will make around it. Watch people's eyes as
they are reading your work and get an idea where they are
looking. Note down the pattern of their glances and see if
you can reconstruct it when you are back at your desk with
the layout.

Jumping through a layout, the eye goes in order through
the pictures from largest to smallest, from most colourful to
least colourful, and eventually to the text. You can help this
landing on the text by leading the eye in a simple curve—if
eye movement continues in the same trajectory it will hit
the start of the text once it has left the smallest image.

Of course, the eye gets interested in an image as well
and takes a stroll through the focal points and textures
within it. It leaps from flashes of intense colour to a brief
exploration of shadow areas, so understanding the interest
areas within an image is also necessary. A number of
introductory art books will deconstruct an image and the
eye flow through it in a discussion of its composition.

The skimming of the reader continues through a layout
from element to element in a hierarchy and a path. If you
are in doubt as you get further down the hierarchy, assume
the eye flow from any point to be to the right and down.

This phenomenon is how text can be lost or hidden in
plain view. Particular placements can mean the eye will
simply not get back to the areas of the layout that are called
the 'fallow' areas, unless something extreme is done to
attract them there.

Eye flow is one of the difficulties for layered image/text techniques because the eye is not only reading through the imagery, but also reading foreground and background. In many cases, the eye is expected to wander over the same area twice, focusing differently to catch the juxtaposed message (because the image will register first).

If you need to correct eye flow, change the size relationships of your images and alter their alignment. If there is a lot of backwards reading, sometimes a mirror image of the layout will correct it—in the same placement relationships, just swap everything on the right to the left.

Dominance

Some layout elements are dominant, some assume dominance and some have dominance thrust upon them.

Pictures dominate a layout—and coloured pictures assume more importance than black-and-white ones. If there is a picture in a layout, readers will look at it first. So that's where they land in your layout and their 'eye flow' starts. If it is on a right-hand page, you may have just lost the left-hand page, unless you somehow drag the reader's attention back to the left (in a backwards motion). Be aware of the eye's movement through your design: What will it see first and where on the page is it? Does it move logically— using standard eye flow—to the next place or is the eye rushing around higgledy-piggledy? Does the eye have a resting spot or somewhere to concentrate for an extended period? Has the eye moved around the page so much that it longs to get out? Has it stopped at all the information points? Does the reader remember what the major pieces of information were? Is the reader enjoying the contrast of details and the overall form?

There are very few examples of designs where pictures do not overpower type. This is the reasoning behind the classic advertising format: a picture at the top, a headline underneath, followed by the body copy, and usually finished with a logo or coupon in the bottom right-hand corner. If the headline was placed above the picture, it may not be noticed because the reader's attention is already further down the page (on the picture).

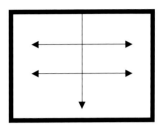

Reading on screen
Readers scan a screen, reading down the centre with a left–right scanning motion. In this way, they can quickly access needed information from short paragraphs, dot point lists, headings, links and graphics.

DOING IT SMARTER
Faces
People pictures are most important. Faces are even more important. And the eyes have it! Think of mass market magazine covers—usually a face with text crowded around it. In extreme closeups, the eyes are the most beguiling features of the cover.

Even implied faces have attraction. Think about your car: the headlights are the eyes, the grille is a nose and the bumper bar is the mouth. Does your car smile at you? In layout terms, this subliminal smiling 'face' creation can make strong designs.

Simplicity

The value of a 'simple' layout is its strength. This is often a comparative value, because a majority of layouts do not have this simplicity and absolute logic that is achieved through both vertical and horizontal simplicity in the layout. For example, extensive indenting can have the effect of complicating your layout vertically. Review your indents and limit them. The persistence of any element—even a 5 mm paragraph indent—quickly establishes another 'invisible' vertical line, complicating your layout. Each tab has the same effect.

In newsletters, the layout is often complicated horizontally where stories finish at different depths in different columns. Try to have fewer of these 'invisible' lines or breaks running across your layout.

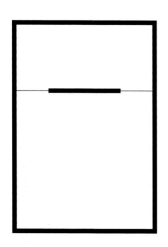

The most striking layouts also tend to rely on recognition of basic shapes, such as square, triangle, circle... These basic shapes need not be obvious. Disguise them through an understanding of implied line and shape. Strengthen the layout by using the standard or pure geometric shapes: circles rather than ovals; squares rather than rectangles or rhombuses; equilateral rather than isosceles triangles.

There is another consideration here. The audience will perceive curves and rounded shapes as friendlier than sharp points and crisp lines, which can be seen as harsh. And curves turning upwards at both ends are 'subliminal' happy faces.

Let's go back to our previous example, the placement of one line of text on an A4 page. If you now place that line about one-third of the way down the page, you create an implied rectangle above the line and an implied square below the line. This is a stronger layout option, because the square is a more pure shape than a rectangle.

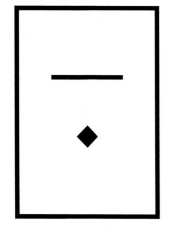

Then if you placed a logo like the Commonwealth Bank's diamond centred about a two-thirds of the way down the page, you would create an implied triangle where the logo is connected by invisible threads to the beginning and end of the line of text below. If you then work the spacing between the two elements to create an implied equilateral triangle, you create a stronger layout statement. The diamond-shaped logo would also give you the point of the triangle—super-strength!

But the structural lines within a layout do not have to be parallel only—or even straight! Many successful layouts use irregular shapes and curves, using fewer structural lines and placing elements in harmony with existing curves. Usually, this recognition that you can use an existing structural line instead of creating a new one will improve a layout.

There are meanings implied by design decisions that are purely visually communicated. If you use a design technique thinking it's simply good to look at without understanding the visual conventions you have used and what they are saying, you may be communicating incorrect meanings to the reader.

For example, if you bleed something off the page or crop in close to something, you are implying that the image is moving off the page or too large to be contained by the 'frame'. This can be very dynamic.

Graphing conventions used in picture layout will imply the simultaneity of events, creating a hybrid visual form of a graphed storyboard. This technique is used in the layouts for *Snowboarder* magazine to capture some of the spirit and dynamism of snowboarding, effectively capturing the fourth dimension (time) in the two-dimensional space of a page.

DOING IT SMARTER
Dummy text
For rough layouts, use actual headings and possibly the first words in an opening paragraph, but replace the real text with 'dummy' text. Dummy text is just gobbledegook that looks like text, but it encourages clients to consider the design effect of the type without being distracted by the content. Your client or boss will then focus on the design and not the minutiae of spelling and proofreading detail.

Snowboarder magazine uses graphing and storyboarding techniques to capture the dynamism of snowboarding in a layout style they call a 'sequence pictorial'.
Publisher: Morrison Media Services
Publication: *Snowboarder*
Art director: Graeme Murdoch

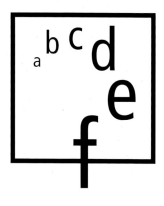

Type over an image limits its ability to be perceived as a window showing reality. The type anchors the image into the book, limiting its effectiveness. However, you can balance this 'con' with the 'pro' that type over an image also gives greater penetration to the text message.

If type starts small and gets larger and darker throughout a line of text, it is akin to musical notation, and the effect is that of a *crescendo* (getting louder). The opposite is also true—if type gets smaller and dies away it is mimicking a *diminuendo*. This can be a volume thing or a 3-D thing—the type could also be seen to be advancing or receding into the distance.

Size and colour also have an impact on where in the visual space we see type and images. There are three dimensions in visual space, and so we see foreground, middleground and background. If something is smaller, muted or paler, it recedes. If something is larger or brighter, it advances. Anything that overlaps something else implies it is 'forward'.

READ MORE ABOUT IT

Robin Williams, *The non-designer's design book: Design and typographic principles for the visual novice*, Peachpit Press, Berkeley, 1994, ISBN 1 56609 159 4.

Lori Siebert and Lisa Ballard, *Making a good layout*, North Light Books, Cincinnati, 1992, ISBN 0 89134 423 3.

John Bowers, *Introduction to two-dimensional design: Understanding form and function*, John Wiley & Sons, New York, 1999, ISBN 0 471 29224 9.

Bryan L. Peterson, *Using design basics to get creative results*, North Light Books, Cincinnati, 1996, ISBN 0 89134 651 1.

Alistair Campbell, *The designers lexicon: The essential illustrated dictionary of design, print, and computer terms*, Cassell & Co., London, 2000, ISBN 0 304 35505 4.

Roger C. Parker, *The makeover book: 101 design solutions for desktop publishing*, Ventana Press, Chapel Hill, North Carolina, 1989, ISBN 0 940087 20 0.

Roger C. Parker, *Looking good in print*, 4th edn, Coriolis, Scottsdale, Arizona, 1998, ISBN 1 56604 856 7.

Marcelle Lapow Toor, *Graphic design on the desktop: A guide for the non-designer*, 2nd edn, John Wiley & Sons, New York, 1998, ISBN 0 471 29307 5.

Unity

Embracing diversity in design techniques and styling has created a visual palette of infinite variety. This very diversity makes it difficult to select the most appropriate form that a message should take because we also recognise that the visual menu reflects the tastes of a diverse human population of message receivers. This has resulted in the current situation where often disparate design styles exist side by side.

Irrelevant arguments about what is good and what is bad are aired in design magazines and public forums, irrelevant because it's all good and it's all bad, depending on where you stand in the diverse marketplace.

But one of the design principles that most seems to be missing is that of unity between elements. Due to the fractured marketplace—and the fractured design field that reflects that fractured marketplace—unity in a design sense has been lost somewhere.

But what is 'unity' in graphic design terms? Unity is in the details. For example, when choosing rules to place between lines of text or to surround photographs, there is a good technique that subtly brings unity to a design. If you choose the stroke thickness of the crossbar of a capital A in the typeface that appears closest to the rules, it means your underlines or photo borders relate to the typeface they are seen with, bringing a 'unity' to those elements. Consistency in captioning style, heading style and text placement in relation to images all help to create a harmonious layout, a comfortable logic system.

Unity is in type selection. You can save time by using a few typefaces consistently—and, by doing so, also achieve unity. They look like they belong together because you set up the expectation that they will recur. In multipage layouts in brochures and feature articles, this type consistency means establishing the fonts throughout the piece, not just using them once. The title face may come back in pull-quotes or drop capitals or photo captions, but it doesn't have to come back in the same weight. It might just come back in the italic version or the bold version or small capitals.

Unity is in image editing. Crop photographs in a range of similar sizes (say, only three: a square, a vertical rectangle and a horizontal rectangle) so there is a visual rhythm created in the layout or the whole publication that also reinforces that the photographs belong. There might be

'All visual form is made up of three categories of components: elements, characteristics and interactions. Visual elements are dots, lines, planes and volumes, and each element possesses characteristics of size, shape, texture and color. These elements and characteristics are directed by principles of visual interaction, which are position, direction and space.'
John Bowers in
Introduction to Two-dimensional Design: Understanding Form and Function

Unity is achieved in this catalogue through repetition in the text block shape of curves taken from the images.
Client: Australian Exhibitions Touring Agency
Publication: *Contemporary Silversmithing: Connections across National Boundaries*
Designer: Maureen MacKenzie-Taylor
Studio: Msquared Research Assisted Design

Design dynamics

to vary your layouts

☐   Balance:
  –   symmetry/centring
  –   asymmetry
☐   Line (and implied line)
☐   Shape (including the shape of text)
☐   Colour and tone (dark/light values)
☐   Scale (relative size of elements)
☐   Contrast (big/small, dark/light)
☐   Texture, pattern and repetition
☐   Unity and alignment
☐   Space

In *Using Design Basics to Get Creative Results*, Bryan L. Peterson discusses design dynamics in this set:

☐   Format
☐   Elements
  –   line
  –   type
  –   shape
  –   texture
☐   Structure
  –   balance
  –   contrast
  –   unity
  –   value (tone)
  –   colour

a photographic attitude too: photojournalism, studio set-ups, detail photography—these styles might create sets of images that imply a consistent image selection and editing approach.

Unity is in space. 'White' space can have a unifying effect on disparate elements. Of course, space does not need to be white—it can be any area of colour that doesn't have a pattern, image or text in it. Similarity in the way you choose to structure space into your layouts can bring unity to a multipage project. Do you normally put space around the edges or just at the bottom of the layout?

Unity is in colour selection. There can be a colour 'attitude' to a piece, where you try to achieve a colour balance between the images and the text. In book covers and posters, where there is a colour photograph, it is often a unifying decision to select colours for the type, background, border and any symbols or single colour graphics that come from somewhere in the image, thereby unifying image and type. Subliminally, we feel the text and layout elements belong with the photograph. In photo selection, discard photographs that do not have a similar colour palette to your main photograph and instead use photographs that complement its colours.

Unity is in proximity or alignment. When you align elements of a layout, the grouping that results may operate as a single entity. So the positioning of four square-cut photographs, in an aligned stack of two on two, creates a larger square within the layout. Even with a group of different sized and shaped elements, close proximity can generate a 'group shape' that may become the foreground element in your layout. Viewers will find connections and assume connections when objects are aligned, juxtaposed or positioned in close proximity.

While it does not have to be too rigid, remember there are benefits to unity. In magazines, the benefit is that you can find the articles between the advertisements. In feature articles or an ad campaign, the identification of like characteristics signals the continuation of the story. In corporate identity programs, the similarities signal a unified organisation and enable you to rely on a level of branding that means you are jumping off with the new story—a whole slew of information is already known about the organisation and doesn't need repeating.

So embrace diversity but appreciate the value of a unified front for some tasks. There are times when unity achieves more.

Graphic detailing

A visual logic system can operate in a design that makes it an 'entity'. This logic system involves consistent application of styling and appropriate decision making on text and image hierarchies and font selection, but also an individual-ising—and unifying—component that could be termed 'graphic detailing'.

You will need to create a unified design entity for each client and often for each project. If your project is a Web site, a publication, an advertisement, a corporate identity or a film title, creating a unique visual system will help it achieve a stand-out quality, and make it harder for your competitors to duplicate. It is creating a 'house style' for layout and design decision making that reflects the uniqueness of that project.

Graphic detailing entails using visual references to unique characteristics of your project. It also involves subtle repetition of those references. It is seeing a chance for individualisation in the smallest details or seemingly most mundane aspects of a design. It saves time because you do not need to create new graphic devices to enliven your layout; simply use the ones you already have. But more importantly, it gives an inner strength to your layout because of the resonances that subtle reiteration can have.

You will be surprised how effective this technique can be. It is often a design ingredient that you don't actually notice until it's pointed out, but you respond to the design and wonder why some designs don't work as 'logically'.

Finding the 'unique' characteristics of the job can be as simple as looking at the letters in the title. If you choose one of the more interesting letterforms in the title and then convert your chosen letterform to paths in your illustration package, select maybe just a curve or angle from the top or bottom of the character. Depending on how you then scale that feature and where you place it in the layout, it might give you a path to which you can snap a title or headline. It could give you a unique shape with which you could crop a photograph. It could become a curved or angled margin that your column of text could contour down. It could become the dividing line between two fields of colour in the

Dingbats
If you want a circle, equilateral triangle or square, consider using the Zapf Dingbats font instead of the drawing tools in your program. Because they operate as a font, you must be sure you have removed general font variations such as baseline shift, italicising or horizontal scaling because they will affect the draw of the character. (*Hint:* You can use horizontal scaling to create an oval out of a circle dingbat, an acute-angled triangle out of an equilateral triangle dingbat, and a rectangle out of a square dingbat. You can then italicise them for fun—and even rotate the text block.)

In many cases, it is faster to resize a typeface than to redraw, enlarge or reduce a drawn element. You can alter the position of dingbats minutely because they operate as a font, so alignment can be fine-tuned using leading, baseline shift, tracking and kerning controls.

A letterform might be used as the basis for a layout

background. You could step and repeat it, and then colour between each, to create a pattern of coloured stripes down your page. All of these possibilities can arise simply from a feature of a letterform from the title!

The fact that a tiny detail like this can provide a rich variety of graphic options means you do not need to create new graphic devices. Simply recognise and use the ones you've already chosen.

Within images, too, there are details that can be recropped and featured elsewhere or used for backgrounds. They might be ghosted to provide a pale but related background for the layout. They might be repeated and distorted into a pattern or texture. You might use the negative version. There are colours that can be duplicated for display text. There are infinite possibilities.

But let's assume you decided that all the photographs in your report would be cropped into squares. The square becomes a graphic device within that layout as a result of that decision. So reiterate it. How? Use squares instead of bullets in dot-point lists. You could also put all pull-quotes or chapter headings into a square. Your folios could be contained in a fine ruled square placed equidistant from the top and outer trim, creating an even more subtle square of blank space. In bar charts, the bars could be a stack of square boxes instead of a rectangle. Your colour codings would have square samples of colour in the key. You could justify your text and fill square text blocks. In a sans serif title, you could customise the letter *i* by replacing its circular dot with a little square. Okay, these really are the details—but they have resonance.

Part of effective corporate identity design involves this type of detailing, using pieces of your existing corporate symbols, logos and colour palette. Maybe you can use stripes that mimic a diagonal line in your symbol to fill borders and strips of colour in the backgrounds of brochure covers and other corporate paraphernalia. In a series of report covers, you could use enlargements of details taken from the symbol to create the base layout.

It can be as simple as a slight colour variation in the background that subtly reinforces the symbol. This reinforcing is the layout secret. If you then incorporate a band of, for example, diagonal stripes that reinforce the diagonal from the symbol, you are creating a design ground that is 'exclusive' to your organisation. Another client could

BEFORE

detail

AFTER

detail

Subtle refinements like a dot on the *i* can reiterate a chosen theme: in this case, the use of squares. Also note the altered alignment.

use those same graphic devices (diagonals and subtle details) because they are not, of themselves, exclusive. But their use elsewhere will not have the same resonance that they will have if you use them. Worse still, if accidentally used by a competitor, their material may be perceived as emanating from your organisation.

Balance

Balance is achieved when the elements in a layout are comfortably related to one another and the different weight of the elements has been distributed evenly across the area of the page. Imagine an adult and a child on a seesaw. For balance to be achieved, you must place the adult and the child carefully in different positions.

An element's size, shape, colour and tone determine weight in a layout.

A symmetrical layout will always be balanced unless you add a rogue element. In asymmetrical layouts, balance is much more complicated and you use other dynamics to achieve it.

Symmetry
Designed around a central axis, symmetry will always balance, but it can be too predictable. For 'predictable', read 'boring'. This traditional Western design style always creates a balanced design because the elements are reflected around a central axis, meaning the 'weight' of each element is evenly balanced on either side of the centre line. The symmetrical layout is static. It will always look neat—and is a good default design if you're running short of time—but is just a bit boring or bland. This is the result of the main structural interest being a downward centre line.

Vertical centring
Try to remember to lift the elements to 'optical centre'—which is slightly above physical centre. This is achieved easily by putting a larger margin measurement at the bottom of the layout than at the top. It avoids the feeling that the text block or print area might have 'slipped' down the page. This is also the reason that title pages normally have the title placed in the top half of the page.

DOING IT SMARTER
Edge detail
Fine trimming and registration slows the job on press and finishing processes—avoid complexity and detail on the trim edges of your designs. Avoid lines, rules or borders that run parallel and very close to the trim edges, because if the trim is slightly out, the parallels will look wrong.

Physical centre

Optical centre

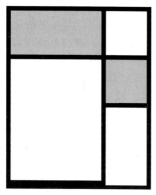

Piet Mondrian's work with areas of flat colour (*above*) demonstrates clear techniques for creating balanced layouts (*below*).

Asymmetry

Asymmetry is inspired by Eastern design traditions. Asymmetrical layouts are much more involving for the viewer than symmetrical ones. The response to an asymmetrical design is a physiological response as well as an aesthetic one. Asymmetrical designs are interesting designs for your eyes. Your eye responds by travelling to and fro across the layout. This eye movement is a physical involvement and is part of our perception of increased dynamism within these layouts.

For balance within asymmetrical arrangement, the Japanese have developed a modular approach to layout in architecture with their arrangement of *tatami* mats, which is also used in screens for room division. The *tatami* mat is a rectangle created from two squares. In combination, *tatami* mats will create balanced patterns that are not necessarily symmetrical.

Asymmetry fascinated Piet Mondrian (among others) in the early 20th century. Using the methods explored by Mondrian can create a strong interrelated layout.

Balance is complicated in asymmetrical layouts because the relationships between the elements are dynamic. There is 'tension and movement' created by positioning. For example, a large black-and-white photograph at the top left of a page might be balanced by a small red logo at the bottom right of the page. The weight distribution here is not only to do with size but also to do with the comparative 'weight' of the elements' attraction value—the red has stronger attraction value and is therefore 'heavier' than its size alone indicates.

Freestyle layout

'Organic' or 'free-form' layout is mostly used on posters, packaging and advertisements. Often you'll sketch a layout and keep sketching until you can see the completed design in the scribbles you have made. Then, sitting at the keyboard with trusty mouse at the ready, you convert the scribbles into your final piece. This is the ideal working method—establish what you want each element of the design to achieve and then translate that, massaging text and image to fit your idea. Details, of course, are not worked out so much in the sketching phase.

Free-form design might answer a particular project more effectively than the often rigid grid structure that many designers adopt. For brochures, pamphlets, handbills, packaging, stationery, covers and posters, consider using freestyle or free-form design.

With freestyle, you can size and place images and text according to their level of importance and their image quality, and interrelate them by juxtaposition or layering. Remember that the viewer or audience will need to get some information from your design, so don't disguise the information or hide it. Help the viewer to understand.

Having the maximum flexibility that free-form offers allows you to place pictures directly where the text refers to them. You also have the ultimate in flexibility for text massaging. You can vary line lengths and leading according to what is most readable for your chosen typefaces, without the limiting structures of modules or grid-based column widths. Pictures, too, can be whatever size is most logical or interesting for the image without having to conform to column widths or modules. Free-form implies an asymmetrical layout.

In most designs, there are places where small changes could be made to improve the accurate retrieval of information. With free-form design, there is the flexibility to do some fine-tuning of type and image sizing and placement, all the while maintaining an interesting design that follows the logical flow of information, rather than a pre-ordained presentation system like a grid.

There are drawbacks to free-form design. It is so flexible that some people find it hard to start. And you don't want to make decisions that allow yourself or others to procrastinate any longer. That flexibility can also make it hard to stop (there is always a little more tweaking you could do). Unfortunately, computers encourage this, regardless of the layout style you choose.

In order to use this technique successfully, you need to have decision and experimentation time—and sometimes that is just too hard to find.

Free-form layout can work in publication design but is rarely used. Grids are faster for production of multipage documents and usually make it easier to control the layout for consistency and general flow through the document. Magazines, however, sometimes use free-form layout in a feature section.

A small element can dominate or balance a larger element in asymmetrical layout.

Layout practice
Using a group of elements such as a picture, some text and a heading, create a series of designs that explore the interrelationships of those elements. Create a layout that is image-dominant where the image is probably larger. Can you make an image-dominant layout where the image is smaller? Try a text-dominant layout as well. These are often difficult, but a hint is to keep the image minute and the headline huge and use interesting type selection.

Try varying the text size (a larger point size will fill more page area) and varying the number of columns, and their width. Columns on the same page do not have to be the same width. Also try to make the text and the image each have exactly the same area in the layout.

You could try a space-dominant layout where your elements float in space. Then try to give a particular character to the layout: jolly, traditional, sophisticated, modern, lively, restrained, even boring! (If you can make a design intentionally boring, presumably you can avoid it later!)

According to André Jute in *Grids: The Structure of Graphic Design*, there are three purposes of a grid:

According to André Jute in *Grids: The Structure of Graphic Design*, there are three purposes of a grid:

- Repeatability, particularly important in:
  - multipage documents
  - a series of documents
  - corporate identity
- Composition
  - to blend linear text with illustration
  - to arrange size, shape and balance of elements
- Communication
  - finding given elements in the same place
  - as a guide to important elements.

DOING IT SMARTER
Breaking a grid

Grids need not be followed slavishly. Indeed, it can be very dynamic to 'break the grid'. It is important to remember that you are breaking something, so it needs to be established before a break can have its full impact.

You can break a grid by bleeding a picture—it is said to 'bleed' if it continues off the page—or having a contoured picture break into a margin. You can also break a grid by contouring type around an illustration, creating a runaround. Give a comfortable zone around the illustration (in most cases, 3–5 mm is 'comfortable') so the type does not limit the illustration.

Grids

To bind elements within a layout and to achieve a visual consistency over a series of layouts, designers often use a grid. A grid is an invisible structure that underlies a layout. Elements such as pictures, text, headings and logos are positioned in the layout in relation to the grid. Nearly all publications, and many advertisements, use a grid.

There are sound financial reasons for using a grid scheme, because the grid simplifies a number of production decisions and controls the production. This is why it is important to develop a grid that enables, rather than a grid that disables. You need a grid that will give you the flexibility of application that you will need in future applications of that grid, not just the initial task.

At its simplest, a grid can just be the four margins surrounding a text area. Don't forget that the bottom margin should be larger than the top margin to accommodate the optical centre.

Pages are designed to be read together, so always create a double-page grid. The page layout will usually be reflected on the spine, though left-hand and right-hand page layouts can differ according to the type of publication.

Avoid numerous indents, as each indent creates a new text element. In multicolumn setting, try to align material in blocks horizontally—across the page—so the horizontal layout will remain strong. This can be done with a series of standardised cross-rules on your grid or even a grid that is broken into modules—they will streamline layout decisions.

A grid system strives to achieve unity. However, we have become so used to breaking the grid that we often break it before it's been established. This will often weaken a publication.

Some grid systems actually work against unity because they are too flexible. The grid systems that allow 2-, 3-, 4-, 6- or 8-column widths on any page tend to make it difficult to establish unity within all but the largest publications where there is a chance that the diversity will be appreciated.

Grid systems often are created by determining column possibilities across the page size. However, to further enhance the structure and bring greater unity to the publication, a series of horizontal page divisions is often created. These give particular points on the page for pictures, captions or headings to hang from. They bring a strength to the publication. They are sometimes called 'flow lines'.

Mixed column grids
On the same template, this grid will accommodate 2-, 3- and 4-columns.

At their simplest, they can be a mathematical division of the column depth, a series of cross-rules placed at regular intervals. This option tends to be used for newsletters and newspapers where the variety of material is wide.

They can be modular for ease of placement of photo-graphs, diagrams, logos and text. Headings can be devised to work in a particular size of module. Then it is simply a case of playing with a jigsaw—fit all the pieces into the page using leftover space for alignment.

For brochures and books, though, the cross-rules are often customised for the particular publication, and there may only be a few well-placed cross-rules that perform specific tasks in the publication.

DOING IT SMARTER
Picture box and rule sizing in unjustified text setting
When your text is unjustified it has an optical width narrower than the maximum text width. To take account of this in picture layouts, the column width of picture boxes is narrower by 5–7 mm in order for the picture to sit more comfortably in the unjust-ified text.

Similarly, if you are placing rules below or above headings or captions in unjustified text, use the optical column width for the width of the rule, not the full column width. Rules will also be 5–7 mm shorter.

A modular grid
created by regular mathematical subdivisions of the columns

Customised divisions
designed to accommodate publication-specific content blocks

DOING IT SMARTER
Corporate grid relationships

You might decide that, for your corporate identification to be consistent across all materials, a coloured band will appear in the top quarter of any shape. So whether it is a badge, the Web site or the letterhead, the top quarter of each shape will be coloured and contain the corporate identification.

Further from this, alignment of logos or symbols is often detailed by measurements taken from the symbol itself. Usually this ensures that the logo is not crammed into spaces that are too small for it. Often it is a placement issue where a particular measure, which could be half its width, is placed above and to the left of the symbol. A quarter of its width might be placed to its right before any type is set.

Using relationships with your elements like this can create a coherence that is simple to maintain across varying sizes, formats and requirements.

READ MORE ABOUT IT
Allen Hurlburt, *The grid: A modular system for the design and production of newspapers, magazines and books*, Van Nostrand Reinhold, New York, 1978, ISBN 0 422 23598 4.

Allen Hurlburt, *Layout: The design of the printed page*, Watson-Guptill Publications, New York, 1977, ISBN 0 214 20674 2.

André Jute, *Grids: The structure of graphic design*, RotoVision SA, Crans-Pres-Celigny, Switzerland, 1996, ISBN 2 88046 277 0.

Formats

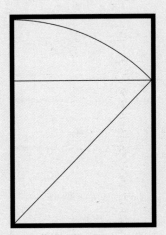

International paper sizes

are based on the ratio 1:√2 or about 1:1.4 (*left*).

There are three series, called the A, B and C series.

The base sheet for the A series is A0 which has a total area equal to one square metre.

The sheets divide proportionally into their smaller sizes (*right*).

International sizes A, B and C series, DL

2A0	1682 × 1189 mm					
A0	1189 × 841 mm	B0	1414 × 1000 mm	C0	1297 × 917 mm
A1	841 × 594 mm	B1	1000 × 707 mm	C1	917 × 648 mm
A2	594 × 420 mm	B2	707 × 500 mm	C2	648 × 458 mm
A3	420 × 297 mm	B3	500 × 353 mm	C3	458 × 324 mm
A4	297 × 210 mm	B4	353 × 250 mm	C4	324 × 229 mm
A5	210 × 148 mm	B5	250 × 176 mm	C5	229 × 162 mm
A6	148 × 105 mm	B6	176 × 125 mm	C6	162 × 114 mm
1/3 A4	210 × 99 mm				
DL	110 × 220 mm				

Other stationery and publication measures

Foolscap	337 × 206 mm
Quarto	260 × 206 mm
American quarto	279 × 216 mm
American foolscap	330 × 216 mm
Magazines	270 × 207 mm
Paperbacks	198 × 128 mm
	178 × 110 mm
Large format	234 × 153 mm
Business cards	55 × 85 mm
	50 × 90 mm

Other product measures

CD jewel cases	
Back cover	118 × 149
i.e. 137 mm + 12 mm for 2 spines	
Booklet	121 × 121 mm
Floppy disk labels	70 × 70 mm
Video covers	115 × 196 mm
Spine	28 mm
Movie posters	
Single sheet	1008 × 688 mm
Day bills	650 × 330 mm
Bus shelter posters	1.8 × 1.2 m

Custom sizes can be created for any of the above.

DOING IT FASTER

Formats

Reuse icons, style sheets and templates. If you have created icons for one document, keep them in a library or drag them between documents. Do not recreate them each time you need them.

Likewise, if you have created a new template for a page size different from your usual, save it somewhere (on a floppy or even your hard disk if it's likely to become a regular project format) where you can access the template when you need it again.

Saving just a short period of time, such as that used to create the page margins and column guides, can speed your production. You've done it once, don't waste it.

You may find it handy to have an A4 landscape page and an A4 portrait page at the ready...and a few other standard sizes:

- a six-panel, 1/3 A4 pamphlet template;
- a four-page, three-column, A4 newsletter template;
- a template for correspondence;
- invoice;
- orders; and
- other regularly used forms.

Measurement preferences

Page measurements, margins, picture boxes and text area are now often expressed in millimetres. Text area always used to be expressed in picas and points. A pica is 12 points or approximately 3.5 mm. This option is still usually available to you in your 'preferences' set-up. But because of the advent of computers and desktop publishing, page divisions are now often expressed in millimetres. However, type measurements, leading and the space measurements within a text block are still expressed in points. Text indents and tabs though, which were previously specified in picas or points, are now often expressed in millimetres, in order to fit with the page divisions.

Margins

Generous margins make a book feel easy to read. Traditionally, the *inside margin* (called the *back margin* in traditional book terminology) is about the same as the *top margin* (the *head*); the *outside margin* (the *fore edge*) is slightly larger; and the *bottom margin* (the *foot*) is the largest.

The inner margins are smaller than the outer margins so the text areas in a double-page spread are seen to be more evenly spaced. If they are specified as half the outer margin, the inner margins create a band of space equal to the outer margin. But there is an optical illusion created by the folding of paper at the spine, so the inner margins are usually two-thirds to three-quarters the specification of the outer margin. Of course, inner margins will need to be larger to accommodate binding techniques like ring-binding, side stapling and perfect binding.

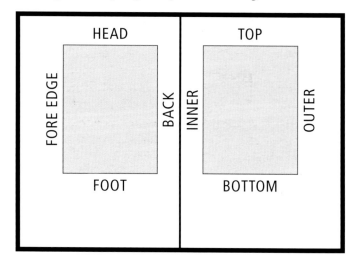

Columns and gutters

Columns are usually set with 5 mm gutters between. Use more space if the column is justified than if it is unjustified. If space is limited, you might choose to run a fine vertical rule between justified columns in order to separate them appropriately.

Columns within a publication can be of equal width, or unequal as in this book—and this is largely determined by the style of the publication and the information it contains. A side column can be useful for commenting on the main text, incorporating headings and images, or summarising and drawing attention to the main content. If columns are of different widths, in many grid systems they will be related proportionally.

Multicolumn layouts are used if the manuscript is made up mostly of short paragraphs. Long paragraphs in a narrow column measure make the text look daunting to read.

Page depth

There are two choices for page depth. You can keep all the elements on your page consistently spaced or keep the bottom line of your page consistent by altering the spacing throughout the page to maintain it. In both cases, you usually define the maximum page depth by creating the bottom margin in your document set-up. But in the case of variable page depth, you can reduce or extend your text block as required.

Variable page depth

Variable page depth maintains constant spacing between elements but the page finishes on or above its maximum text depth line. The top line of text remains constant and the text hangs from that line like clothes on a clothesline. Variable page depth is a convenient way of avoiding 'widows' and 'orphans' and other awkward page breaks.

Footnotes still sit at the bottom of the grid. It is even more desirable to have variable column depth in publications that have two or more columns, as artificially evened-out columns on the same page usually look disgusting, due to the distortion in their vertical space distribution.

DOING IT SMARTER
Making a style book

A style book documents, in one place, all the production and design decisions to date in the production of a book, magazine, newspaper, newsletter or larger scale work like a series of publications or a corporate identity. It should include a hard copy or written description of:

- typographic style sheets
- templates, grids and master pages
- editorial style sheets
- colour palettes and swatches
- standard graphic elements like rules, picture boxes, symbols and other page furniture
- illustration preferences and stylings
- paper stock specifications
- print specifications
- suppliers' names, addresses and phone numbers
- sample copies.

The style book enables easy replication if the file is lost or temporarily unable to be accessed or if a new producer needs to prepare material in the same style.

DOING IT SMARTER
Widows and orphans
A widow is the first line of a paragraph that has been left at the foot of a column or page by itself. An orphan is the last line or, worse, the last word, in a paragraph that has been taken over to start a new page or column by itself.

To avoid these two unfortunate circumstances, a paragraph with three lines or less should be taken over to a new column or page. That is, only a four-or-more-line paragraph can be broken, provided the break takes at least two lines and leaves at least two lines.

Jason Grant of Inkahoots Design Studio, speaking at *Sydney Design 99*, noted: 'A picture is worth 1000 words —and 1000 words for what it omits.'

DOING IT SMARTER
Picture selection and text interaction
Selecting imagery to support text is a skill in itself. The interaction of images with text is a complex piece of design manipulation. To practise the technique, choose an image and a word that when seen together make someone laugh, sad, angry, nostalgic. Four concepts. Isolated.

To work with basic interaction of text and image, start with book covers with usually not more than two levels of text—title and author— and select an appropriate image. Posters are also a good starting point. Gradually increase the complexity and the interaction of the different elements.

Constant page depth
Constant page depth indicates that pages throughout the publication will always start and finish at the same points. This is achieved by artificially stretching the spacing between elements of the page. This means adding or subtracting space around headings, paragraphs, tables, illustrations and, on rare occasions, between lines of text. Unless it is prepared with extreme care, the manipulation of text like this should be avoided. However, this is the 'classical' style of page make up, but the fine skills that perfected it are rare these days.

Avoid your computer's vertical justification operation. If you want your pages to be a constant page depth, make the spacing decisions yourself. It is time-consuming, but will also ensure that the alterations are not too obvious. Your computer is not nearly as considerate.

Imagery

Images should add dimension to the text that cannot be achieved in any other way. The illustration should complement the text and be, at least, relevant, and preferably enhance the reader's understanding.

To decide where images should or could go, read the manuscript and jot down ideas for images in the margins. The positioning of images should also lend pace and variety to the document.

No image is preferred if the only option is a poor image. The quality of any illustrative material will not be improved by reproduction techniques.

It takes planning, and in many cases research, to find an appropriate image with excellent reproduction quality. Photo libraries and archival institutions are good initial sources.

It is advisable to seek the services of a professional illustrator or photographer if the material you require does not exist, is not readily available or would have greater impact if it were consistent and original.

When placing an image into your layout, be aware that images usually create a square or rectangular shape on the page. They also have a tonal level. Even though they will vary in tone, they can be reduced to a basic tonal level which is usually seen if you squint at the image.

They may also be 'contoured', where they make a complex shape on the page because the subject is cut out from its frame. When you squint, this shape will also 'reduce' to a basic form—circle, triangle, oval, rectangle, square or trapezium. This becomes the layout element for balance purposes.

Photographic imagery is one of the strongest elements in a design because, since television brought moving pictures into our homes, our society has become reliant on visual information. Imagery was always the strongest element in a design—even in illuminated manuscripts, the pictures are the first things we notice.

It would be foolish to deny the greater attraction of the image over type. So use images carefully and look at what information they are giving. Photographic images have had such power because traditionally they have been 'real'—they were recognisably a slice of reality captured in a single image. However, with image manipulation, the strength of that implied 'reality' has been eroded.

When you analyse a photo, what should you look for? Does the subject stand out from the background? Whatever the subject of a photo, it is usually best for that subject not to compete with its background. It may mean the photographer has chosen a simple background (as in controlled studio portraits—black or white or mottled back cloths) or has separated the subject from the background by focusing carefully so the subject is in focus and the background blurred. In portraits, a photographer will often backlight a person's hair to create this separation from the background.

Is the photo in focus? If not, what part of the photo is in focus? If the subject is moving, sometimes it will have moved just out of focus and there will be a tree in the background perfectly in focus. This is fine if you want a photo of a tree. But not necessarily appropriate if you wanted a portrait of an Olympic cyclist.

Does the photo have a full range of tone? In black-and-white photography, are there a solid black and a pure white somewhere in the photo, and a complete range of greys in between? In colour photography, is there a solid black somewhere and a pure white somewhere with a representative colour range between?

Is the photo colour-correct? Does it have a colour 'cast' where there is the unwanted effect of seeing the image as if through a filter of one particular colour? Is there a yellowy tinge like indoor shots taken without flash on outdoor film? Often, colour film will have a predisposition to produce a particular colour cast.

CHECK LIST

Images

- [ ] Photographs
- [ ] Drawings
- [ ] Paintings
- [ ] Photographs of 3-dimensional illustrations
- [ ] Digital illustrations
- [ ] Cartoons
- [ ] Symbols
- [ ] Pictograms
- [ ] Maps
- [ ] Diagrams
- [ ] Graphs
- [ ] Flow charts
- [ ] 'Found' material or mock authentic material such as old letters, faxes, telexes, telegrams, tickets

Out of focus?

Don't necessarily discard a photograph just because it is out of focus. You can use it—differently. You don't necessarily have the luxury of being able to shoot it again, so adjust your thinking of how you can use it.

Photos that are out of focus usually look in focus the further away from them you get. In publication terms, this means reduce the image. If it's just a question of soft focus, where the photo is just slightly out of focus all over, it may need to be reduced only slightly. The more out of focus, the smaller you will need to reduce it. And don't worry, as small photos still get attention.

Image manipulation programs give you the ability to improve the clarity of an image with 'unsharp masking'.

The 2-Ls cropping method

Take a sheet of light card about A4 in size (mid-grey is a good colour if you have a choice) and cut out the centre, leaving about a 30 mm frame. Then cut two corners that are diagonally opposite each other, to create two L-shapes. By overlapping them and sliding them left to right, up and down, you can alter the size and shape of the frame. You can see how a photograph looks in square, vertical or horizontal rectangular formats—just by moving the two Ls.

But more than this, when selecting photographs for a project, select ones that will look as if they were specifically created as a set. There should be a certain consistency of subject matter or attitude to the subjects. It can be to do with where the focus is or a specific method of lighting the subject—soft or harsh, dappled or pin-lit, bright or shadowy. There might be a particular point of view. The colour set might be limited in some way or manipulated to have a similar palette. Equally, you might choose photographs that have a particular grain or texture or use a filter that gives them a consistent texture. You might use cropping techniques to help the photographs fit a consistent format.

READ MORE ABOUT IT

Peter Bonnici and Linda Proud, *Designing with photographs*, RotoVision SA, Crans-Pres-Celigny, Switzerland, 1998, ISBN 2 88046 353 X.

Tim Daly, *Digital: photography: A user's guide to creating digital images*, New Burlington Books, London, 2000, ISBN 1 86155 273 4.

Catharine Slade, *The encyclopedia of illustration techniques*, Simon & Schuster, Sydney, 1997, ISBN 0 7318 0599 2.

Terence Dalley (ed.), *The complete guide to illustration and design techniques and materials*, Chartwell Books, Secaucus, New Jersey, 1980, ISBN 0 89009 316 4.

Steven Heller and Teresa Fernandes, *The business of illustration*, Watson Guptill, New York, 1995, ISBN 0 8230 0545 3.

Terry Jones, *Instant design: A manual of graphic techniques*, Architecture Design and Technology Press, London, 1990, ISBN 1 85454 838 7.

Cropping

Deleting unwanted or distracting areas of an image is called cropping. Cropping can change the shape of an illustration or zoom into a small area of it and refocus attention. This is perhaps the designer's single most effective tool in using photos. It can change a horizontal photo to a vertical one, alter the subject matter of the photo and improve the composition of a poor photo. It can also destroy an excellent photo (and some photographers will not give reproduction clearance for a photo if it will be cropped).

Cropping enables you to delete half the photograph to highlight a particular piece of information. You might want to highlight the office furniture for a catalogue and delete the workers who are in unfashionable clothing. Cropping also enables you to fit a predetermined layout shape, as sometimes the layout is created while you wait for a photo to be supplied.

It also means that you can alter the appearance of a photograph by cropping it radically. What might have been

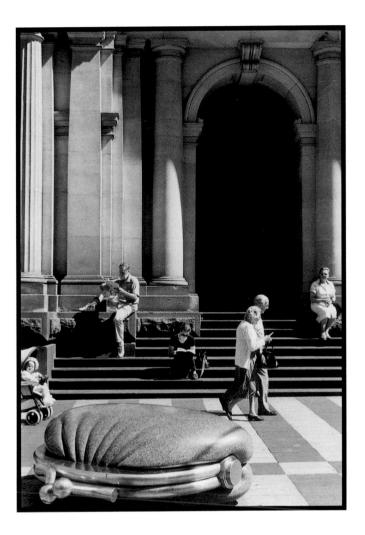

Picture cropping

By cropping, you can create four pictures (*below*) from one original image (*left*).

an ordinary snap can become a dynamic image by creative cropping. By deleting one element in the foreground, you may be able to alter the visual structure of the image enough to lend it greater drama. Let the reader become involved in the picture.

With the 2-Ls method, you can see what the photo looks like when cropped diagonally. Try it with a portrait and see what happens to the profile of a face when it is tilted upwards and downwards in the frame—doesn't that begin to have an effect on how you perceive the person who is portrayed?

Scaling

Scaling is a technical process where you find out how much area to leave in your layout for the image you want, or you have allowed a certain area in your layout for an image and you need to decide which part of the selected image to use.

Sources of photographs and copyright

If you do not have any, photographs can be accessed through image libraries. Charges for the use of an image usually depend on:

- the number of copies that will be reproduced and distributed
- the size or area the image takes up in your layout
- whether it is used on the cover or inside the publication.

Photographers may sell images they have shot previously, or you can commission photographs to be taken specifically for your project. Make sure you brief the photographer on what you actually need, and the format you need it in, such as slide, print, transparency or digital file.

Ask to see a portfolio of the photographer's work before commissioning. This is the same for illustrators—make sure that their style is the style you want before you sign a contract or a commission.

Remember also that you often purchase the image only for the specific use you have negotiated. Any further reproduction from that image without renegotiating rights is infringing the copyright of the work.

The image belongs to the originator of the image—the photographer or illustrator—unless they assign the copyright to you or a third party (such as an image library) or give you unlimited usage. You will usually pay more for unlimited usage or copyright purchase.

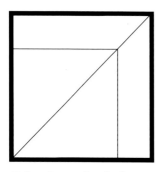

Enlarging and reducing on the diagonal

To scale an image, use its diagonal for enlargement or reduction calculations. Where the cropping is known, the column depth can be determined by moving along the diagonal until the column width is reached. Measuring from that point down will tell you the depth.

If the final size is known but the cropping needs to be done, you can use the same technique.

DOING IT SMARTER

Calculating percentages for enlargement or reduction

To calculate a percentage for either enlargement or reduction, divide the measure you want (from your layout) by the measure you have (from the original image) and multiply by 100. You can use either the vertical or horizontal measure—or the width of a person's eyes if you want to get faces looking the same size—as long as you measure the same part of the image.

You will also need to include an image credit line (usually in very small sans serif type up the side of the image or the page on which it appears). In many publications, image copyrights have a separate listing in the acknowledgments or credits, referring to the image's position on the page and the page number on which the image appears. The credit will usually include both the originator of the image and the name of the image library from which it comes.

Image libraries will limit the number of times an image can be purchased and decide if the resale of that image to the next person who requests it will have adverse effects on the last sale. If so, they will not release the image. However, if the two markets are different enough, and the likelihood of the image being recognised or diminishing the return to either of the purchasing parties is not at risk, they will release the image for other users. For example, if the image is for an annual report that will be released in Australia, the image may also be released for an advertisement in central America.

Clip art

Many companies release volumes or selections of 'useful', 'standard' illustrations, photographs and backgrounds on CD-ROM or in slide or hard-copy form. Unfortunately, the wide availability and widespread use of these illustrations can make them less effective.

Another problem with clip art is the compatibility of one image with another. For example, illustrations will often have conflicting drawing styles, which can sit uncomfortably with each other. For unity in an ad campaign or through a publication, you will probably want stylistic continuity.

Alternatively, the most successful thing you can do with clip art is to design your layout and style around a diversity of imagery sources. This can create its own difficulties, since it means you may have to find optional pieces for one spread, because the styles are too similar. Fortunately, with image manipulation programs, you have the capacity to alter images stylistically.

If you use clip art, crop it or combine it to create a 'new' image. In that way, if the studio next door bought the same CD, your use of the image will be different from theirs.

DOING IT FASTER AND CHEAPER
Limit picture scalings
Choose a scaling that will fit the majority of your photographs and then draw one picture box. Multiply it by duplicating, and position the clones. Even if some of the photographs are landscape format, you can rotate the box by 90° from a portrait position to the landscape. By carefully specifying the runaround on the original box, you can place the clones anywhere and the text will consistently wrap around the boxes.

This will save you money, too, because the person who produces your scans can scan a batch of images at once, minimising the time spent on the scanner.

Mostly, your purchase of clip art pays the fee for unlimited use of the image. (Note that this is not the case with image libraries where you pay for each use of the image. You may also find an image is not allowed to be cropped.)

Cartoons

Cartoons can enliven text. But check before you commission a cartoonist—does the client organisation really want a hard-hitting 'editorial' cartoon, or does it want simply a funny picture?

If you choose a well-known cartoonist and leave it in their hands to illustrate a particular aspect of the text you have supplied, you can expect to pay them for the image, even if you choose to not use it in the final production. Ascertain how much leeway for interpretation your client organisation is prepared to give. Most cartoonists understand there may be limitations or particular requirements and are happy to comply if adequately briefed.

Diagrams, graphs and charts

Diagrams explain complex processes, phenomena and relationships with an easy-to-understand clarity. By recognising patterns and hierarchies of information, a diagram designer is able to simplify and communicate the hidden or even the abstract.

By taking a lead from techniques such as mapping, a flow chart evolved—where a process becomes the journey. There may be twists and turns in the path. You may have to repeat a particular sequence. There may be sub-processes operating concurrently nearby. It can all be mapped or staged in the familiar form of a diagram.

When creating a chart, the first requirement is to select the nodes (towns on a map) and then create the links (access routes). Then you might start relating the nodes to each other by differentiating different processes with colour, shape and size (some towns have particular facilities or higher population density). The sorting process attempts to make the clearest, least complicated explanation of the connections and relationships between the nodes.

Then there is the choice of diagrammatic representation. Which graphing styles could be used? Which will give the most appropriate understanding?

And then there is the unexpected connection. What about an exploded diagram of an organisation instead of

---

Tony and Barry Buzan in *The Mindmap Book* list the skills available to all of us that are used in the mapping process they describe (not a bad list to consider when creating diagrams, graphs and charts):

☐ Language
  – words
  – symbols
☐ Number
☐ Logic
  – sequence
  – listing
  – linearity
  – analysis
  – time
  – association
☐ Rhythm
☐ Colour
☐ Imagery
  – daydreaming
  – visualisation
☐ Spatial awareness
  – dimension
  – gestalt (whole picture)

READ MORE ABOUT IT
Tony Buzan with Barry Buzan, *The mindmap book*, rev. edn, BBC Books, London, 1995, ISBN 0 563 37101 3.

an organisation chart? Why not a recipe card for a manufacturing process? What about a map of your brainstorming
session (actually, that's a technique called 'mindmapping' by
Tony Buzan)?

Graphs are one of the most misused and misunderstood
communication techniques. They tend to be used to hide
information rather than to clarify it. They can instantly
convey a message, but are so easily manipulated that the
message conveyed can be quite erroneous. However, graphs
and charts in the right hands are a technique for making
the complex clear.

Graphs should contain accurate information and
compare relevant and appropriate data. If you need to
prepare a graph, find out what is supposed to be understood after reading the graph. Most graphs start as tables of
numbers with multiple columns of statistical information.
You may be able to delete whole columns from the table if
you know the intention of the author in providing a graph.
This will simplify and amplify the graph's message. The
audience needs to be able to see accurately in only a glance
what the graph is communicating. For example, we do not
read area accurately unless it is in rectangles or squares that
relate to each other.

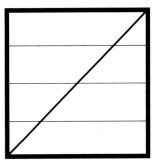

A standard line graph

A graphing convention that confuses information,
despite being a convenient technique for graph drawing
purposes, is the use of exponential axes. When you are
comparing amounts that are very small with amounts that
are very large—as in 'exponential growth'—it is convenient
to show this in a sliding scale where the axis divisions get
smaller as they increase.

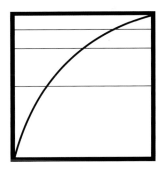

A distorted graph
showing the same information using
an exponential scale

As readers, we do not dwell on graphing and examine
detail, so we assume that the axes are evenly divided. If you
have huge numbers to compare with tiny numbers,
consider showing this in other ways that will enable people
to accurately see the magnitude of the difference.

Think about the impression people reading the graph
should gain from a glance. Will they see the contrast more
clearly by producing a different style of graph?

If you are producing graphs—usually to convert tables
into a form more easy to read—choose the appropriate
graphing style for the information. For percentages,
consider pie charts. For increasing amounts over time,
choose a line chart or bar chart. For showing the connections in a process, consider a flow chart.

Optical and actual area
It is difficult to read comparative area in graphing. It is easier to read the dimensional variation than the mass variation.

50%

25% area

50%

25% area

50%

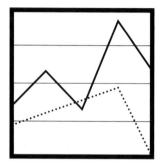

Line charts

Line charts show quantities over time. The progress of time is conventionally represented from the past on the left to the present on the right. Line charts can compare two or more lines, but the fewer lines the better.

Colour coding the lines works. In single-colour reproduction, keying the lines works better than tonal variation in the lines. Combining colour coding and line keying can work but you may get too many levels of information if you need to resort to that.

It can be helpful to run a series of evenly spaced background lines off the left axis to enable more accurate reading of the graphed values.

Pie charts

Usually based on figures that have been converted to percentages, a pie chart shows a whole divided into its parts. In annual reports, there can be a temptation to compare pies of different sizes with the justification: 'This year's pie was smaller than last year's.' It is unwise to compare pies of different sizes, as people do not accurately read the comparative area of circles. In most of those pie charts, the main information to be communicated is based on comparative distribution and, if featured with last year's pie, the difference in distribution, possibly showing a priority shift or even showing maintenance of the status quo. The comparative size of the pies can be compared in a separate figure with a different graphing form, such as a bar chart.

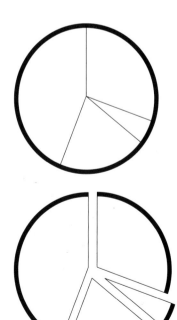

Consider the size at which the final pie will be reproduced when you decide into how many parts it will be divided. Avoid slices that are too thin—they are difficult to key clearly.

Colour coding the slices works, or tonally coding the slices in single-colour reproduction. Introducing line and dot patterns into the slices rarely works because the patterns do not have enough area in narrow slices to clearly establish which pattern they are. 'Exploded' pie charts tend to distort sizes and are consequently less accurately read. Three-dimensional pies tend to confuse information. And combining a pie chart with pieces that are different heights due to a vertical graphing process—effectively bar-charting a pie—is fascinating, but totally confusing for the reader.

Bar charts

Showing comparisons of quantities, bar charts have a high recognition of actual figures—particularly if a few well-chosen rules establish some standard divisions of the numerical axis.

Sometimes it is desirable to read the exact figures, in which case each bar is labelled, either centred inside the bar at its top, or in the space directly above the bar, centred on the width of the bar.

Subdividing a bar into its component parts can work, but can also become confusing. It might show the variation in priorities in funding between different years, but will need some explanation or discussion in the text because the reader will not always accurately read the information.

Colour coding and tonal coding of bars works.

Avoid three-dimensional bar charts, because accurate readability of the actual figures is lost, which is one of the bar chart's strengths.

Variations of bar charts, such as horizontal bar charts and building the height or length of the bar with a pic-togram that represents what the bar is graphing, provide opportunities for increasing the visual attraction of the bar chart. For example, when comparing male and female participation rates in sports, you could prepare a horizontal bar chart that moves out from the centre labels with males moving numerically to the left and females moving to the right. This would demonstrate any imbalance visually.

3-D graphs

In all graphing styles, it is best to avoid three dimensions. The third dimension often only confuses the information. A graph is produced to clarify or put figures into perspective, to give an idea of trends. Bevelled edges are about as adventurous and intrusive as the third dimension needs to get.

CHECK LIST
Key lines
(Most important to least important)
1   Bold continuous line
2   Fine continuous line
3   Dashed line
4   Dot-dash dotted line
5   Dotted line

3-D confusion
where your reader is unsure which line gives the correct figure.

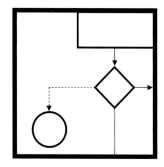

Flow charts

Flow charts show a process in sequence and can be very effective. They can incorporate optional paths and often use straightforward graphic symbols like arrows to propel the reader accurately. Used in manuals and handbooks, they are often more easy to comprehend than narrative text or numbered sequences in text. They do not need to use the original flow-charting coded shapes of diamonds signifying a choice between optional paths, rectangles for answering statements, and circles for completion. They do generally incorporate connecting lines, numbering, arrows and colour coding as required.

Flow charts are used in the planning of multimedia and use icons and shapes to indicate which media is used in which page in the program. Site plans for Web sites are also often based on the principles of flow charts.

Organisation charts

Hierarchy and connections, lines of authority and areas of responsibility are often shown in organisation charts. They are often based on a simplified flow-chart style. Authority is generally depicted from highest authority at the top to least authority at the bottom.

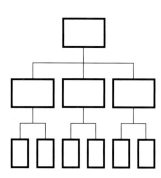

Another option which can be successful—particularly with layered captions, that may indicate a division title, a name, a position title for each person on the chart—is to make the authority move from highest authority at the left to least authority at the right. This can accommodate alignment of divisions and simplify the fitting of all the people onto the chart when the lower authority levels kick in.

Often, designers will centre the text contained within the blocks of the chart, but there can be problems where there are disproportionate amounts of information in blocks at the same level of hierarchy, e.g. where you need to accommodate 'Human resource development' and 'Operations'. Always design the block based on the longest heading but also consider how the shortest heading will look. Will you vertically centre each heading in its box or will you align all top lines? Vertical centring will often make each box look better, but alignment of the lines usually makes the chart as a whole look better.

You might try a variation where, using connecting rules and arrows only, you connect type in columns, avoiding the need to plan the blocks.

In photographic organisation charts, which are increasingly popular, try to keep the scale of all the heads the same and the background colour even. This is easy if all the people portrayed are photographed on the same day, by the same photographer, against the same background, from the same distance. But if you are dealing with photographs supplied by individuals, try to make the distance from the left of the left eye to the right of the right eye the same when scaling all the photographs.

Sequence diagrams
Staged sequences can describe the evolution of the world or the creation of a publication or how your client's new product will get to market. Using a numbered sequence of pictures or pictograms that describe each step in the process, a visual representation of the process can clarify a task for a team, educate a novice in the area, or introduce a new skill in a logical manner. The sequence will often have a series of descriptive captions below each of the pictures.

The captioning might also have timeframes allocated. Time can be represented by a clock face or a digital clock readout (in the case of, say, a recipe) or by a calendar or seasonal references for longer processes.

Sequence diagrams are used in project management. The critical path method is widely used. Time progresses from the left, where a project starts, to the right, where a project ends. Horizontal bars represent each of the stages and can be layered to show concurrent activities.

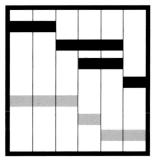

The program evaluation review technique (PERT) diagram is similar in principle but uses numerically staged events and links them with arrows, indicating where two processes need to culminate before another can begin.

Exploded diagrams
Assembly instructions often 'explode' the parts being assembled and show how they connect and interconnect with arrows. The assembly is often numbered in sequence as well. The illustration is often a realistic uncluttered line drawing in either perspective or axonometric projection.

This style of diagram is used to show the floor plans of multilevel buildings and even Web site plans, as well as its more familiar role in model aeroplane construction.

DOING IT SMARTER

Animating or staging diagrams, graphs and charts

In Web sites, television and multimedia, diagrams, graphs and charts need to move. In bar charts, the bars can grow; in line graphs, the line can travel its course; pie charts can spin. But diagrams and processes often need more attention. The chart will have been broken into stages or sections or modules, so focus on building each module and then integrating in the full chart. In this way, you might have a simple structure that takes you to a further level of detail when you click on an element. Readers can create their own path through the information, much like they do with a site.

Don't forget to use the animation techniques and 2-D movement techniques to help the diagram maintain attention on screen. You might develop a character that will guide the reader through the information. You might incorporate sounds and video of the process. With virtual reality (VR), readers can be walked through a museum or trade show on screen without having to read a map in the traditional manner.

READ MORE ABOUT IT

Nigel Holmes, *Designer's guide to creating charts and diagrams*, Watson-Guptill, New York, 1991, ISBN 0 8230 1338 3.

Peter Wildbur, *Information graphics: A survey of typographic, diagrammatic and cartographic communication*, Trefoil Publications, London, 1989, ISBN 0 86294 110 5.

Trevor Bounford, *Digital diagrams: Effective design and presentation of statistical information*, Cassell & Co., London, 2001, ISBN 0304 354074.

Walter Herdeg (ed.), *Graphis diagrams: The graphic visualisation of abstract data*, 4th edn, Graphis Press Corporation, Zurich, 1981, ISBN 3 85709 410 9.

Peter Wildbur and Michael Burke, *Information graphics: Innovative solutions in contemporary design*, Thames & Hudson, London, 1998, ISBN 0 500 01872 3.

Paul Mijksenaar and Piet Westendorp, *Open here: The art of instructional design*, Thames & Hudson, London, 1999, ISBN 0 500 28170 X.

Molly W. Joss, *Looking good in presentations*, 3rd edn, Coriolis, Scottsdale, Arizona, 1999, ISBN 1 56604 854 0.

Tim Harrower, *The newspaper designer's handbook*, 4th edn, McGraw-Hill, Blacklick, Ohio, 1998, ISBN 0 697 32720 5.

Harry Mills, *Artful persuasion: How to command attention, change minds and influence people*, MG Press, Sumner Park, Queensland, 1999, ISBN 0 908722 91 5.

Contrast

Contrast can be the most powerful technique used in a layout, particularly contrasting:

- scale (size variation)
- tone (dark against light) and/or colour
- texture.

Contrast is an overriding design element. So much of the success of a layout is to do with effective deployment of contrasts, such as using contrasting typefaces, images and groupings of elements. This is one of the most useful design techniques.

Scale

The interaction of shapes with one another can be dynamic if you contrast the size of various elements. This is the basis of the design principle called 'scale'. The scaling of elements can have a distinct effect on your message.

Contrasting scale is the single most useful technique for improving a layout that is not working. Making one element larger and reducing the other elements to sub-servient roles will always help a boring layout by adding implied dimensionality.

Tone

Light or dark. Positive or negative. White or black. In black and white (or any other single-colour work—the black is a single colour printed on a white paper), you always have three colour options: the colour of the paper (white); the colour of the ink (black) and tones of the ink colour (greys) created by reducing the solid colour to a halftone or stipple.

To create an interesting tonal layout, identify the tonal average of your photos and text blocks. You do this naturally when you are deciding to reverse a headline or caption out of a photo—or whether you'll just overprint the image. If you can reverse out comfortably, it is a dark photograph; if you will need to overprint, it is a light photograph.

Boring layouts are layouts where everything reduces to a grey soup. You need the interplay of dark areas and light areas to interest the eye. Illustrations and photographs will reduce to an average tonality. Night shots usually have an overall dark tone. Shots of the Sydney Opera House at midday usually have an overall light tone.

Contrasting scale
A layout with two elements is often made more dynamic by altering their scale (or their size relationship).

But look at an alpine tourist brochure. The snow and sky will probably reduce to light, but the forests will usually reduce to very dark. With such well-defined contrasts in a single photograph, consider the picture area not as a rectangle filled with a mid-grey (an average of those two areas) but as an abstract pattern of light and dark. When you crop the photo, decide how the light and dark areas of the illustration will work in your layout. Do the lights and darks set up directions within the illustration? Can you use the directions they set up to lead to another layout element?

Typecolour

You can alter the tonal value of type (referred to as its 'typecolour') by creating bolder text or using a chunkier typeface, which gives a darker tone to the text block. Usually body text has a light-grey tone. Leading and tracking also affect typecolour. If there is more space between the lines or the letters, more of the background colour can be seen, which, if it is white, makes the text block appear lighter. You can check their tone by squinting at the elements— the famous 'squint test'.

Contrast the tone of text blocks with the tone of other text blocks or illustration areas.

Typecolour also helps define the shape of a text block. Usually text falls into vertical strips—light-grey rectangles. However, when you contour your type around an illustration or centre the text, you are dealing with different light-grey shapes in your layout.

Repetition, pattern and texture

Repetition creates logic within a design. It is the technique behind the principle of consistency in a publication.

You repeat text attributes to enable clear communication of a hierarchy of information. You might prepare your style sheet in order to consistently present particular information in specified type treatments. You can repeat a style or technique of illustration for unity. You might repeat a particular set of colours or specific textures to bring continuity to the job. Sometimes, repetition of line width around headings or as photograph borders is enough to identify that a particular design has come from a particular company. Even repetition of a particular scale relationship between two pictures in each of a series of advertisements can create a recognisable style.

But repetition of a visual element can also create texture and pattern. It can be ordered repetition of recognisable elements creating a pattern or random repetition of an abstract unit creating a texture. In pattern formation, you can create a pattern with photographs, illustration or type. The complexity of the pattern depends on the sequence you develop in order to repeat the original image. You may choose a small element simply duplicated in a line, then duplicate the line and place it underneath, continuing the duplication until the desired pattern exists. You might duplicate and flop or turn the original image to create a more complex sequence.

Creating patterns

A pattern can be created when you repeat anything. 'Anything' means illustrations, photographs (or bits of illustrations and photographs), type, punctuation marks (spaced lines of tabbed full stops will create a background pattern) and, of course, 'anything' includes dingbats. All those little stars and snowflakes, ticks and crosses, leaves and flowers, squares, triangles, circles and diamonds, can be used individually or in groups to create a multitude of patterns.

The pattern can be a simple, repeated symbol that makes a border or rule. It can then be copied and repeated in tightly leaded lines to create a security background for cheques.

Direction

Many shapes also imply a direction. For example, triangles tend to point somewhere. Rectangles tend to have a vertical (downward if it's a text block—because we read down) or horizontal (pointing to the right if it's a short text block—because we read across) stress. Only squares and circles are static.

Think of the classic photo of Uluru—horizons that seem to stretch forever from the central monolith. This is establishing a really powerful horizontal line within your layout. You can use that line and mimic it with, say, a long thin headline or a number of horizontal layout elements. Alternatively, you can use the contrast of strong vertical elements (text blocks, rules and other illustrations).

Borders and rules

Borders and rules should largely be avoided, as they are text distractions and can break the flow of information. However, they can help establish an old-fashioned feel or help organise material in complex spreads.

There are many decorative and illustrated borders and rules that can recreate the feel of early Australian theatre and 'Wanted' posters, country catalogues and Edwardian concert programs.

When using rules, it is important to remember that they are separation devices, so they will create the impression that material between them is linked. Bold or strong rules are used as section dividers; lighter rules separate within a category. Rules can separate information layers in tables, contents lists, indexes and even in multideck headings, but this separation can be achieved more efficiently with spacing and type attributes.

In lists, rules might be used to separate items, but note that the placement of a bold rule is above a bold heading to visually keep the heading with the text that follows it. When creating the style sheet for this sort of rule, specify the rules as 'rule above' each level of information.

There is little place for rules in layout—they are more an affectation of styling. Similarly, boxes are more usually achieved with colour change than with borders. Borderless tinted boxes or boxes and photographs with fine (0.25 point) ruled borders are less intrusive.

DO	**DON'T**
Vegetables	**Vegetables**
Asparagus	Asparagus
Broccoli	Broccoli
Carrot	Carrot
Fruit	**Fruit**
Apple	Apple
Banana	Banana
Cherry	Cherry

Space and pace

In a layout, balance is determined by placement of design elements within space. Many people are frightened of 'gaping holes' in the layout, but space is an incredibly forgiving design element—it is truly your friend.

If you have been found guilty of leaving space in a layout, you may well have been told that it is 'wasted'. It rarely is. Space is a dynamic layout element. It can guide the reader's eye through a page. Space is essential for accentuating the dynamics of scale and contrast, and provides a resting place within a layout. It can provide an area of calm in a dynamic design, which serves to heighten the dynamism, because you create a greater contrast between the busy and the relaxed, the fast and the slow, the loud and the soft.

Space—an area without a picture or text, but occasionally with a background colour or even a faint texture—can 'balance' a difficult design. Space is used to separate levels of information, highlight and support a heading hierarchy, and as rest area for the eyes.

The more space around a heading, the more importance the heading will assume. It is possible to set a heading in type smaller than the text of a story. If the heading is given a large area of space in which to float, it will be read first. You may have seen a 'blank', full-page newspaper advertisement that has only a small text area like a classified ad floating in the centre. Bet you read it!

In publication design, layouts with generous space provide a marked contrast to layouts where the page is filled with text and images.

In Web site design, to avoid having the reader scrolling through empty layouts, there is a tendency to fill all the screens, but this can have an adverse effect. Readers can become tired of the site and exit prematurely. Build the experience by pacing its delights. Document design is entertainment design—even more so in electronic documents with sound, movement and interactivity.

Predominantly 'white', or empty, layouts contrast well with busy layouts. This contrast—achieved partly through the distribution of space between stories—is one of the determinants of the 'pace' of the document. Pace in documents is best understood using the metaphor of a stage musical. Start with an overture. In a Web site, this is the splash screen or entry sequence. In a book, it is the cover, endpapers and maybe a frontispiece.

Audience members might read the program. In a Web site, this is the home page and site plan. In print, this is the contents list.

Then the show starts. It contains a series of big production numbers, separated by smaller numbers, ballads, duets and dialogue scenes that bring a rhythmic structure to the whole. The Web site, then, has major sections, multimedia-heavy scenes and text-only documents, small specialist sections and brief updates; video, sound, animation, text and graphics. The book has colour sections, heavily illustrated parts and sparsely illustrated parts, appendixes and even inserts; text, images and graphics.

I'm
the
smallest
type
on
this
page:
bet
I
got
your
attention!

'Build a book like a body moving in space and time, like a dynamic relief in which every page is a surface carrying shapes, and every turn of a page a new crossing to a new stage of a single structure.'
El Lissitsky quoted by
Lewis Blackwell in
20th Century Type: Remix

According to Karel van der Waarde in *Visual Information for Everyday Use*, readers assume relationships between different graphic components based on their:

Proximity

☐ Physical proximity implies an informational connection.

☐ Physical separation implies an informational separation.

Similarity

☐ Similarity implies a functional connection.

☐ Difference implies a functional differentiation.

Prominence

☐ Prominence differences imply hierarchical (status) differences.

Sequence

☐ The visual sequence implies the sequence of information.

There could be an intermission. In a Web site, this might be a community forum or chat line. In a book, this might be a part title, chapter or part summaries, or a full-bleed, double-page photo.

At the end of the show, there are the curtain calls, leaving the theatre and buying the souvenir T-shirt. In a Web site, there is the exit sequence, the credits and copyright information, the visitor registration form and the on-line shop. In a book, there is the conclusion, the colophon that describes production technicalities, the verso title and acknowledgments that list the production personnel, and sometimes an order form or registration card for catalogues from the publisher in the same subject area.

In theatre, comedy is placed to heighten—or lighten—tragedy. The juxtaposition of contrasting elements is equally effective as an entertainer or 'pacer' in document design, too. In magazines, the 'songs, scenes and choruses' are replaced with regular columns, news items and feature articles respectively; articles can be light or serious, text or picture spreads. Feature articles often use different layout devices to achieve an identity of their own, and the deployment of space is one of those devices.

In some publications, margins and chapter breaks are the only rest area. In novels, this is fine. In newspapers, it is probably fine. In magazines, it is unwise. Rest areas, as they are on highways, exist for a reason. If you are tired—and you can be visually tired—you should stop and rest. Advertisers and publishers do not want you to close the magazine; they want you to continue on your journey—so rest areas should be provided. Some articles provide this service. Sometimes, full-page or double-spread, full-bleed pictures can do it. Sometimes, just having a bit of extra space in a layout is enough.

If in doubt, rely on space—large, empty, clean space. It can bind disparate elements together and help stylistically different combinations sit comfortably within reach of each other. Space also contrasts texturally and tonally with the elements of your layout because it is usually white and gives your layout the highlight area for that important tonal range. So do not underestimate the importance of some 'empty' areas in a layout.

Traditional and modern layouts

Most text designs will fall into either the traditional (Italian Renaissance) or modern categories. 'Modern' in this sense is not 'fashionable', 'trendy' or even 'contemporary', but a specific styling from the mid-20th century. Greatly influenced by the Russian Constructivist and the Dutch *De Stijl* designers early in the century, Bauhaus teachers taught it and it was refined by the Swiss. It became the dominant international corporate style.

For 'traditional', read 'classical', as it is the style based on Italian book and type design from the Renaissance. It has been the dominant styling used for books since and can lend an olde worlde atmosphere to advertising and posters.

Both styles are used for annual reports because they give particular visual clues to how an organisation wishes to be seen.

The modern style says an organisation is forward thinking, at the cutting edge, a bit of a risk-taker, even casual or brash. But it can sometimes be stark and harsh. Most manuals, magazines and reports, all forms and nearly all corporate identity programs are based on the modern format.

The traditional style, by contrast, implies the organisation has roots and a solid foundation, it values where it has been and can be trusted and respected. Be careful to avoid being seen as pompous or, worse, backward. Most books, some manuals and nearly all wedding invitations are based on the traditional format.

Although it seems bizarre to say designs fall into these two categories, you will find that they are fairly easy to spot once you know the styles. But to create a uniquely flavoured design, substitute ingredients: mix in serifs or scripts where sans serifs are specified; or add more line rules and typefaces to spice up the layout. Contemporary designers do not follow these styles as rigid rules, more as guides. They usually create a distinct hybrid.

READ MORE ABOUT IT

Suzanne West, *Working with style*, Watson-Guptill Publications, New York, 1990, ISBN 0 8230 5872 7.

Traditional layout

Create substantial margins that relate to each other, from smallest to largest: the top, the inside, the outside and the bottom margin. The margins should look generous. The page number should be centred on the text block and roughly central in this bottom margin.

Choose a good, strong serif typeface (Bembo, Garamond, Times, Baskerville, Palatino or another classic font), and prepare your text with italics for stress when necessary. Loose-tracked small capitals can be used occasionally for stress or headings within the text. Indent paragraphs by about 5 mm, with no extra space between them.

Justify the type, leading it generously, and centre the capital letter headings. Headings might need a little tracking as well.

Initial drop capitals on chapter opening pages and printer's flowers or dingbats centred at the end of the chapter will add a traditional feel. A few fine line rules and lots of capital letters for headings and first lines will also help. If you can get ligatured character pairs and swash characters, which are sometimes available in a 'specialist' or 'alternative' font, it will add to the traditional detailing.

Place the text in your page layout to fill each page to a constant page depth—the bottom line as defined by your bottom margin. Put some extra space around your headings. Remember that more space above a heading than below it will keep the heading with its text.

Images, in the classic form, are on separate pages with centred captions in tracked small capitals below the image.

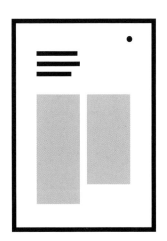

Modern layout

Create light margins, keeping the top margin and side margins much the same. The bottom margin should be slightly larger. Then divide the text block into two or three even columns, each separated by a narrow gutter.

Prepare your text in a sans serif typeface with an extensive font family (Helvetica, Univers, Frutiger, Gill Sans or Futura will have the range of light, medium, bold, extrabold and italics that are required). Type should be formatted flush left unjustified, avoiding hyphenation as far as possible, and leaded generously to separate the sans serif lines for easy readability.

Use blocked paragraphs—not indented—and separate them with half to one line space. (This is now usually reinterpreted to be 5 mm indented paragraphs with no indent in the first line after a heading.)

Be creative with your headings, carefully avoiding the use of capitals, but being generous with the use of different point sizes and weights. Headings often hang from the top margin line and are separated from the text by a space, which creates a text drop line further down the page. The headings will mostly be bolder than the text and italics are usually avoided, except for stress within text. Sometimes you might use the occasional line rule or bar in association with a heading, often taking it to optical column measure and placing it above the heading.

Fill each column comfortably to a logical paragraph break, but don't fill to the bottom, just let the text hang.

Images should also hang from the text drop line. Images will probably conform to one- or two-column standard scalings and might be positioned according to a strict grid for placement. Captions are often in italics the same size and leading as the text.

Four ways to save a failing design

There are times when your design—like your hair—simply looks dull, boring and lifeless. On such design bad-hair-days, don't throw out all that work and start again. Do a bit of judicious design teasing and moussing. Look at the design with a new set of eyes. Imagine someone else did the design and you have the job of fixing it up.

There are four good techniques for fixing an ailing design, which are relatively quick and work wonders. But note that if you are working on a publication and it's looking boring, you don't have to enliven every page—occasional breaks in a publication are sufficient. Every page does not have to be dynamic and new.

Increase tonal contrast

A design that looks grey can be very boring. Text blocks reduce to grey tone if you squint at them. The 'squint test' is the clincher—if it is boring to squint at, then it's boring to look at. What the squint test shows you is the interaction of the tones on the page.

Fix your tonal contrast. Get some dark and light areas happening in that grey base. For dark, choose a darker typeface for some headings (such as an extrabold). Perhaps use a reverse—where the type is white on a black block. Use a dark stripe somewhere (bleeding off the side of the page or down the side of photographs). Then add some light—some large white type can be reversed out of a photograph, or a logo could be reversed out of a dark stripe, or simply keep a larger area of white space below the main heading or create bigger margins.

Redistribute space

Many people are scared of leaving a blank area in a design, fearing that it makes them look inept because they couldn't fill the page neatly and their layout looks like something's missing. On the contrary—this area is called *space* or *white space* (even if it's black) and can have a wonderful effect on the liveliness and vibrance of a layout, partly because space has the effect of increasing the tonal variety, but also because it becomes a layout element that interacts with picture blocks and text blocks. So manipulate space.

Space can be added to a margin to increase the layout's feeling of space. This can be done by hanging type and pictures from an invisible line across the top part of the page and letting the columns fall to a natural length, leaving the space at the foot of the page. Alternatively, you can put a slab of horizontal space across the page by having an area at the top where headings sit and then a drop before text can start. In a multicolumn format, you might leave one of the columns blank for vertical space.

If the page is full and it looks like there is no space to redistribute, try altering the setting from justified to unjustified—it will immediately open up the page. Also, you can reduce the size of the pictures to get some space. You can reduce a heading size but keep the space around it the same, giving the illusion of more space.

Alter scale relationships

One of the best fixes is to alter scale (the size relationships within the layout). Basically, the contrast of little with big is dynamic and visually interesting.

If there are three pictures in a layout, make one picture big and the others very little. Not just little—very little. The one that is big might be so big it bleeds off all four sides, forcing you to place the little ones somewhere on top of it.

Don't forget that type can work that way, too. What about an enormous title that has little tiny pictures floating in it? What about large body copy (the main body of text) with a tiny heading? (It can work, but it's tricky.)

Repeat something

You can enliven a layout simply by repeating some of its existing elements—logos, images, even type. When you repeat them, you can create a pattern. Or you can alter their sizes and use scale variation. This works well with logos and photographs, particularly if you use a technique called ghosting where you fade the logo or image until it's like a shadow. It can then float behind the text or the solid version of itself. This effect of different layers gives dimension to the design, which is why it works as a fix.

Typography

Handling type is the special skill of the typographer. It is sensitivity to the forms of the alphabet and numerals that other mortals use carelessly every day in handwritten memos and even in electronic mail. It is a tradition that goes back to the scribes who were the official carers for our fledgling letterforms.

The difference between a good piece of design and a great one is often the level of expertise in the selection and use of type. Type must be appropriate to its subject, its message and the illustrations that surround it—and the reader's experience of type.

Typefaces can have many associations for a reader. There are typefaces we read as a child; those that recall a bygone era; those that feel traditional and others that feel modern; type that says, 'This is news'; type that is romantic; faces that are quirky and others that are serious. The 'personality' of a typeface can be related to historical or emotional associations, or simply a reflection of our experience of type.

One of the exciting things about the personal computer and desktop publishing (DTP) is the discovery that there is a whole new world of 'typography' out there—something experienced from our earliest years, so often taken for granted, but also misunderstood. Although it is exciting, it is also a concern because we soon find that using type is not as easy or as intuitive as we expect.

Using type on a personal computer is very different from using a typewriter. Typesetting, or the simulation of it we call DTP, uses different formatting techniques to achieve similar but superior results. Even when an original typed manuscript was re-keyed by a typesetter, typing for publication has always had more refinements than simply keying-in the text, because typeface designers had many more characters available to them in a type case or on a computer than would fit on the typewriter keyboard.

'Type is about much more than questions of legibility or readability. Fashions and technological change are just part of the backdrop. What makes typography fascinating, and an essential enquiry for anybody involved in design, is that this activity is a manifestation of our search for greater efficiency and greater power in the written word. It reveals personalities, politics, and economic factors, along with advances in science. It is a celebration of humanity, and a vital and subtle indicator of values.'
Lewis Blackwell in
20th Century Type: Remix

Mechanical spacing & constant character width

Typewriting

Mechanical spacing and constant character width are aspects of typewriter fonts like Courier.

DOING IT SMARTER

Spell-checks and proofreading

Use spell-checks regularly, particularly as you are typing and before you transfer the text file into a page layout program. But don't forget to fully proofread the final text. A spell-check is better than nothing, but it is not as accurate as a good proofread.

DOING IT FASTER

Keyboard shortcuts

Use as many keyboard (and extended keyboard) shortcuts as you can remember. Selecting from a menu every time is time-consuming. Using rulers and toolboxes also helps, but the keyboard shortcuts really streamline document production.

Typography immediately says that the information presented is more important than handwriting or type-writing because only something that needed to be seen as complete was set in type. This is why people are so much more critical of draft text and letters in a 'typeset' form—an error becomes magnified. If a politician handwrote, or typed in the Courier typeface, a letter that had a spelling mistake, no one would mind. In Times Roman, that same mistake simply confirms our suspicions and demonstrates the sender's incompetence. And if they're this incompetent just getting a letter right, how much more incompetence is hidden from our view? Don't throw away that Courier font just yet—it can save you.

If the text has the appearance of typesetting, it should exhibit all the other hallmarks of typesetting. If it doesn't, readers may perceive it as unprofessional and sloppy. There are a number of areas where you can establish a professional styling within text:

- punctuation styling is different between typing and typesetting
- italics are used for stress within text instead of underlining
- heading handling is different because with typesetting and DTP there are options which were not available in typing
- by using columns, rules, colour, boxes, variable spacing and other graphic elements.

With the vast capabilities many word-processing and DTP programs contain, many users are tempted to use a number of techniques that were previously used sparingly. Now it is so easy to click on the menu or key-in the command that some users are no longer considering the wisdom of using techniques such as drop-shadows, type set around a circle, outlined type, contoured text, boxed text and even justification.

All these capabilities are needed on occasion, but not as regularly as they are being used. It is just like the smorgasbord of typefaces that are available which are there to give variety and flexibility to typography. They were never intended to be used in the same document at the same time.

Considering the manuscript

How will the document be used?
Will it be scanned or read continuously? Is the reader tired or alert, relaxed or stressed?

Does the reader want to read it?
Is the reader motivated or reluctant?

Is it information?
Are there enough headings to indicate specific areas of interest?

Is it instruction?
Can it be read in order and followed clearly? Will it be translated into multiple languages? Is there enough room for the increased text area of many other languages? What production requirements does its use imply? (For example, you may need a printed surface that can be wiped clean in a kitchen or a garage.)

Is it reference material?
Are specific areas of interest clearly labelled and logically ordered?

Is it entertainment?
Will the reader be unnecessarily distracted from a sustained read?

Is it familiar?
Has it a recognisable form to streamline usability like that of a dictionary, a TV guide or a novel?

Creating text interest

Subheadings
For people who scan to quickly find what they need

Columns
To make the information look easier to approach—smaller blocks of text; more accessible paragraphs

Space
To give the reader a place to rest

Pictures
To stimulate, and to break the text

Colour
To stimulate the eye and to add depth to the text—this can also be achieved with tones and tints of black

Boxes and rules
To separate text and to arrange it into more manageable blocks—this also guides the reader through material

References, links and footnotes
Streamline the text for readers who do not want to read 'irrelevant' material; but also provide for readers who want more information

Various type sizes and treatments
To indicate the relative importance of the information as determined by the author or editor; to make the visual presentation more attractive

READ MORE ABOUT IT

Robin Williams, *The Mac is not a typewriter*, Peachpit Press, Berkeley, 1990, ISBN 0 938151 31 2.

Robin Williams, *Beyond the Mac is not a typewriter*, Peachpit Press, Berkeley, 1996, ISBN 1 201 88598 0.

Erik Spiekermann and E.M. Ginger, *Stop stealing sheep: And find out how type works*, Adobe Press, Mountain View, California, 1993, ISBN 0 672 48543 5.

Jeff Bellantoni and Matt Woolman, *Type in motion: Innovations in digital graphics*, Thames & Hudson, London, 1999, ISBN 0 500 01914 2.

Stefan Rögener, Albert-Jan Pool, Ursula Packhäuser and E.M. Ginger (eds), *Branding with type: How type sells*, Adobe Press, Mountain View, California, 1995, ISBN 1 56830 248 7.

John Miles, *Design for desktop publishing: A guide to layout and typography on the personal computer*, Imprint Publishers, Sydney, 1987, ISBN 1 875132 00 7.

Jan V. White, *Graphic design for the electronic age: The manual for traditional and desktop publishing*, Xerox Press, Watson-Guptill Publications, New York, 1988, ISBN 0 8230 2122 X.

Jill Yelland, *Typo survival kit: For all type emergencies*, 2nd edn, Press for Success, Perth, 2000, ISBN 0 646 28070 8.

Kate Clair, *A typographic workbook: A primer to history, techniques, and artistry*, John Wiley & Sons, New York, 1999, ISBN 0 471 29237 0.

Robin Williams, *The non-designer's type book: Insights and techniques for creating professional-level type*, Peachpit Press, Berkeley, 1998, ISBN 0 201 35367 9.

Type categories

It helps to have an appropriate language to talk about type. Type falls into five main categories: serif type, sans serif type, scripts, specialty or display typefaces, and symbol or picture fonts.

READ MORE ABOUT IT

Christopher Perfect, *The complete typographer: A manual for designing with type*, Quarto Publishing, London, 1992, ISBN 0 316 90326 4.

Gordon Rookledge and Christopher Perfect (rev. Phil Baines), *Rookledge's international typefinder: The essential handbook of typeface recognition and selection*, 2nd edn, PBC International, Glen Cove, New York, 1998, ISBN 1 870758 03 X.

Philip B. Meggs and Roy McKelvey, *Revival of the fittest: Digital versions of classic typefaces*, RC Publications, New York, 2000, ISBN 1 883915 08 2.

Ken Garland, *Illustrated graphics glossary: Of terms used in printing, publishing, photography and other fields of interest to graphic designers, their clients and their suppliers*, Barrie and Jenkins, London, 1980, ISBN 0 09 141511 X.

Stanley Morison, *A tally of types*, Cambridge University Press, Cambridge, 1973, ISBN 0 521 20043 1.

Eric Gill, *An essay on typography*, 5th edn, Lund Humphries, London, 1988, ISBN 085331 509 4.

Jan Tschichold (trans. Ruari McLean), *The new typography: The first English translation of the revolutionary 1928 document*, University of California Press, Los Angeles, 1998, ISBN 0 520 07147 6.

Alexander Lawson, *Anatomy of a typeface*, Hamish Hamilton, London, 1990, ISBN 0 241 13267 3.

Hermann Zapf, *About alphabets: some marginal notes on type design*, The MIT Press, Cambridge, Mass., 1970, ISBN 0 262 24010 6.

Allan Haley, *Alphabet: The history, evolution and design of the letters we use today*, Thames & Hudson, London, 1995, ISBN 0 500 27835 0.

Allan Haley, *Typographic milestones*, Van Nostrand Reinhold, New York, 1992, ISBN 0 442 23642 5.

Friedrich Friedl, Nicolaus Ott and Bernard Stein, *Typography: When, who, how*, Könemann Verlagsgesellschaft mbH, Cologne, 1998, ISBN 3 89508 473 5.

Allan Haley, *Type: Hot designers make cool fonts*, Rockport, Gloucester, Mass., 1998, ISBN 1 56496 317 9.

Sebastian Carter, *Twentieth century type designers*, Trefoil, London, 1987, ISBN 0 86294 076 1.

Lewis Blackwell, *20th century type: Remix*, Laurence King Publishing, London, 1998, ISBN 1 85669 116 0.

Spencer Drate and Jütka Salavetz, *Extreme fonts: Digital faces of the future*, Madison Square Press, New York, 1999, ISBN 0 942604 74 1.

Rob Carter, *American typography today*, Van Nostrand Reinhold, New York, 1989, ISBN 0 442 22106 1.

Steven Heller and Louise Fili, *Typology: Type design from the Victorian era to the digital age*, Chronicle Books, San Francisco, 1999, ISBN 0 8118 2308 3.

Wolfgang Weingart, *My way to typography: Retrospective in ten sections*, Lars Müller Publishers, Baden, 2000, ISBN 3 907044 86 X.

Serif typefaces

Serif type has 'little feet', like the type you're reading at the moment. If you were drawing the letters by hand, the individual movements of a calligraphy pen that make up a letterform are called *strokes*. Serifs are the flicks—mostly small horizontal strokes—at the start or the end of each character stroke.

Serif type is believed to be the most readable type for continuous text, which is why many magazines, books and newspapers use serif type for body copy. For extended reading, it is more comfortable which explains why fiction paperbacks—motivated, narrative reading with few headings or other interruptions—are always in a serif typeface.

Serif typefaces are often associated with tradition and can lend an air of authority to text. Many of the 'big name' classical serifs like Bembo, Times, Baskerville and Garamond have been around for centuries and immediately conjure up a feeling of tradition, which is exactly what many companies want to project, particularly at annual report time in a recession.

Serif types usually have strokes of different widths. Look at a capital A—the left stroke is thin, the right stroke is thick and the crossbar is thin. This is because typeface designs were based on the writing of scribes which was produced with nibbed pens.

The problem with variable stroke thickness is that it can make small type and reversed type a problem. The fine lines might drop away when they are printed. Avoid using serif typefaces on gloss paper, in reverse, or at very small sizes because their serifs and thin strokes can disappear.

Note: Slab serif typefaces can usually be used in a manner similar to the use of sans serif typefaces, because of their apparently even stroke thickness—even their serifs are as thick as the strokes.

Variable stroke thickness

Times new roman

Original fonts

Why spend money on original fonts? Why not use the many lookalike font clones that are available in cheap font sets? This is not font piracy (where you copy a font that someone else has paid for). This is where a new font is released and becomes so popular that other font companies create lookalike fonts in order to keep their customers from changing to a new supplier. But they don't pay the original font designer or buy the original drawings from the original font producer—they redraw their own version. It happened with Helvetica, which is available as Megaron, Helvetia and Geneva. It happened with Palatino, which is available as Palatio, Palladium and Andover.

It's happening still, although there is a new twist in the legal definition. In a 1998 US case, it was upheld that although the designer still can't copyright the font design itself, the software program that defines the font can be copyrighted.

But what's wrong with it, aside from dubious ethics and dodgy principles? Why is it worth the money to get the original?

Most designers would acknowledge that the original font contains nuances that most redraw copyists appear to have been unaware of or ignore. This nuance is most often found in optical correction. The designer of a font will often draw a geometrically and measurement-correct letterform only to find through tests and close observation that, when our eyes see that character, we perceive it incorrectly. We may thicken one part of it or see an oval where a circle is desired.

Optical correction of a font means that capital letters are different measured heights even though they appear the same height. An *O* or a *W* are actually taller by measuring than an *H*. An *A* is somewhere between the two. This is to do with the alignment of characters on the baseline where, for example the points of a *W* actually sit below the line to ensure that the letterform appears to sit comfortably. Similarly the curve of the *O* sits below the line. The *H*, having no curves or points, sits on the exact baseline.

Incidentally, this is why, when people use Letraset or other rubdown lettering systems, they often end up with wobbly lines—unless they use the Esselte Letraset alignment system that takes account of it.

But in font design, there is also optical correction of stroke thicknesses. Particularly in *S*, but also surprisingly in *I*, and any straight strokes, the actual shape of the stroke is full of nuance. Rarely, even in the most deceptively geometrically constructed sans serif font, is there a straight line, due to optical correction. Most straights are, in fact, subtle curves that come in at the waist of the straight stroke and fan out at the top and bottom.

The mistake made by many font redrawers was to trust their eyes!

So you will miss the nuance, but who cares as long as it looks okay? And it probably will look okay at text sizes up to about 12 point. But when won't it look okay?

This is where the digital font revolution has really made an impact. All those original nuances become obvious in enlargement. But so do any of the font redrawers' short cuts. If you've tried to enlarge a poor font, you will know the problem—it looks ugly, ungainly and lumpy. Points are often not sharp and smooth curves can have an unsightly kink in them.

This is often an indicator that they were scanned and redrawn from a printed character that had gained thickness due to inking in the printing process. It also means that the originally finely tuned contrast between the medium and bold versions of a face can also be lost.

The other testing that an original font designer will do is to do with how particular character pairs set and the overall texture of the new font in text setting. This is all to do with interletter spacing and character kerning.

The redrawer will not have spent the same amount of time as the originator in the detailing of those combinations and the testing of the setting, so often uneven setting results with a redrawn font. This is okay if you are prepared to do the kerning and letterspacing yourself, but how much actually gets done that should?

Originators of a font will also spend more time creating the full font requirements for high-end publishing—they will often create an expert set and sometimes foreign language font sets to match.

Serif typefaces

All typeface examples are shown in 18 point.

ABCDE abcdefg 12345
Century schoolbook Morris Fuller Benton 1924

ABCDE abcdefg 12345
Garamond Claude Garamond 1530

ABCDEFGHIJ 12345
Trajan Carol Twombly 1989

ABCDE abcdefg 12345
Baskerville John Baskerville 1754

ABCDE abcdefg 12345
Goudy old style Frederic Goudy 1915

ABCDE abcdefg 12345
Times new roman Stanley Morison 1931

ABCDE abcdefg 12345
Bodoni Giambattista Bodoni 1798

ABCDE abcdefg 12345
Palatino Hermann Zapf 1949
Optional names for *Palatino: Palladium, Elegante, Andover, Paladio, Patina, Malibu*

ABCDE abcdefgh 12345
Bembo Francesco Griffo 1495

ABCDE abcdefg 12345
Galliard Matthew Carter 1978

ABCDE abcdefg 12345
Cheltenham Bertram Goodhue 1896

ABCDEFGH abcdefgh 12345
Matrix Zuzana Licko 1986

Serifs

Bracketed serif

I

Times new roman

Modern serif

I

Modern no. 20

Slab serif

I

Rockwell

Slab serif typefaces

ABCDE abcdefg 12345

Rockwell Inland Typefoundry 1910
Optional names for *Rockwell: Stymie, Memphis, Cairo*

ABCDE abcdef 12345

Clarendon English Fann Street Foundry 1845

ABCDE abcdefgh 12345

Italia Colin Brignall 1975

Sans serif typefaces

'Sans serif' is a French term, which means 'without serif'. Sans serif types used to be called 'grotesques' and that's the way some people prefer to think of them.

Though sans serif type is considered to be less readable than serif type, it is the most legible type. When you learn the alphabet, you are taught sans serif shapes because they are the basic or 'pure' forms of the symbols, and therefore the most legible or easiest to recognise letterforms. You were probably taught to read using sans serif type.

Its greater legibility is one of the reasons that sans serif type is used for headlines, billboard advertising and numberplates, and for signage on highways, at hospitals, in airport terminals and car parks.

However, as typefaces for text setting, they are considered 'modern', like the architecture of Le Corbusier. If you want a futuristic or contemporary look, sans serif type can help. This is probably because the 'big name' sans serifs like Futura, Helvetica and Univers were developed in the mid-twentieth century and sat comfortably with Art Deco's geometric designs and its development into streamlining and, later, the international style.

Sans serif can look more informal or 'friendly' than serif type, although some perceive the 'clarity' of a geometric sans serif to be 'clinical' or 'distant'.

Sans serif type also has the appearance of constant stroke thickness. If you look at the capital A, all strokes appear to be the same width. Because of this, they work at very small sizes and in reverse—good news for people who need to put photographers' credits up the sides of photos, write 'Registered trade mark' under a logo, or use any other fine print.

This is Rod.
This is Janette.
See Rod and
Janette run.

Futura

Tiny type
Sans serif type remains quite readable at even 3 or 4 point. You should use wider letterspacing at such small sizes.

Constant stroke thickness

Transit

Sans serif typefaces

ABCDE abcdefg 12345

Helvetica Max Miedinger 1957
Optional names for *Helvetica: Newton, Triumvirate, Helios, Swiss,*
Geneva, Megaron, Claro, Vega

ABCDE abcdefg 12345

Univers Adrian Frutiger 1957

ABCDE abcdefg 12345

Frutiger Adrian Frutiger 1975

ABCDE abcdefgh 12345

Meta Erik Spiekermann 1991

ABCDEF abcdefgh 12345

Gill sans Eric Gill 1929

ABCDE abcdefg 12345

Optima Hermann Zapf 1958
Optional names for *Optima: Chelmsford, Optimist, Musica, Oracle, Zenith*

ABCDEFGHIJ 12345

Lithos Carol Twombley 1989

ABCDE abcdefgh 1234

Franklin Gothic Morris Fuller Benton 1905

ABCDE abcdefg 12345

Friz quadrata Ernst Friz 1965 (a hybrid serif font, used as sans serif)

ABCDE abcdefg 12345

Futura Paul Renner 1927

ABCDE abcdefgh 12345

Template gothic Barry Deck 1990

ABCDEFGHIJKL 12345

Avant garde Herb Lubalin 1970 CAPS ONLY

Compare a serif typeface with a sans serif

Notice the serifs at the end of the stroke and compare the thickness and stress of the strokes.

So

Times new roman

So

Transit

Serif versus sans serif

Arguments rage about which style of type is superior. Some people like to quote readability tests and all sorts of statistics to back up their claims. But the fault with much of the testing is that it starts from the assumption that serif and sans serif types are interchangeable—that you can set up your type specifications (which include the size of type, the leading and the length of each line) and simply change the typeface and run the test again. But you don't specify a holiday based on your car's limitations, and then change to an airline booking, without altering your schedule and costing.

Each typeface category has tasks it performs well— and there will be some tasks it will not perform well. It is not usually the typeface at fault, but more what the user does with it.

Scripts

Script typefaces tend to mimic handdrawn or calligraphic type. The letters are often linked to each other, hence the self-explanatory subdivisions of script called *connecting scripts* and *non-connecting scripts*. There is also a subset called *blackletter* based on Gothic pen letterforms which was the form of the movable type Johannes Gutenberg invented for his Bible published in 1455.

In nearly every case, script typefaces should be used only in lower case with initial capital letters.

A mistake often made with wedding invitations and other traditional uses of script faces is to choose a swirling copperplate script typeface, which is often difficult to read. Script typefaces can be used effectively but usually need to be larger than 14 point and used for titles, and headings such as 'The Wedding of Jennifer and Matthew', 'The Signing of the Register', 'The Exchange of Rings'. But when it comes to readability, consider pairing them with a classical serif which often works well with the traditional scripts and blackletter fonts associated with weddings.

Contemporary scripts and casual scripts usually work better with sans serif typefaces.

Script typefaces

ABCDEFG abcdefghi 12345
Zapf chancery Hermann Zapf 1974

ABCDE abcdefgh 12345
Snell roundhand Matthew Carter 1965

ABCDEFG abcdefghij 12345
Kaufmann Max R. Kaufmann 1936

ABCDE abcde 12345
Brush script Robert E. Smith 1942

ABCDE abcdefg 12345
Mistral Roger Excoffon 1955

ABCDE abcdefg 12345
Sassoon primary Rosemary Sassoon 1990

ABC abcde 1234
American uncial Eisner and Flake

ABCDEFGHI abcdefghijklmno 123456
Erikrighthand Erik van Blokland 1991

ABCDEFGH abcdefghijklm 12345
Justlefthand Just van Rossum 1991

Blackletter typefaces

ABCDE abcdefgh 12345
Old English Morris Fuller Benton 1901

ABCDE abcdef 12345
Fette fraktur Wagner and Schmidt 1875

ABCDEFG abcdefghijk 12345
Wilhelm Klingspor gotisch Rudolf Koch 1925

Specialty and display typefaces

Specialty typefaces can have letterforms that have been adorned in some way. They are usually relegated to titling and can lend atmosphere to a piece of text.

Avoid clichéd typeface choices in this category, such as using letterforms with icicles on them for refrigeration contractors and flame letterforms for 'red hot' sales—the novelty has worn off and is less than successful.

Many decorative typefaces do not have a complete font set. They may have only capitals, numbers and selected punctuation marks. Often they aren't extended into a family, so you will rarely find an italic or a bold.

Symbol and picture fonts

There have always been dingbat fonts. They haven't always been called that, because it's the American word used to describe a font of symbols. Europeans used to call them *pi fonts* (after the mathematical symbol *pi*—π), *symbol fonts* or *fleurons* (or, in England, *printer's flowers*). But what do they do? Whatever you call them, they come in handy for:

- dressing up a pull-quote
- setting mathematical equations or formulae
- creating a border
- making some interesting bullets for a series of dot points
- decorating a title page
- producing a piece of feature typography.

On forms, tick boxes are outlined squares. On business cards and in *Yellow Pages* advertisements, instead of using the word 'telephone', telephone symbols are often used. On coupons, the scissors along the broken line are found in dingbat fonts. There are many pointing tools (hands, arrows, aeroplanes) that are used on pamphlets to highlight product features and prices. In magazine and newsletter pull-quotes, chunky opening and closing quotes are sometimes dingbats.

There are some other uses you can put them to— particularly as they are now installed on your computer and can be used as you would use any other font. They can be italicised, outlined, reversed, tracked and kerned, enlarged or reduced, overlapped (horizontally by tracking, vertically by changing leading, or, with even greater freedom, by layering different text blocks), condensed or expanded (using horizontal scaling), and their baseline can shift.

Specialty or display typefaces, symbol or picture fonts

A B C D a b c d e 1 2 3 4

Broadway engraved Morris Fuller Benton 1929

ABCDEFGHIJ abcdefghijklmn 12345

Playbill R. Harling 1938

ABCDEFGHIJK 12345

Neuland Rudolf Koch 1923

ABCD ABCD 1 2 3 4

Copperplate gothic Frederic Goudy 1901

ABCDE ABCDEFG 12345

Typeface six Neville Brody 1986

ABCDE ABCDEFG 12345

Typeface seven Neville Brody 1986

ABCDE abcdefg 12345

Fur extra rounded Paul Sahre 1993

ABCDEFGHIJ abcdefghijklmnopqrs 12345890

Industria inline Neville Brody 1990

ABCDE abcdefg 12345

Beowolf 23 Erik van Blokland and Just van Rossum 1990
This random font will construct a slightly different letterform each time.

Specialty or display typefaces, symbol or picture fonts

Osprey Stephen Farrell 1993

ABCDE   abcdef   12345

Verdana Matthew Carter 1996
This font was developed as a free-to-air font for the World Wide Web.

★ ☆ ➢ ♠ ♥ ♣ ● ■ ▲ ☞ ❦ ✈ ✄

Zapf Dingbats Hermann Zapf

ΑΒΧΔΕ αβχδεφγ ≤°∞ℑ♠

Symbol font

Decorated initials

If you need an angled oval, you can condense a circle by slimming it down with horizontal scale, then italicising it and, if necessary, rotating the text block to the desired angle. However, it's quicker and easier to do that with a drawing tool.

Picture fonts have been released by some font producers and are able to be distorted with type commands in the same way. Picture fonts compete with clip art.

With these symbols and pictures available as a font, they have the attributes of any computerised font—they are much more flexible than dingbats used to be.

Typefaces, families and fonts

The naming conventions of typefaces are similar to how we name one another—there is a family name and given names to distinguish each of the family members. In type nomenclature, the family name comes first. That is the name of the typeface—Helvetica, Palatino, Garamond, Frutiger. This is followed by the name of the family member or *font* (or the English preference, *fount*)—bold, medium, light, italic, etc. A 'font' is one set of capitals, lower case, numbers, punctuation marks, symbols and special characters.

Often, many fonts will exist within one typeface design. The typeface is developed like a family—there is a set of characteristics (based on the genetic make-up or the type equivalent of the DNA of the originally drawn version) that the resulting family members share. It might be a geometric detail, a particular shape of serif, a particular method of generating a stroke or a more complex curve that recurs.

Each of the fonts is then given a name that describes its difference from the original. If it leans to the right, it is called *italic* or *oblique*. If it is slimmed down, it is called *condensed* or *narrow* or *compressed*. If it gets wider, it is called *expanded*. If its strokes get thicker and it looks darker, it is called *bold*. If the strokes get even thicker, it is called *extrabold* or *black*. If its strokes get thinner, it is called *light*. If its strokes get even thinner, it is called *extralight* or *thin* or *fine*. There are other variants, often self-explanatory, such as *outline, inline* and *shadow*.

With all these variants taking the family name as well, the original face is often given a font title—it could be called *medium* or *roman*. If there is a font drawn between the medium and the bold, it might be called *demi* or *book*.

DOING IT SMARTER
Type families
Develop your awareness of the capabilities of a type family by using only one typeface and its variants. That is, don't rely on different faces to create a hierarchy of information. Insist that only one typeface (and its family members) be used.

DOING IT SMARTER
Readable text type
Develop awareness of readability requirements for text setting by setting short pieces of fiction. Effort is not expended on selecting heading attributes, but focuses on the details of creating good text—type selection, leading, tracking, justification, line length, etc.

Expanded font sets

A specialist set or expert set will mostly include:

☐ small capitals that are slightly thicker and stockier than the capitals so that they are the same optical weight and spacing as the lower-case characters

☐ titling capitals that are slightly slimmer and narrower than the normal capitals

☐ an oldstyle number set as an alternative to the normal aligning numbers

☐ full set of diacritical marks for foreign language setting

☐ more ligatured character combinations

☐ 'true' fractions

☐ optional swash capitals for display setting

☐ optional ampersands

☐ a selection of dingbats in the style of the font.

A font

Scala Martin Majoor 1990–98

ABCDEFGHIJKLMNOPQ RSTUVWXYZ

Capitals/upper case/majuscules

abcdefghijklmnopqrstuv wxyz

Lower case/minuscules

ABCDEFGHIJKLMNOPQRST UVWXYZ

Small capitals

1234567890   1234567890

Oldstyle/text/non-lining numbers   Lining/display numbers

-	—	——	•	&	#
Hyphen	En rule	Em rule	Bullet	Ampersand	Hash

Æ æ Œ œ	fi fl	ß	$	¢	£	¥	€
Dipthongs	Ligatures	Eszett	Dollar	Cent	Pound	Yen	Euro

ç ñ å ä â á à ˘ ‐ ·	1	@	©	®	TM
Diacritical marks/accents (L–R: cedilla, tilde, ring, umlaut, circumflex, acute, grave, breve, macron, dot)	Dotless i	Commercial 'at'	Copyright mark	Registered mark	Trade mark

+ = < > − ÷ ≠ √	¼ ½	%	°	π	Σ Ω Δ μ
Mathematical symbols	Fractions	Per cent	Degree	Pi	Greek symbols

:	;	?	¿	!	¡	\	/	/
Colon	Semicolon	Question	Opening question	Exclamation	Opening exclamation	Backslash	Fraction bar	Solidus/ slash

,	•	…	*	†	‡	§	¶	‖
Comma	Full stop/ period (US)	Ellipsis	Asterisk	Dagger	Double dagger	Section marker	Paragraph marker	Parallel lines

' '	" "	‹ ›	« »	„	′ ″	( )	[ ]	{ }
Single quotes	Double quotes	Single guillemets	Double guillemets	Base quotes	Foot and inch	Parentheses	Square brackets	Braces

A sans serif type family

ABCDE abcdefg 12345

Frutiger light Adrian Frutiger 1975

ABCDE abcdefg 12345

Frutiger light italic Adrian Frutiger 1975

ABCDE abcdefg 12345

Frutiger roman Adrian Frutiger 1975

ABCDE abcdefg 12345

Frutiger italic Adrian Frutiger 1975

ABCDE abcdef 12345

Frutiger bold Adrian Frutiger 1975

ABCDE abcdef 12345

Frutiger bold italic Adrian Frutiger 1975

ABCDE abcdef 12345

Frutiger black Adrian Frutiger 1975

ABCDE abcdef 12345

Frutiger black italic Adrian Frutiger 1975

ABCD abcde 12345

Frutiger ultrablack Adrian Frutiger 1975

ABCDEF abcdefghijk 12345

Frutiger light condensed Adrian Frutiger 1975

ABCDEF abcdefghijk 12345

Frutiger condensed Adrian Frutiger 1975

ABCDE abcdefghi 12345

Frutiger bold condensed Adrian Frutiger 1975

ABCDE abcdefghi 12345

Frutiger black condensed Adrian Frutiger 1975

A serif type family

Roman

Times new roman

Italic

Times italic

Bold

Times bold

Bold italic

Times bold italic

Ampersands

Times new roman

Goudy

Scala italic

Palatino italic

When you first start to use type, the safest thing to do is to stick with a good strong type family. Usually a text typeface will have a set of four variants, i.e. the type nuclear family—the original typeface, the bold, the italic and the bold italic. With this basic family, you can create cohesive type layouts because the letterforms will work comfortably together because of their similar design attributes.

When type was made of little metal characters that were placed together in lines by hand, each size of the typeface had to be cast in metal—so 'font' described one set of characters at a specified size. Unlimited, digital sizings were not available: only sets or 'fonts' of 6, 8, 10, 12, 18 and 24 point sizes and a limited range of larger sizes were available. Now, due to digital scaling, size is not an issue, so a font has come to mean the particular collection of characters that makes up a type family member.

Type nomenclature

millimetres   centimetres   points   picas   inches   **Measurement systems**

Type size

Type sizes are described in *points* (abbreviated as *pt*).
There are 72 Anglo–American points to an inch or roughly
3.5 Anglo–American points to a millimetre. In Australia,
the French–European Didot point system is not used to
measure type.

The 'point size' is the body size of the type measured
from the top of the ascender to the bottom of the descender.
In some typefaces there is a distinct difference between the
height of the ascender and the usually smaller cap height,
so type is mostly measured from the ascender line rather
than the cap height.

Most people can comfortably read text type in sizes from
9 point to 12 point, with the most popular being 10 point
and 11 point. For children's books or material for the aged,
text size should be larger and start at about 14 point.

x-height comparison
Each *x* is from the
48 point font

X

Times new roman

X

Transit

x

NuptialScript

Type selection
Develop your typography skills
by excluding illustration (or
photography) from your design.
Illustration has such a dominant
effect in a design that it can be a
crutch for a poor designer. Take
away the illustration to extend
your typographic skills.

Usually, a sans serif font can be set a point size smaller than a serif font. It is all to do with the *x-height* (the height of the lower-case *x*) and its relation to the ascending and descending characters that surround it. A serif *x* will mostly be smaller than a corresponding sans serif *x*.

On a narrow measure, 9 point might be necessary, but on a wide measure, it is best to increase the size to 12 point. These choices will determine the number of characters on the line.

All other type decisions are made following text font selection and the text size and text leading decisions.

Type selection

One of the safest ways to produce a cohesive text treatment is to select a type family and use its variants exclusively. One family member—usually the original version—is chosen to be the basic font. Its designer determined that this font is best for text setting. It usually is.

All decisions on text width, leading, spacing, indenting and headings are made based on that selection. It should be legible and easy to read, which often means it is free from decoration and unusual letterforms.

Often an organisation will choose a typeface that becomes its 'corporate' typeface—all materials produced by the organisation are effectively identified by the use of that type family.

There are even families designed with matching sans serif and serif typefaces. Using such extended families gives a 'corporate' cohesion to text and, because of the similarity in curves, weight and stroke thickness, removes the difficulty of finding compatible typefaces.

The Stone family includes:

Sans

Stone sans Sumner Stone 1987

Informal

Stone informal Sumner Stone 1987

Serif

Stone serif Sumner Stone 1987

Compatible typefaces

To avoid the 'ordinary' or 'boring' look of a single typeface used through a publication, you can add interest by adding a second 'special' typeface. It works best when the second face is used sparingly. This retains the interest in it on the occasions when it is used, possibly for headings, running heads, pull-quotes or captions.

Think of one face as the 'special' and the other—probably the text typeface—as the working face. You can then use the variants of both families for various tasks within the text.

The secret of successful combination of typefaces seems to be the ability to maintain several contrasts between them. It is best to use at least two of those contrasts when selecting your 'special' and your 'worker'. The stronger the contrast, the more effective the combination will be. You can contrast:

- their form—serif, sans serif, script or decorative
- their weight or typecolour—reversed, bold, medium or light
- their scale—large or small
- their spacing—wide or narrow
- their direction—roman or italic
- their shape—condensed, normal or expanded
- their case—capitals or lower case.

Another guide here is to choose typefaces from different type categories, with no more than one face from any one category on a page. Use their variants, but maintain a minimum of two contrasts between each combination. This gives not only compatibility but also flexibility.

But there are also times when the contrast might be too great or the differences may be in conflict. For example, it is often unwise to use an italic serif font with a script typeface because their letterforms will clash. Also consider the effect that one typeface—and its associations—will have on another. For example, contemporary script faces are often too 'casual' to sit comfortably with traditional serif typefaces because their associations are different and there is a lack of logic in their proximity to each other. It is a very special elderly relative who will sit comfortably in a group of loutish youths.

CHECK LIST
Type compatibility
The most successful technique for selecting two types that will complement each other is to use at least two contrasts between them:

☐ **Form**
SERIF vs SANS SERIF
Decorative vs Normal

☐ **Weight**
LIGHT vs **BOLD** vs `REVERSE`

☐ **Size**
LARGE vs SMALL

☐ **Spacing**
W I D E vs NARROW

☐ **Direction**
Italic vs Roman

☐ **Shape**
CONDENSED vs NORMAL vs EXPANDED

☐ **Case**
CAPITALS/UPPER CASE vs lower case

DOING IT FASTER
**Measuring optimum
line length**
In order to quickly decide how wide
your columns could be without
counting, find a type catalogue that
presents settings of the lower-case
alphabet of each font in different
sizes. Simply measure the setting of
the lower-case alphabet in the size
you intend using and multiply it from
1.5 to 3 times to determine the range
for optimum line length. Then
consider whether your format or
grid allows a line length within
that range.

DOING IT SMARTER
**A personalised type
catalogue**
Create your own type catalogue by
typing up the alphabet in all caps and
then in lower case, a set of numbers
and punctuation marks. Caption it
with font and size information.
Duplicate it numerous times,
selecting the size options you are
most likely to use, remembering to
revise the caption. Print it out. Then
select the whole page and allocate a
different typeface and print it out,
too. Do this for all the typefaces you
have and generate new pages when
you invest in a new face.

Legibility and readability

We read best what we are used to reading. It's best to avoid
idiosyncratic typographic features, because they can be
unwelcome distractions to a reader. Don't make long text
documents harder to read—it's difficult enough as it is to
get people to read them.

Because people have a finite amount of time to spend
reading, there is an emphasis on the speed and accuracy of
their comprehension. This puts great importance on the
ability to achieve clarity of letterforms and to maintain
correct emphasis within the text. What you do with your
chosen typeface to enable the reader to find and understand
the material being presented is paramount.

A major inhibitor to smooth reading is inconsistency. Be
consistent in:

- headings, once you have established an appropriate
  hierarchy
- the style for references and cross-references
- spelling
- punctuation
- the structure of information.

READ MORE ABOUT IT
Rolf Rehe, *Typography: How to make it most legible*, Design Research
    International, Carmel, Indiana, 1984.
Colin Wheildon, *Communicating or just making pretty shapes*, 3rd edn,
    Newspaper Advertising Bureau of Australia, Sydney, 1990.

Line length

Optimum line length is generally considered to be between
1.5 and 3 alphabets or, given the alphabet contains
26 letters, 39–78 characters (which is sometimes rounded
up to 40–80 characters) or, for people who prefer a single
figure to a range, 60 characters. It largely depends on
which publications you read.

The range is more useful than the absolute. The number
of characters per line in various typefaces and formats will
change, so you will not be able to achieve the absolute of 60
in every setting, and that does not necessarily mean that
your readability is compromised. A range also implies that,
if you go beyond the range, you are entering potentially
difficult areas.

In any case, line lengths that are near the upper limit
will need more leading than those near the lower. This
enables readers' eyes to accurately and consistently drop to

the starting point of the next line without doubling (where you read the same line twice or even three times).

In narrow columns, there are a few standard techniques to increase the number of characters to a comfortable reading level:
- reduce the point size of your type
- select a condensed or narrow typeface
- use the italic font, which will mostly set narrower.

Another consideration is the written style of the text. If the manuscript has many long words, such as a scientific or technical paper, and long sentences and paragraphs, it does not lend itself to narrow, multicolumn setting; if it has short paragraphs and lists, or dot points with short entries, it will.

Leading

When printers used metal type, they inserted thin strips of lead between the lines of type to separate them. The term *leading* (pronounced 'ledding') refers to the space between lines of type. This space is generally measured from the baseline of one line to the baseline of the next, so it is nearly always larger than the point size of the typeface.

If there is no leading between the lines, the text is 'set solid'. Solid setting has the potential for the descenders of one line to touch the ascenders of the next, which upsets the word shape and inhibits readability. You need some leading in all cases where readability is paramount, particularly in text setting.

Auto-leading refers to a default setting that places an extra 20% of space between the lines—if your text is set in 10 point Times Roman, the auto-leading is 12 points (which means there are 12 points from one baseline to the next).

It often helps to imagine how this was achieved with metal type. Type is measured from the top of the ascending characters—like *d*, *h* and *k*—to the bottom of the descending characters—like *g*, *y* and *j*. Using the same example, you would have a line of Times that was 10 points deep with a 2 point wide piece of lead between it and the next line of 10 point Times.

Leading is now measured in points from baseline to baseline (which is the sum of the body size of the type and the width of the imaginary lead strip between the lines). It is then expressed as the size of the body 'on' the measurement from baseline to baseline.

Leading between
LEAD
lines of type

The amount of leading required is determined by the interrelationship between the x-height and the number of characters that fit in the measure. The longer the line, the more leading it will require. Conversely, with short lines, less leading will be required.

Sans serif type usually requires more leading than serif type. This is related to the x-height of the letterforms—usually sans serif typefaces have a larger x-height than serif typefaces.

As a rule of thumb, you should be able to fit a minimum of an x-and-a-half space between your x-heights.

With a serif face, the minimum recommended leading is one extra point on the size of the face. For example, 10 point Times with 1 point of space between the lines is called '10 on 11 point Times' and written as '10/11 pt Times'. The leading is entered as '11 points' even though, in the past, it would have been a 1-point lead strip placed between the lines. As a rule, leading for a serif font will be between 1 and 4 points on the size of the font—using 4 on a long line length. Using the same example, if you had 60 characters in a line, the appropriate specification might be 10/13 pt Times. If closer to 80 characters, it may be 10/14 pt Times.

With a sans serif face, the minimum recommended leading is 2 extra points on the size of the face. Leading for sans serif will vary from 2 to 6 extra points on the size of the font, again using more on a longer line.

If you do not feel confident enough to make leading decisions, auto-leading is a good guide, but not infallible, as it is also mostly based on the appropriate leading for a serif face.

As a further example, if you set 10 point Times Roman with 12 point leading and then changed the typeface to the sans serif Helvetica, you could alter the size to 9 point Helvetica but keep the 12 point leading (which is greater than the auto-leading for 9 point, at a comparative leading of 133%).

If you apply leading more generously, you create a lighter looking text block which can be a useful technique to remember for varying the tonal arrangement within a layout.

Minimum leading

As a general guide, the minimum requirement is an x-and-a-half between lines of x-height in both serif and sans serif type—or 2.5 times the height of an x.

Minimum
leading

Extreme leading

You might leave a line space or more between lines, e.g. '10/24 pt Times'. As a display setting style for advertisements or annual reports, it can be quite effective. Some designers interweave headings, footnotes, even other paragraphs or a second column of text through the wide linespacing.

It can be a most effective technique but has drawbacks; it relies on a reader being able to identify the typeface variation. Maximising the contrast seems to be the easiest way to ensure that both levels of information are read. This is best done with colour, weight of font, or an entirely different typeface.

Negative leading

In display lines that are set in capitals, a negative leading is often allocated, i.e. leading that is smaller than the body size of the type, e.g. '10/8 pt Times caps'. This is done to avoid the distance that occurs when there are no descenders to fill the gap. Without the descenders, the space between the lines can separate the lines too much, particularly if the second line is a continuation of the first and not a separate heading.

In extreme cases, you may want the lines of capitals to touch. Trial and error is the best way to determine the amount of negative leading for this. Make sure your laser printer gives you an accurate depiction; sometimes what looks accurate on a laser printer will not look so accurate when produced from an imagesetter.

You can use this technique to make a cohesive heading shape with lower case as well. It is often used when centring two- or three-line headings in an oval shape. Ensure that descenders from above don't crash into ascenders from below. You may need to massage the line breaks in order to avoid a crash or even use optional characters (the dotless i [ı] is sometimes useful to avoid a descender from the line above). You might also 'interpret' your centring, creating a more asymmetrical arrangement of the lines to avoid any clashes.

When using extreme leading,

Extreme

you may offset headings and other

leading

text elements like footnotes, cross-

creates

references or links by placing them

cross-readings

between the lines of the main text.

Capitals set solid in 18/18 pt Scala are changed to 18/15 pt Scala to better shape the three-line title.

BEFORE THE — DAY'S — END —

AFTER THE — DAY'S — END —

A title set solid in 18/18 pt Scala looks uneven in this three-line setting due to the descending *y*, capital *E* and ascending *d* that fill the second linespace—creating an optical illusion of those lines being closer. While the second line has a capital *D*, the first line has no descending characters so the leading between the first and second lines was reduced by 2 points to 18/16 pt Scala to optically correct the title.

BEFORE

The
Day's
End

AFTER

The
Day's
End

DOING IT FASTER
Kerning
Don't fiddle with kerning at rough or draft stage—if at all.

Uneven leading within a heading

In a multiple-line heading set in lower case, such as those that sometimes appear on narrow pamphlets, you will need to alter the leading for each line of the heading so that it will look optically even. The optical distortion usually occurs when there is a line that has no descenders. The space between it and the next line will often look inordinately large, so you need to move the next line up a few points until it looks even.

For this to work, make sure that each line break is established with a line return, otherwise any leading change will flow through the entire heading.

Letterspacing

Letterspacing is usually achieved by a combination of optical and mechanical spacing. Optical spacing achieves the look of there being similar space between characters but takes account of the letterforms and their counter spaces. You can use a combination of techniques to achieve this. For instance, imagine a number of jellybeans that neatly fit between each letter so the blank area or white space takes the same number of jellybeans, despite their odd distribution around some lettershapes. Another technique is to determine the optical edge of the letterforms and then mechanically space them.

Mechanical spacing puts exactly the same amount of space between letters, but it is measured from the right of the first letter to the left of the following letter, regardless of the letterform. This means some letter combinations will look further away than others.

Letterspacing controls are at your fingertips in most page layout programs, and the terms most often used to describe letterspacing techniques are tracking and kerning. They are not interchangeable terms—in most programs you will encounter both because they have different functions.

Kerning

Letters are usually spaced so there is the appearance of even space between them, but in some combinations of letters, the spacing remains awkward. *Kerning* is the respacing of specific pairs of letters that are causing uneven spacing within a word. Although this does not usually need to be used in text setting, it is often worth the trouble for titles, logotypes and headings. Kerning is usually required in setting where there are capitals such as T, A, V, W and L.

Kerning alters the space between any combination of two characters, i.e. how the first letter relates to the second letter. Place the cursor between the two letters and reduce or enlarge the space with the kerning controls until it is optically correct.

Most fonts include specified kerning pairs that are automatically applied to particular character combinations, according to the font designer's wishes. These usually include problem letters (T, L, A, V and any letterforms with weird space distribution around their shape) and how they will set with each other and any lower-case letters that follow. For example, will the *a* sit under the crossbar of the *T* in *Table*? In capitals setting, will the L sit neatly under the T in ALTER? Will the A and the V overlap in AV?

You should bother with kerning only in display type, because it is time-consuming and few clients can afford the time it takes you to tweak it. But consider editing your fonts so your kerning preferences are saved and automatically applied.

Tracking

The mechanical method of letterspacing is called *tracking*, which evenly distributes more or less space between each letter. Some text designers have a preference for tightly spaced characters; others prefer 'open' or 'loose' spacing.

As a general rule, the larger the type, the tighter you can track. Many programs do this automatically. However, tracking capabilities are occasionally handy for respacing a headline, logotype or title.

Tracking alters the amount of space between each letter in the whole word, heading or text block. Select the word or line and go to tracking commands. Less space between the characters makes the word narrower and is called 'tight'; more space between the characters makes the word wider and is called 'loose'.

Often, tracking decisions are aesthetic, but there are readability issues here. As type gets smaller, there needs to be more space between the individual letters—the spacing cannot be mathematically reduced like the characters themselves. There needs to be slightly wider tracking as the word shrinks.

This problem is often highlighted in logos where they are fine on cover designs but do not work in running heads, or they may be fine on a letterhead but hard to read on the

DOING IT FASTER
Kerning preferences
If possible, edit the kerning pairs in each of your fonts to suit your personal preferences. Save them and they will be applied automatically.

side of a building—the spacing may be at fault. Some organisations have logo artwork for reproduction at different sizes so those readability and reproduction problems are resolved.

You will often need to use looser tracking when you set a word or some text in small capitals. To approximate the same grey as the text block, tracking of small capitals usually needs to be looser than the surrounding text.

Very loose tracking is sometimes used in all-capitals setting as a display technique. Rarely do we wide-track lower-case letterforms, although it is becoming more accepted through occasional use.

If there is very wide spacing in a heading and the heading spills onto the following line, the 'rule' is to have at least the same amount of space between each letter as between the lines, so increase the leading.

If you loose-track bold type, you alter its weight on the page. If loose tracking erodes that importance, the page looks duller (because of the lack of contrast) and the relative importance can be lost.

If you tight-track bold type, the letterforms will often overlap, which can create legibility problems. Used in large sizes, overlapped letterforms can create interesting hybrid shapes, but you have to be sure your audience can be bothered trying to decipher the message.

Street signage—or better still, highway signage—contains some valuable lessons when it comes to readability. You can apply them to shop signs, posters, or even Saturday morning garage sale signs.

If you analyse a highway sign at close quarters, you'll find that there is a very significant amount of letterspacing in road signage. This is for precisely the same reason that you use very loose tracking on 4 point type—when type is small, you need exponentially more space between the letters, and at the distance from which you start reading a highway sign, it is very small type.

If readers will be across the room or down the road, extra letterspacing will help them read the message.

Capitals tracked wide in 18/18 pt Scala are changed to 18/28 pt Scala to better shape the three-line title and avoid vertical groupings. Also note the kerning of the apostrophe.

BEFORE

T H E   —
D A Y ' S   _
E N D   —

AFTER

T H E   _
D A Y ' S   _
E N D   —

Using type variation

To show relative importance within text, there are a number of standard type variations that can be used. Each decision will have an impact on a reader's comprehension of the text, as type variations imply a particular level of importance due to their traditional role in typography.

Bold type

Bold type is 'heavier' in *weight* than text fonts. This is achieved by thickening the strokes of the original font's letterforms. Thickening makes bold fonts appear darker. The level of relative darkness of a font is referred to as its *weight* and how it is set on a page determines its typecolour or tonal variance to the other type around it.

Weight variation is often used to add life to a page layout or to help define levels of information contained within text. Darker text tends to jump out of a page of ordinary text and grab the reader's attention (which makes it perfect for indicating the location of specific information, as a heading does, or for warnings). The choice of a bold font is all to do with the resulting patterns of tone that are created on a page by the areas of type.

In a heading hierarchy, bold type is the strongest (with the exception of a reversed block of text)—and is therefore reserved for the most important information. Bold headings within a text area will stand out because of the contrast between bold type at its heavier weight and the lighter text type. It is easier for readers to find the section they want to read.

Because bold type is a thickened version of the typeface, the counters (i.e. the enclosed spaces within letters such as the loop of the *e*) are correspondingly smaller. This can make the letters a bit difficult to distinguish, so it is wise to track bold type a little looser—but only fractionally, because the more space you put between the letters, the lighter the typecolour will appear to be, and you must not lose the benefit of the weight change.

Typefaces like Helvetica, Frutiger, Gill and Univers (notice they are all sans serif) mostly come with an extrabold or black weight. This weight is particularly handy—its contrast is very sudden when compared with the text weights and can be impressive.

However, if overused, bold type can be too distracting and can inhibit reading, but, judiciously used, it can

DOING IT SMARTER
Typeface associations

Create 12 layouts that show type contrasts for the pairs of words listed below. Each layout should be in a 60 mm square (but can be any size you want). Select a typeface for each word and choose the way you set it: In capitals? What spacing? In bold or italic? On an angle or upside down? Reversed out of black to white? Tracked? What size? Not only should these design decisions help to convey the meaning of each word, they should also depict the difference between the two words.

This is not just a type selection exercise. Use layout to help communicate the difference in meaning as well. Use repetition, reversing, centring and other formatting options. Run one word through the other or explore other forms of dynamic placement in an asymmetrical layout.

To increase the complexity of this exercise, use a typeface only once. This means that for the 12 examples, 24 typefaces must be chosen. If you have used Helvetica extrabold, don't use Helvetica again—find another sans serif type that will work as you want.

This is a great exercise if you are working on book titles and advertising headlines, or feature articles in newsletters, magazines, Web sites or e-zines.

The words to be contrasted are:
- big/little
- fat/thin
- dark/light
- happy/sad
- out/in
- old/young
- rich/poor
- up/down
- fast/slow
- east/west
- beautiful/ugly
- powerful/meek.

enhance meaning by giving appropriate importance and it can add the dark tones to a page that help the page to live.

Reversed type

When you change the colour of type to white on a black background, it is called a reverse. It is like a text negative.

It is better to reverse a bold font. This helps the type when it is printed. You may have noticed that black type tends to thicken slightly when it is printed; when it is reversed, the black background is thickened, making the white type spindly and more difficult to read. If you use reversed bolder type, it will often look like the same weight as the text because of this optical illusion.

It is also better to reverse a sans serif typeface. The same slight thickening of the background of a reversed area tends to make the narrow strokes of serif type and the serifs themselves thinner—and, in some cases, they disappear altogether—which makes the type more difficult to read. To avoid this problem, type that is reversed out of black, a solid colour or a photograph should be sans serif.

It is better to track reversed type a little wider (or 'looser') than if it were not reversed. This helps the definition of the individual letters and aids readability.

Comparing italic forms

Scala regular

a

Scala italic is an italic form

a

Helvetica

a

Helvetica italic is an oblique form

Italics

Aldus Manutius, a Venetian printer and publisher of the Renaissance, first used italics in 1501. He developed them to fit more words into the small page of his pocket editions of classical literature—and you can still usually fit more words to a line if you set italics, because the characters are often narrower than the roman font. Francesco Griffo, the typeface designer in Aldus's studio, based his italic design on a popular slanted handwriting style of the day.

Physically, italics lean to the right and are a redraw of the roman font to which their name corresponds. When comparing a roman serif typeface with its italic version, you will notice that some letterforms are different, particularly the lower case g/g and a/a. The italics are often more calligraphic in appearance which makes them a logical choice for headings with a difference.

In sans serif typefaces, the italics are often just an *oblique* version of the roman font, i.e. they are the same character shapes slanted.

Italics should have the same weight (or the same tone on the page when you squint at them) as the roman font. Because of this, the use of italics through text does not interrupt the texture of the page, which means they are perfect for stress within a text block.

Avoid setting italics in all capitals. In fact, when Aldus used them in 1501, all the text was set in italics except the headings which were set in roman capitals and the first letter of each line which was a roman capital letter—there were no italic capitals.

The readability of the text is not sacrificed when you use italics. In testing, there has been no significant difference in the speed and accuracy with which people read italics when compared with the readability of roman letters.

Quoted material used to be cited in italics and still can be if desired. Italics are regularly used for the captions to photographs or diagrams and for cross-references. They are also traditionally used for specific text functions:

- When you are quoting titles of magazines, newspapers, books, films, plays, long poems, operas, musical works (those with specific non-musical titles only), ballets, shows, paintings and television programs, it is customary to use italics, thus: *Australian MacWorld*; the *Financial Review*; Sally Morgan's *My Place*; *Priscilla: Queen of the Desert*; David Williamson's *Emerald City*; A.B. 'Banjo' Paterson's *The Man from Snowy River*; Peggy Glanville-Hicks's *Nausicaa*; Peter Sculthorpe's *Kakadu* but Peter Sculthorpe's Piano Concerto; Graeme Murphy's *Nearly Beloved*; David Atkins's *Hot Shoe Shuffle*; Margaret Preston's *Illawarra Lillies and Waratahs*; and *Water Rats*. However, when citing an article, episode of a television program, short poem or song title, it is customary to use quote marks, not italics, thus: 'Makeover' from *Desktop*; *Bananas in Pyjamas* 'The Big Parade'; Judith Wright's 'Bora Ring'; 'Solid Rock' from Goanna's *Spirit of Place*. Also note public service preferences for citations: Hansard but *Commonwealth of Australia Gazette*.
- On the occasions that you need to quote the name of a vehicle, usually a ship or an aircraft, it is a convention to use italics for the name of the vessel. For example, HMAS *Success* or the *Fairstar*; Kingsford Smith's *Southern Cross*; or even the starship USS *Enterprise* from *Star Trek*.

CHECK LIST
Titles or names
that are set in italics:
- ☐ Books
- ☐ Magazines
- ☐ Newspapers
- ☐ Plays
- ☐ Operas
- ☐ Films
- ☐ Television programs
- ☐ Long poems
- ☐ Musical works
- ☐ Paintings
- ☐ Sculptures
- ☐ Artworks
- ☐ Acts of parliament (when full title, including date; shortened forms are in roman)
- ☐ Legal documents
- ☐ Ships
- ☐ Trains
- ☐ Aircraft
- ☐ Genus
- ☐ Species
- ☐ Subspecies
- ☐ Varieties

- Foreign words which are not regarded as anglicised are set in italic, but use them sparingly. Many expressions are considered to have entered English, such as cafe, consomme, cliché or résumé (note the acutes so the word 'résumé' is not confused with the word 'resume'). The *Macquarie Dictionary* will not italicise any foreign words or phrases that it lists which means they can be considered part of written English and need not be italicised. If it doesn't appear in the *Macquarie*, use italics.
- Scientific names like *Acacia flavescens* (yellow wattle)
- In military histories, the enemy's formations are cited in italics.

Note the following details of plurals and punctuation for italic usage:

- She handed me a few *Sydney Morning Herald*s.
  (roman *s* for plural form)
- Have you read the *Age*'s book review yet?
  (roman apostrophe, roman *s*)
- Have you seen Tom Roberts's *Bailed up*?
  (roman question mark)

In fact, use italics wherever you would have used underlining in typewriting.

Italics can be used as a separate voice in text and are sometimes used in fiction works for thoughts or a second narrative. In the same way, they can be used for editorial notes to the reader [*like this one*] because they separate the voice of the information from the main voice of the text—a sort of ancient hypertext.

Capitals/upper case

When the Romans conquered Greece, they took what they liked and improved on it. And that's exactly what they did with the Greek alphabet. The Romans refined the letter-forms to a point where the alphabet looked very much like it does today. But all this development was only in that part of the alphabet that we call 'capital' letters or 'upper case'.

Now, think of gods like Zeus and Jupiter, goddesses like Athena and Minerva, think of ancient buildings like the Parthenon and the Pantheon. 'Capital' is an architectural term, which describes the decorative top of a column. Atop the capitals is a strip of marble that is inscribed with the name of the god or goddess to whom the building is dedicated, and these are literally 'capital' letters.

Stonemasons cut them to precise specifications, so that each letter would have its correct width in comparison to the others.

The relative widths of capitals were defined as part of their essential character for optimum shape recognition, so the M and O were wide, the S and V were medium, and the I was very narrow.

That is why typefaces with letterforms that do not follow these width interrelationships are often less legible; correct character relationships enable recognition.

Of course, we now use a 'double alphabet'—capitals and lower case, or if you prefer the correct Latin terminology, majuscules and minuscules.

The concept of big and little letters really came from the monks who were scribbling copies of the Bible and got bored. They started embellishing the first word of a section with large initial letters and similarly with the first letter in important names. But, skipping a fairly long and involved story that would take us from Greece and Rome to Ireland (where a heap of monks toiled, developing an alphabet called 'semi-uncials' which was like our little letters), France (where the lower case we know today was developed at the court of Charlemagne and, incidentally, named 'Carolingian minuscules'), and Germany (where two gentlemen put the two alphabets together and put serifs on the little letters so they'd match the capitals), we find that, at the end, we have developed a code of use for capitals and lower case and a fairly complicated code called 'punctuation'. Both codes help us to communicate in written form.

CAPITALS SHOULD BE AVOIDED IN CONTINUOUS TEXT BECAUSE THEY SLOW THE READER DOWN. THIS IS BECAUSE CAPITAL LETTERS CREATE WORDS THAT HAVE A RECTANGULAR SHAPE AND WE CANNOT RECOGNISE THE SHAPE OF THE WORDS AS DISTINCTLY AS WE CAN WITH lower-case words, which have a more quickly identified individual shape due to their particular combination of ascenders and descenders. This helps us to read lower-case words more quickly.

Capital letters are used to signify a proper noun—'naming' words such as Australia, *The Design Manual* and Whitbread.

You might also have noticed how capitals in a paragraph jump out. Capitals appear to be more important so they can be used for information that needs to be brought to the reader's attention urgently. But there are other techniques

Proper nouns

that take an initial capital letter:

- Names
  - people
  - organisations
  - products
  - places
- Titles
  - publications
  - stage shows
  - films
  - musical works
  - visual arts works
- Public service preferences
  - specific references capitalised
  - generic references in lower case

For example: Note the capitals in Department of Foreign Affairs and Trade, but no capitals when simply referring to 'the department'.

that achieve the same result. Bold or italic fonts are often better suited than capitals.

Capitals are usually reserved for short pieces of information such as titles, headings and logotypes.

These days, although it is preferred to set headings in lower case with an initial capital, titles on covers are often set in capitals to make the title a solid block—a rectangle is often an easier shape to use in a layout. That's why we often relegate capitals to what we call display setting, where the shape of the letters and words is more important for its design implications than its readability. After all, the difference in the time it takes to read one word in capitals and the time it takes to read the same word in lower case is negligible.

Often, a heading in capitals can be reduced in size, but sometimes this leaves the heading looking squashed. To counter this, use looser tracking with headings set in all capitals.

All-capitals headings also work well reversed to white in black boxes. That still needs a bit of loose tracking and normally a bolder typeface for easy printability. This creates one of the strongest heading styles, because the black box has such a powerful impact on the layout. Usually, as a result of this, the reversed heading is not used for headings that occur quickly after one another—that can chop up the page too much.

Because of their clear shapes and defined widths, capitals are more easily recognised forms and considered to be more legible. Lower-case letters are often based on a circular stroke that inhibits that recognition factor. Compare A with a and *a*: the triangular capital letterform is more distinct in a grouping. But lower-case letterforms are considered more readable because the distinguishing characteristic of ascender and descender combinations enables us to recognise the word shape more quickly.

Minimal and maximal capitalisation
Minimal capitalisation is where only the first word and proper nouns in a title take an initial capital. Maximal capitalisation is where all major words in a title take an initial capital. It is problematic because of the definition of 'major words' and the resulting uneven look to the text.

Maximal capitalisation has been used in the title of this book. Note how the title has then been detailed: auto-leading has been altered to negative leading to better group the lines; and the capitals have been optically aligned, with the cross-bar of the *T* allowed to 'hang' in the margin.

BEFORE

The Design Manual

AFTER

The Design Manual

All main words in a title or a heading used to be capitalised:
- The Namatjira Works on Paper
- *For the Term of His Natural Life*
- An Analysis of Sculthorpe's Symphonic Works

But with minimal capitalisation, only the first word and any proper nouns in a title or heading will be capitalised. So the above examples would reduce to:
- The Namatjira works on paper
- *For the term of his natural life*
- An analysis of Sculthorpe's symphonic works

Although it is optional how much capitalisation you use, the trend towards less punctuation implies dropping capitals to lower case where possible. This book uses minimal punctuation in its further reading reference lists, for example, but note that in text, titles take maximal capitalisation. The Vancouver referencing system also uses minimal capitalisation.

Typographically, capitals break up text passages by disturbing the even texture of lower-case text. This is also the reason for typing only one space after a full stop in a paragraph—the capital that starts the next sentence is easy to find so doesn't need the extra space.

Small capitals
In a specialist set, small capitals are a redraw of the font where the small capital height is slightly higher than the x-height of the face and the small capitals are close to the same width of the lower-case letters.

In packages where small capitals are drawn from the font matrix for standard capital letters, you should set the height or vertical scaling to about 66% and the width or horizontal scaling to about 85%. This will create small capitals that are scaled closer to the dimensions of a true small capital font—where the small caps are a squat version of the real caps.

In display type, where you might be using capitals beside small capitals, it is often worth playing with the weight of the fonts. A true small capital font will have a comparatively thicker stroke that matches the standard font stroke thickness. If you are scaling your small capitals, you might try using the demibold font or bold font to match the character width of the initial capital. Alternatively, use a lighter font for the initial capitals.

It is preferable to use small capitals in text setting where you want to set a word or phrase in full capitals. This will not interrupt the text flow or 'jump out of the page'.

Small capitals may even be used for all-capital abbreviations such as personnel position references, post-nominals, and state, department, organisation and company names that appear in text: CEO, PA, MBA, VC, ACT, NSW, WA, SA, NT, TAS, VIC, QLD, UNSW, DSS, NRMA, RACQ.

Some fonts also now have 'petite' capitals which are the same height as the x-height.

Raised and drop caps

A raised initial capital.

Raised and drop capitals

Sometimes in a layout the positioning of some graphic elements requires that a text block go in a position that does not follow a logical reading flow. A raised or dropped cap is a graphic device where something is needed to drag the reader's attention back to the text, particularly if there is a picture or heading to the right of the text block.

IN ORDER to redirect the reader's attention to the text block, we use a device of colouring and/or making a graphic element of the initial letter of a text block. It is usually quite low in the hierarchy on the page: we see pictures, headlines and then drop or raised capitals. They are used to lead us into the text.

A two-line drop capital aligned with the cap-height of the first word and the baseline of the second line.

Raised capitals are certainly the easiest to use—they have the same effect but you simply change the size and font of the capital as desired. The text simply flows on using the same baseline. The increased height needs to be taken into account by adding more space above the paragraph.

A three-line drop capital aligned with the x-height of the first line and the baseline of the third line.

Drop capitals can have a 2- or 3-line drop. Their size is determined by the size of text and its leading. Usually the drop cap aligns with the x-height of the top line of text and sits on the baseline of either the second or third line of the paragraph.

Care should be taken that unintentional cross-readings do not occur, as readers notice the featured letters in order of their dominance: in this case spelling 'RIR'.

Sometimes the rest of the first word of the paragraph is set in capitals to ease the reader into the smaller size, in which case the drop cap is set to align with the cap height. You will probably need to track the first word a little looser and kern it carefully into the initial drop cap so it runs smoothly into the word.

Drop caps might also have text set to run around them rather than leaving a white block of space for them to sit in.

Some designers overuse the technique and can come

unstuck. You might spell presumably unintentional words across a layout or down a layout with strong random initials. They also tend to cancel each other out, becoming just a decoration and losing their importance in redirecting the reader's gaze.

READ MORE ABOUT IT

Geoffrey Rogers, *Editing for print*, Macdonald and Co., London, 1985, ISBN 0 356 10787 6.

Baden Eunson, *Writing at work*, John Wiley & Sons, Brisbane, 1996, ISBN 0 471 33564 9.

Shirley Purchase (compiler), *The little book of style*, AusInfo, Canberra, 1998, ISBN 0 644 38296 1.

George Stern, *Choosing your mark: A guide to good expression and punctuation*, AGPS, Canberra, 1995, ISBN 0 644 42663 2.

Style manual for authors, editors and printers, 5th edn, AusInfo, Canberra, 1994, ISBN 0 644 29771 9.

Constance Hale (ed.), *Wired style: Principles of English usage in the digital age*, HardWired, San Francisco, 1996, ISBN 1 888869 01 1.

Punctuation marks

The accurate detailing of punctuation is a part of professionally presented text. If it is inconsistent or incorrect, it makes your client or organisation look incompetent or, worse, inept.

The rule of thumb for editorial correction is that, while you may have personal preferences, many options are acceptable, provided that they are consistently applied.

The current practice is leaning towards minimal punctuation, minimal capitalisation and minimal text interference. That said, you would again find personal preferences often win out. But readability and understandability are the main determinants of how much punctuation to use.

Spacing punctuation marks

Punctuation marks nearly always immediately follow or precede that which they punctuate.

Question and exclamation marks, commas and full stops, semi-colons and colons do not have a space before them, and they have only one space after them—never two, as typists were taught.

Apostrophes have no space either side, unless they follow a plural (e.g. 'She could never remember her uncles' birthdays.'—the birthdays of many uncles) or unless they

Different spaces

There are spaces achieved in lines of text with indents and tabs—either preset or customised. And either tracking or kerning can customise spacing between letters. However, there are other spacing options.

The normal space bar is pressed once for a space between words. It will vary in width in justified settings and also allows lines to be broken at that point. But there are times when you do not want a line broken at that point, e.g. in the middle of a phone number, code or number, or after initials in a name. In these instances, use a *non-breaking space*, which is a different keystroke.

In listings, you sometimes want to space some text slightly further away from an entry, such as prices in menus or page numbers in contents lists. You can use an *em space* or an *en space* (which are the same widths respectively as the em and en rules).

A *fixed space* or *thin space* (called a *punctuation space* in America) is the width of a comma and often used instead of a comma in numbers. Because it is a 'fixed' space, it will not increase or reduce in size when used in justification.

In display setting, punctuation marks will sometimes be reduced—which, in the case of apostrophes and quote marks, will also require them to be re-positioned. They are then kerned and 'hung' in the margin for an improved optical alignment of the text block.

BEFORE

'Okay,'
he said.

AFTER

'Okay,'
he said.

indicate that the beginning or ending of a word is missing (' 'Allo, 'allo, what's goin' on 'ere, then?').

Opening quotes are preceded by one space but no space follows them. Closing quotes do not have a preceding space, but are followed by a single space.

If punctuation marks were spaced, they would leave gaps within the texture of the type and interrupt the typecolour.

Minimal and maximal punctuation

These two addresses demonstrate one of the most important principles to remember about modern punctuation: reduce it to bare essentials. Compare:

Mr DW Whitbread	Mr D. W. Whitbread,
PO Box 3127	P. O. Box 3127,
Weston Creek ACT 2611	Weston Creek, A.C.T., 2611.

Note that it is also acceptable to space initials if desired:

D W Whitbread

Excluding sentences and poetry, do not put punctuation at the ends of lines because the line return is enough to make the distinction. However, in text where you might run the address within a paragraph, you would punctuate it like this: Mr DW Whitbread, PO Box 3127, Weston Creek ACT 2611.

Street names do not include possessive punctuation—so 'King Georges Terrace' is not punctuated to 'King George's Terrace'.

Also recognise the modern practice for referring to Australian States and territories without full stops: NSW, WA, SA, NT and ACT. This is largely because Australia Post computers do not like punctuation in the final line of addresses, which always includes the reference to the State. So 'VIC' is preferred to 'Vic.' for Victoria; 'TAS' is preferred to 'Tas.' for Tasmania; and 'QLD' is preferred to 'Qld' for Queensland.

Acronyms and initialisms

Like States, in acronyms and initialisms we delete full stops: UNSW, WHO, NAB, BHP, CSR, ALP, USA, UK, OHS, HRD, HOD, ASIO.

Note the following exceptions, which, although they are acronyms, are set with an initial capital only: Qantas, Anzac, Unesco.

Full stop/full point/period

Full stops appear at the end of sentences, immediately following the last word. Only one space follows them and then the next sentence starts. 'Period' is the US term.

Full stops should not appear in logos, no matter how strongly an advertising agency argues the case. They should rarely appear in headlines, and if they do on the occasion that the headline is a sentence, they should be reduced in size and kerned to make minimal impact on the text. A full stop on a headline has been found to be a disincentive to continue reading the body text that follows it.

Full stops should be used in lists when the dot points are in sentence structure, and on the last point when the list is a continuation of a lead-in phrase.

Full stops are used to divide the parts of a Web URL and to signal abbreviations but are not used in contractions.

On the occasions where you are tempted to key three full stops, replace them with a single keystroke called the 'points of ellipsis'.

Contractions/abbreviations
Where the last letter of a contraction is the final letter of the word that has been contracted, the contraction does not have a full stop. Note these examples:

- 'Pty' for 'Proprietary'
- 'Ltd' for 'Limited'
- 'Bros' for 'Brothers'
- 'St' for 'Saint' or 'Street'
- 'Ave' for 'Avenue'
- 'Rd' for 'Road'
- 'Mr' for 'Mister'
- 'Mrs' for 'Missus'
- 'Miss' for 'Mistress'
- 'Dr' for 'Doctor'

but note 'no.' for 'number', which is a contraction of the Italian word 'numero', but takes a full stop to avoid ambiguity.

Abbreviations take a full stop when their final letter is a letter partway through the word, thus:

- 'Inc.' for 'Incorporated'
- 'Dr.' for 'Drive'
- 'Cl.' for 'Close'
- 'Pl.' for 'Place'
- 'Prof.' for 'Professor'
- 'Uni.' for 'University'
- 'Co.' for 'Company'
- 'Cor.' for 'Corinthians'.

There is also a software titling convention that has become a standard naming convention, which is often playful or gimmicky and usually incorporates contraction, particularly of spacing and punctuation, but retains capitals within a hybrid term, thus: QuarkXPress, AusInfo. But note: Westpac (for 'Western Pacific').

CHECK LIST
Punctuation to watch
- Use open (') and close (') quotes
- Single quotes preferred to double
- Only one space typed after a full stop
- No space typed before: % ? ! : ; /)]
- No space typed after: $ / (['
- No space before or after: -
- No punctuation in:
  - addresses
  - dates: 18 November 1989 (but note: Saturday, November 18, 1989, which is US usage)
- No full stops in:
  - logos or headings
  - post-nominals: BEd, PhD, MSc, BA(Hons)
  - abbreviations in capitals: NSW, GPO, AGDA
  - metric symbols: km, g, L, mm

Real quotes

'
  Opening single quote

'
  Closing single quote

"
  Opening double quotes

"
  Closing double quotes

The symbols for imperial measures
for inches and feet:

'
  Foot mark

"
  Inch mark

Smart quotes

Many programs have a preset default
that will automatically replace typed
inch and foot marks with opening
and closing quotes. The ability of
the program to do this is based on
accurate preparation of the spaces
around the marks. If a space
precedes the mark, it assumes you
want an opening quote. If a space
follows the mark, it assumes you
need a closing quote. It will also
assume you want a double quote if
you type the inch mark and a single
quote if you type a foot mark. This
has its problems when it comes to
wanting apostrophes to start a word,
because the default wants to give
you an opening quote mark, not an
apostrophe.

Compare:

'Tis the season

Apostrophe

'Tis the season

Opening quote

Comma

If the text is understandable without punctuation, i.e. it is
unambiguous and reads logically, then don't interrupt it
with punctuation. To this end, we do not use as many
commas as may have been used in the past. Commas
rarely appear in headlines or display text. We also avoid
them if line breaks separate ideas, so the idea that every
line in an address or poem finishes with a comma has
been superseded.

Quotes/inverted commas

In dialogue or quoted text, the preference is for single
quotes for a first-level quotation and double quotes within
a quote. This is probably exactly the opposite of what you
were taught at school. Thus, bearing in mind that less
is best:

- The Professor asked, 'Why is it so?'
- 'Then she said, "I'm 18, okay?" and I admitted her,' the
  attendant explained.

Slash/solidus/slant

The slash or solidus usually stands between two options,
hence 'and/or' and even 'him/her'. This is why it is
incorrect to use the solidus to express a financial year:
'2000/01' implies 2000 'or' 2001. The slash also stands for
'per', hence '$5/adult'. The solidus is used to separate
elements within Web URLs:

  http://www.unswpress.com.au/designmanual/

It can also be used in the expression of dates: 09/01/94.
Note that the use of double figures in this method of
expression creates a more even look than 9/1/94. Also be
aware that this date as expressed is understood in Australia
as 9 January 1994 but in the United States would be
understood to be 1 September 1994. For Web sites and
other international communications, it might be more
appropriate to use a spelt-out date for clarity. In forms it is
becoming more widely recognised that a coding specifying
the sequence is required: 'DD/MM/YY' for Australia and
'MM/DD/YY' for the American preference.

Hyphen

The hyphen is a single keystroke and is used in compound words like blue-green algae.

It has also been used between double vowels when the vowel sound needs to change as in 'co-operate', so you don't read 'coop' as in chickens, but this detail is now passing out of usage, successfully argued by proponents of minimal punctuation, so 'cooperate' is now preferred.

When you break a word at the end of a line to continue it on the next, as in most justification programs, a hyphen is used.

For display setting,
there are a few finer details of their use you might like to consider:

- In large headings, punctuation marks (including hyphens) are often reduced so they are not so intrusive. If they are smaller though, they are raised to correct position for the type using baseline shift.
- Between words set in all capitals you need to raise the hyphen to the centre of the capital letters, because the hyphen is set at the centre of the lower-case x-height.

Compare:

Hyphen	-
En rule	—
Em rule	——
Double em rule	————

En rule

An en rule is about double the length of a hyphen and is used in compound terms and stands for the words 'and' or 'to'. Therefore, the Sydney–Brisbane grand final takes an en rule for Sydney 'and' Brisbane. The Melbourne–Perth rail link takes an en rule for from Melbourne 'to' Perth.

The 2000–01 financial year has an en rule meaning 2000 'to' 2001. The solidus is often incorrectly used in this form (i.e. not 2000/01, as there is no sense of option or 'per').

Spaced en rule
The spaced en rule (space, en rule, space) should be used with compound terms that are compounded. Therefore, the Western Australia – South Australia match is the compound of two compounds and should take a spaced en rule. The Queensland – New South Wales border is a compound term because New South Wales is three words. So the rule is: When one or both the terms have a space within the term, there should be a space either side of the en rule.

Another example of this is in date spans: the weekend of 30 September – 1 October, or 1 July 2000 – 30 June 2001.

For display setting:
- In large headings, punctuation marks are often reduced so they are not so intrusive. You would also probably avoid the spaced en rule in headings.
- In titles, you may like to replace the en rule with a circle or diamond to make the setting more interesting.
- In all-capitals setting, you need to raise the en rule to the centre of the capital letters because the en rule is set at the centre of the lower case x-height.

Em rule/dash

An em rule is double the length of an en rule. It may or may not have a space either side but, if it falls at the end of a line, the line can be broken either before or after the em rule.

Most justification programs will not separate two words that are connected with an em rule unless there is a space. Consequently, at the moment, most magazines and publishing companies have a policy of using a spaced em rule (space, em rule, space) so the rule will break at the end or beginning of a line.

The em rule is not like a hyphen, which appears only at the end of a line in a broken term. The em rule can appear at the beginning of the next line if it does not fit on the previous line.

But when should it be used? There are arguments that the em rule can be replaced by other punctuation marks, specifically commas or parentheses (these round brackets). Often, em rules are used in sets of two—though not exclusively—for a parenthetical statement. If you reread the previous sentence, it could read 'Often, em rules are used in sets of two (though not exclusively) for a parenthetical statement' or even 'Often, em rules are used in sets of two, though not exclusively, for a parenthetical statement'.

For display setting:
- In headings and titles, where possible, em rules are avoided and other punctuation marks, such as commas and parentheses, are used instead.
- In all-capitals setting, you need to raise the em rule to the centre of the capital letters, because the em rule is set at the centre of the lower-case x-height.

Double-em rule
A double-em rule is used in bibliographies and references. It is used in lists of publications where an author or authors may have written more than one book listed in the bibliography. List the author/s for the first entry and then, instead of repeating the author/s for the subsequent entries, use a double-em rule to indicate that they are the same as the previous entry:

> Meggs, Philip B. *A History of Graphic Design*. New York: Van Nostrand Reinhold, 1983.
> ——. *Type and Image: The Language of Graphic Design*. New York: Van Nostrand Reinhold, 1989.

Colon
Colons introduce quotations, summaries and lists, either in catalogue form or in continuous prose. They are also used to indicate a ratio (1:2) and to separate chapter and verse in references to the Bible (Deut. 4:26).

In computing, film and video referencing, they are also used in the expression of time to separate minutes from hours: 12:00 (but note that this is not the practice in general text).

Semicolon
Semicolons can be used between entries in listings where commas would not be clear enough or the entry has numerous parts that already contain commas. A semicolon is thus a separation device. In sentence structures, they are sometimes used in place of conjunctions (words which join two related statements).

Parentheses/square brackets/braces/brackets
Parentheses are the curved 'brackets' that separate ideas from main text (like these).

Square brackets [like these] are often used for editorial asides within text—they indicate another voice. They are also used as the secondary level of bracketing within parentheses in mathematical setting. In display setting, they often work better than parentheses with sans serif and slab serif typefaces.

Braces are the wriggly ones {like these} and are mostly used in mathematics to join two elements of an equation. They are handy for display setting at times as they sit more decoratively with script and traditional serif typefaces.

Proofreading marks

There is a margin mark to draw attention to the error and a text mark that defines exactly where it occurs. At the end of each margin mark there is a solidus or slash to separate it from the next mark if one occurs in the same line.

	Margin mark	Text mark	Correction as it would appear
	r/	Insert	Insert
	#/	Insert space	Insert space
	i/	Mistake	Mistake
Spell out	sp.out/	&	and
	ꝺ/	Delete	Delete
	ꝺ/	Delete and close up	Delete and close up
	STET/	Leave as is	Leave as is
	CAP/	capitalise	Capitalise
	c.+s.c./	Capitals and small caps	Capitals and Small Caps
	l.c./l.c./	Lower Case*	lower case
	itals/	Italicise	*Italicise*
	bold/	Make bold	**Make bold**
	rom./	Make roman	Make roman
	w.f./w.f./	Wrong font	Wrong font
Superior/superscript	sup/sup./	degree o footnote 1	degree° footnote [1]
Inferior/subscript	sub./sub./sub./	$x_a + y_b = z_c$	$x_a + y_b = z_c$
	trs/	Transpose	Transpose
	c.u./	Close up	Close up
	align/	Align	Align
	align/	Align	Align
	align/	Correct alignment	Correct alignment
	run on/	Run on	Run on
Insert	⦂/ ⦂/ ⦁/	colon semi-colon full stop	colon: semi-colon; full stop.
	?/ !/	question exclamation	question? exclamation!
	⸌/ ⸍/ ⸌⸍/ ⸍⸍/ ,/	single double comma	'single' "double" comma,
	s.q./s.q./	Single quotes*	'Single quotes'
	‐/	Hyphenate	Hyphen-ate
En rule*	en/ ⓝ/	2000/01 Sydney-Canberra	2000–01 Sydney–Canberra
Em rule	ⓜ/	You you're kidding?	You—you're kidding?

* Two accepted methods for indicating these changes are illustrated.

Citing the Bible

The punctuation of Bible references is standard: 'John 3:16' cites an individual verse and means a reading from the Gospel of Saint John, chapter 3, verse 16. The colon follows the chapter number and the verse number follows with no space. '1 Corinthians 13:1–13' cites a chapter and means a reading from Paul's first letter to the Corinthians, chapter 13, starting at verse 1 and finishing at verse 13. The first letter is denoted by using the Roman numeral for 'one' which is a capital *i*. Paul's second letter to the Corinthians would be cited: 'ii Corinthians'. The colon follows the chapter number, then comes the starting verse number, followed by an en rule and the closing verse number, with no space either side of the en rule.

To abbreviate the Bible sources, the same citation could read, 1 Cor. 13:1–13. Since verse 13 is the final verse of that chapter, you could also cite this reference, without specifying the verses, as: 1 Cor. 13.

Some Bibles will give a preferred abbreviation guide in the contents listing at the front.

Spell-checks and proofreading
Nothing beats the proofread for fixing errors. Spell-checks can only go so far. A spell-check will not recognise such typos as the miskeying of 'from' to 'form'. Although a spell-check will identify words it doesn't recognise, and this enables you to catch most typos, there is a need for someone to do a proofread for sense and style following the spell-check.

Text formatting

There are five text formatting options available to you, but really only two that are practical for continuous reading. The other three are suitable for display text setting and some specific purposes, but need to be used with care.

Unjustified text

If the lines in a text block remain uneven in length, it is called *ragged right, range left* or, more often, *flush left unjustified.*

The left side of the text is set at a regular point which aids the return of the eye to the next line, and the right side of the text is uneven, ensuring the texture of the type is even. Text that is set flush left unjustified has an even typecolour because the spacing between words is constant. It leaves that extra space at the end of the line, which gives it the ragged look, hence its alternative title 'ragged right'. It even usually avoids the cross-patterning of 'rivers'.

Unjustified text also looks a bit more modern—it was considered an essential ingredient in the Swiss styling that dominated design in the mid-20th century. Other ingredients of that 'modern' style were sans serif type, a multicolumn grid and a generous use of white space.

Flush left unjustified

or

ranged left

or

ragged right

If text is set in narrow columns, it should be set flush left unjustified to avoid the uneven spacing and hyphenation that justification causes but also to give extra 'optical' separation between the columns. The actual measure of unjustified columns is wider than their optical width, due to the space (which would be distributed between the words if the setting was altered to justified) being placed on the right-hand side of the text. The optical width of the column gives the impression of a wider gutter between columns.

However, when people are asked their preference, unjustified text is often disliked because it looks so 'untidy'.

To make unjustified text more even down the ragged right side, you can introduce limited hyphenation either by using judicious hyphenation as a manual process by the editor or designer, or by using a *rag zone*. By setting a minimum line length, any word that sets beyond that length is hyphenated according to the program's hyphenation dictionary.

Flush right and centred settings

There are two other options to consider when choosing unjustified text format: *ragged left, range right* or *flush right unjustified*; and *centred*. These are self-explanatory and, interestingly, best used in a similar manner.

Due to the difficulty of extended reading of either centred or flush right unjustified text, use those styles only for brief, self-contained pieces of information, such as the pieces used in posters, titles or invitations: headlines, titles, names, dates, times, places, addresses. Each line-break should be logical.

It is believed that the difficulty of reading these two styles stems from the fact that the left side of the text is uneven. When reading justified or flush left text, the left side is constant, giving our eyes a standard point to which they can return. This is believed to be essential for comfortable, extended reading.

Asymmetrical/free-form text

There is a free-form text styling that is sometimes used by poets to create a random or unstructured text layout. You may use a set of standard indents for alternate lines of text and allow short and long lines to fall as they will. Asymmetrical text has grown from modern poetry layout and has become a popular option for dynamic display type: magazine article headings, advertising and cover titles.

Flush right unjustified

or

ranged right

or

ragged left

There is a readability issue. Being able to find the start of the next line has been shown to be a reading aid—that is why flush right and centred text formats have been found to be unfriendly to readers. It also partly explains the ease with which we read flush left unjustified and justified text formats—the eye can return consistently to the same starting point for the following lines.

So asymmetrical type layouts are best when made up of self-contained lines of text. But for occasional titles and short bursts of information, such as those in Web sites and advertising, asymmetrical text formatting can be a fresh and dynamic option.

Always consider the overall shape of the text block you have created.

Justified text

Justification is achieved by spreading the space left at the end of a line evenly through the line so that all lines become the same length. Usually this means the word-spacing varies; though in extreme cases the letterspacing varies as well. Basically, it is this extra spacing and the unevenness it creates that are disturbing to the typographer. Justification often interrupts the typecolour of the text—the uneven spacing can make the text block look blotchy when you squint at it. However, justification does lend a traditional feel to a layout, and is almost essential if you want centred headings because it firmly establishes the width on which you are centring the heading.

When text is justified, the left and right sides of each column of type are parallel. If the words and spaces were left to fall naturally, the end of each line would occur at a different point.

So why bother? Many people assume that justified type is 'professional' type. They refer to the traditions built up over centuries of book and newspaper design—but let's face it, those old newspapers were hardly reader-friendly.

In fact, it is only when specifically asked that people even notice the difference between justified and unjustified text—and then they state their preference for justified text because it 'looks neater'. It makes no difference to how effectively they read the text.

Rivers

A 'river' of white space running contrary to horizontal reading rhythm can subliminally distract your reader. It is more likely to occur in justified text—due to the extra space distributed through the lines to justify them. An example is marked.

These two paragraphs have been justified, but not to the same measure as the unjustified paragraphs—they have been optically adjusted for the unjustified formatting.

Books are another matter. If you need to feel like a part of the continuum, justify your text. But do so with an understanding of the craft of justification. It is this craft, a finely honed sensibility to type and its readability, that has largely been lost since the development of computer-generated type (including computer typesetting here as well, not just DTP).

When type was justified by hand, the person setting the type made decisions at the end of every line: Will the line have too much space distributed through it if I don't hyphenate? Will a hyphen be needed? If so, where will it best go in the next word? Can I squeeze the letterspacing of a few well-chosen words to accommodate an extra word in the line?

Hyphenation
It is essentially the process of justification that has necessitated the development of hyphenation programs. It is very convenient, if you choose to have your text justified, to be able to fit a bit of the next word onto a short line. Because of this, justified text will usually save a few lines in column depth.

However, a worst-case scenario is the possibility of a connect-the-hyphens game down the right-hand side of a paragraph. This can be the result of either a poor hyphenation program or a text width that is too narrow for justification.

Once text has been justified automatically, do a quick scan down the right side to seek out strange or overused hyphenation. In most cases, a wise decision to force-hyphenate (typing in a hyphen that sends part of a word back to the previous line) can fix a paragraph.

Sometimes a punctuation mark that is not spaced, such as an en rule, will be ignored as a logical breaking point. If you type in a space on one side of the en rule, it will split the term over the line break.

In many cases, ugly justification or hyphenation can be fixed editorially—a skilful editor will occasionally find a shorter adjective or add a word to 'fix' a line.

Paragraph styling

The distinction between paragraphs is traditionally made as a selection from two options. However, there are often many paragraph stylings contained within the one document. So although you may think your decision is just whether to indent or to block and space your paragraphs, you will have further paragraphing decisions to make.

Indented paragraphs

The most widely used form is the paragraph indent. Simply set a first line indent of 5 mm or as small as 1 em (or the width of the typeface: in 10 point text, this becomes a 10 point indent).

As a layout element, this creates an irregular pattern of white blocks down the side of the grey block. You might choose to introduce more paragraph divisions to keep the pattern more regular. Discuss this with the author or editor.

You might maximise the effect of the random paragraph indents by featuring them: decorative indenting is simply achieved. For example, in justified text, you might do a half-line paragraph indent, which with centred headings reasserts the central axis. In unjustified text in a pamphlet or a press ad, you might do a 30 mm indent that creates a pattern like piano keys down the side of the text block. Sometimes an author or editor will help you to achieve a specific pattern.

Maximising paragraph indents by using them for the indents in lists and as the line used for photo borders reinforces the grid line established by a paragraph indent.

It is better to delete or override the paragraph indent with contoured text or runarounds (so that the runaround doesn't have an unsightly bump where the paragraph indent occurs).

Blocked paragraphs

Reasonably popular with letter presentation and a good one to remember if you have a short letter on your letterhead, the blocked paragraph has no indent and is separated from the other paragraphs by space. This spacing is often achieved with an extra line return, but that is a poor method. The preferred method (because it allows greater options for your text beyond the initial use) is to use the spacing-before-or-after section of a style sheet and allocate a specific space.

DOING IT SMARTER
The squint test
Graphic designers don't necessarily have bad eyesight when they squint at a layout! You can check the tonal arrangement on the page if you look through your eyelashes. The type and pictures recede and appear to become rectangular blocks or free-form areas of grey tone. These areas, some of which will be light and some dark, create patterns, which are like a piece of abstract art.

The full line return, which in text set 10/12 allocates 12 points of space between the paragraph, is too much. A half-line return is better: a 6 point space. Even a 3 point space can succeed—anything less can look accidental.

As a layout element, spaced full blocking can create a disjointed page due to the horizontal white stripes that appear randomly through the grey text block. For this reason, it almost never works in multicolumn setting.

First paragraphs

As a layout consideration, the first paragraph after headings is blocked, i.e. with no paragraph indent. Consider using this blocked paragraph even after indented lists to avoid the look of the paragraph continuing the final dot point.

It is easy to create this first paragraph styling in a style sheet as 'based on' normal text but with the indent deleted.

This is both a typography and a layout issue. Typographically, the indent serves to separate a paragraph from other paragraphs, but we signify the difference between paragraphs and headings with at least a font variation and often a spacing variation, so an indent is unnecessary. As a layout issue, the text block is strengthened if the corner is established in the top left, making a sharp rectangular grey block, rather than a dulled one, which an indent would create.

Consider using a first paragraph styling if a paragraph falls at the top of a column to strengthen the text block on that page. A paragraph that is broken in the middle has the correct effect because it simply continues across into the next column or page with no indent.

Hanging indents

In lists, you specify a hanging indent but do not show it because you set a tab position to the point at which the continuing lines 'hang'. So this odd indent (where the first line is full width and the second and continuing lines are indented) is rarely used in other text setting. Some people use it to give an unusual and attention-getting effect in pamphlets and brochures, like a backwards paragraph indent. It has been used in the 'Read more about it' lists in this book.

Lists

If lists in the text are indented:

- use bullets and align them with the left margin
- align the text entry with the paragraph indent
- do not justify the text.

In legal documents, the lists are numbered and subdivided alphabetically and further subdivided with roman numerals, thus:

1. Recommendation
    (a) First point
    (b) Second point
        i)   First subdivision
        ii)   Second subdivision
        iii) Third subdivision
    (c) Third point
2. Second recommendation

In technical reports, the subdivisions will be numerically coded with paragraph numbering:

1   First chapter
    1.1 First point
    1.2 Second point
        1.2.1 First subdivision
        1.2.2 Second subdivision
        1.2.3 Third subdivision
    1.3 Third point
2   Second chapter

You should as far as possible use dot points for subdivision of text, unless you are describing a process where the sequence—and therefore sequential numbering—is important, such as the steps within a recipe or a description of how to get a refund.

1   Describe step one
2   Describe step two

Dot points

Avoid more than two levels if possible.

Use bullet first then en dash and align as shown to reduce the number of indents/tabs:

- Bullet or symbol on margin; text aligned with paragraph indent
    - dash or secondary bullet on paragraph indent; text indented one more step.

Punctuation options for lists

There are three alternatives in the setting of lists.

In lists with full sentences (like this one):
- Start each sentence with a capital letter.
- Finish each sentence with a full stop.

In lists with a lead-in phrase, long dot clauses and subsets (like this one), you should:
- start each entry in the list with lower case unless it is a proper noun;
- use a dash
    - for a subset of a dot point
    - to indicate a list within a dot point;
- use a semicolon at the end of each entry, except for the last point which takes a full stop.

In lists with a lead-in phrase and dot points (like this one), use:
- lower case
- no punctuation
- a full stop at the end.

Consult a style manual for more detail on capitalisation and punctuation options for lists.

Many people prepare lists with indented dot points like this:

Our products include:
- Apples
    - Golden delicious
    - Granny Smith
    - Fuji
- Oranges
    - Valencia
    - Navel

In the following examples, the layout is instantly improved and, incidentally, stronger because of the reinforcement of the margin and avoidance of secondary tab levels:

Our products include:	Our products include:
• Apples	■ Apples
– Golden delicious	□ Golden delicious
– Granny Smith	□ Granny Smith
– Fuji	□ Fuji
• Oranges	■ Oranges
– Valencia	□ Valencia
– Navel	□ Navel

You can use bullets or any combination of appropriate dingbats as markers.

Tabs

All a tab can do is align text. Tabs control the horizontal placement of text within a line. They are mostly used in producing tables or lists. When used to position headings or the starting line of text, we normally call them 'indents'.

Indenting

Too many indents can make a page look really ugly. Some people go indent crazy, choosing to tab successive levels of information without using some of the other techniques available to them for establishing levels of importance (altering fonts from medium to bold, for instance). It often happens in contents lists.

Compare:	with:	or
Title	**Title**	**Title**
Subtitle	Subtitle	Subtitle
Author's name	Author's name	*Author's name*

Better? Usually, in text and contents lists, it is better to avoid indents if possible and limit yourself to one or two.

DOING IT FASTER

Copy and paste

Use the copy and paste features for lists where you have allocated a dingbat (such as a square) for the dot point instead of a bullet. Copy the dingbat and the tab that follows it, then paste that over each bullet in the list. You will find it is quicker than changing the typeface to dingbat font at the beginning character of every line.

To save you doing this, some programs will allow you to allocate a keyboard command to your character style sheet.

DOING IT EVEN FASTER

Search and replace

Use the search and replace feature for something that needs to change throughout a manuscript. Remember to proofread carefully because this can create some unexpected alterations because you may have removed something unintentionally by doing a universal command.

Tables

In tables and lists it can get much more complex. Take a simple table with some standard tabbing errors:

Product	Sales ($)	Sales (% of stock)
Apple	114	54.4
Orange	255	61.75
Lettuce	12	9.5

or worse, the same table with each column centred:

Product	Sales ($)	Sales (% of stock)
Apple	114	54.4
Orange	255	61.75
Lettuce	12	9.5

Ugly. Even worse, though, is the same table with rules separating the columns:

Product	Sales ($)	Sales (% of stock)
Apple	114	54.4
Orange	255	61.75
Lettuce	12	9.5

Vertical rules in a table may link the wrong information; horizontal rules relate the appropriate information string.

Now, reset the table with correct tabs set (which will align the $ sales on the right, so that the figures align correctly—units above units, tens above tens, and the percentages will be aligned on the decimal point) and a slight improvement in the definition of levels of information (the use of italics for the column headings). The column headings will be tabbed differently from the content of the columns—so there are two tab sets defined because of the third column heading not having a decimal point in it.

Product	Sales $	Sales % of stock
Apple	114	54.4
Orange	255	61.75
Lettuce	12	9.5

Greatly—and simply—improved.

Get to know what your tabbing commands mean. Usually you have left-align, right-align, centre-align and decimal-point-align tab options.

And don't fall into the trap of using only preset tabs (they are usually evenly spaced, left-aligned tabs at regular intervals across your column measure). Preset tabs can be a problem when you import from a word-processing program to your page layout program.

Even in spreadsheet programs, when outputting turn off all the column borders and use type variation and spacing to make the tabular material easier to read.

Footnotes/references/bibliographies

Footnotes appear at the foot of the column or page on which a text reference occurs but can be set beside the text reference in margins or a side column or, in text with generous leading, footnotes can sit between the lines at the point where the reference is made.

Endnotes are set like footnotes but occur in a list at the end of the chapter or the end of the publication.

Reference systems vary but there are two common stylings.

Traditional footnotes

In text: Use these symbols in order, starting anew on each page: * (asterisk), † (dagger), ‡ (double dagger), § (section marker), || (parallel mark), ¶ (paragraph marker).

In text, it has become more usual to use the superior number instead of the symbols. There are three options for numbering: consecutively through the page, consecutively through the chapter or consecutively through the book.

At the foot of the page: The footnote is usually set in the same font but two point sizes smaller than the text size, mostly unjustified even if the text is justified. Sometimes a fine rule (0.18 mm) of about 15 mm in length is used above them to set footnotes apart from the text. The number corresponding with the text superior appears at the left and then a tab, usually set at the paragraph indent of the main text, then the note follows starting with a capital letter and finishing with a full stop. The number of the footnote need not be a superior figure.

Some people use Latin terms such as 'ibid.', 'op. cit.' and 'loc. cit.', but not everyone understands their meanings fully so it is best to avoid them.

Author–date style
In text: The reference is in parentheses and immediately follows a quote or a reference to a particular work. It refers to a bibliography or reference list that contains the full reference to the citation.

> One commentator suggested that the world is flat (Brown 1996, p. 43).

Note the punctuation and the positioning of spaces.

At the end of the chapter or the publication: The bibliography or reference list is organised alphabetically according to the author's family name and the date of the publication:

> Brown, J. 1996, *History of the World*, 2nd edn, West Books, Sydney.

Again, note the punctuation and spacing. (For further information, consult the relevant style manuals.)

Internet, e-mail and CD-ROM referencing
Following the same form as a book reference as far as possible, Internet and CD-ROM references include a reference to the medium in which it was published, a carefully checked, full URL and the date on which the reference was sourced by the person making the citation and the date the last update to the site was uploaded by the site manager.

Boxed text
Boxing text separates it from the rest of the text. It should be done for a reason—either it is more important, it is a distinct, self-contained subject, or it adds dimension to the text that surrounds it. When boxing text, do not crowd it. Make the box fit the grid and indent your text on all sides. The box becomes the dominant visual element in the layout, not the text width.

Beware of giving relatively unimportant pieces of text great importance in the page layout due to being boxed. Also avoid using too many boxes, because each competes for the reader's attention.

Therefore the correct text to place in a box is text with importance and text that stands alone (i.e. it does not need the context of the story to be understood).

You can also box a section of information that is on a tangent to the main article—as you often see in magazines. In an article on the First Fleet, there might be a boxed section on 'The Eora people'.

Vancouver system
The Vancouver system of referencing is preferred to the author–date style by some professions, particularly the medical profession. It features a numerical coding in superscript, which is given consecutively to references throughout the text. That coding becomes the code for all references from that same source throughout the document. References at the end of the document are identified in numerical order. There are many differences to the citation style for references discussed here. For example, when citing titles, there are no capitals except the first word and any proper nouns—not even the first word in subtitles!

READ MORE ABOUT IT
Shirley Purchase (compiler), *The little book of style*, AusInfo, Canberra, 1998, ISBN 0 644 38296 1.

There are some points to remember about boxing text, nearly all of which are to do with the ability of the box to be read out of context.

When boxing dot-point material, always include the lead-in or write a heading so the boxed list stands alone. This applies to the headings of boxed tables and graphs as well.

Don't box the final paragraph in a newsletter or magazine story, which is often only an address with the heading 'For further information'. Because boxed text jumps out of the page, you read the article headline and then the final paragraph, potentially missing the story. The 'For further information' address can be treated differently from the text (maybe indented and in a different weight of typeface) but not boxed.

If you use text in ovals and boxes on the same page, the text that is more important should be in the oval. The oval will be seen as a more important element than the box.

Many times the text in a box is cramped by a box that is tightly stretched around the perimeter of the existing text area. Let the text breathe, i.e. give it some space—a minimum of 12 points or even 5 mm on all four sides from the text to the border of a box and from the box to the surrounding text.

Positioning text boxes in a column
A common mistake is for the text block to be left as it is (same width as the rest of the text and same spacing between paragraphs) and a box superimposed over the section that is to be highlighted. This means the box bursts into the margins and is squeezed between the surrounding paragraphs. The strongest layout element is the box, not the text inside the box, so the box should align with the columns and the text should be indented on both sides. The box will then align with the margins, and the text inside the box will be indented in comparison to the text outside the box.

Consider the colouring of boxed text. Readability tests have shown that, for text, you can have any colour as long as it's black. So let's assume black text. They've also shown that background colours can limit readability, but background colours have an attraction value, which is not to be easily dismissed, so limit the background to 5% or 10% of a colour. Certainly, if you are using tones of black (light grey), don't go heavier than 10%.

A large amount of reversed, boxed text is very tiring to read. If you have a black box and reversed text, remember the text should be sans serif, preferably bold, and it should also be the most important information on the page. Do not reverse a full story, just the first paragraph. You might have a two-tone box where the heading reverses out of a black band and the rest of the box is tinted with black text.

Page furniture

A page pretty much designs itself but, to be distinctive, there are a few page components that can establish a designer's presence:
- heading style and typeface selection
  - chapter openings and part titles
- captions to illustrations and photographs
- folios and running headings
- footnotes.

In books, reports and other long documents, the way you furnish a page determines the success of the design. The pieces of text interact with each other and with illustrations and basic page requirements such as folios (page numbers) to create the overall look of each double-page spread. Those spreads combine to create an interesting document.

So that it remains interesting, build in design features that occasionally appear. They could be decorative chapter openings or title pages for different sections.

You must create design interest in the page furniture because the body text (the bulk of the content) must be kept typographically simple—it needs to be legible and, more importantly, readable.

Captions

As the use of printed images has increased, the power of the photograph caption has increased exponentially. It is now one of the most important pieces of text in a design. As a consequence of this, captions are getting longer and, instead of simply defining the subject of a photo, they now offer opinions and express concepts that previously would have been discussed in the body of the text. Caption wisely.

DOING IT FASTER
Duplicate
Many people will draw rules above each heading in their document. They end up drawing the rule and going to a menu to specify its width every time that heading appears.

That's what duplicating is for. You create it once, duplicate (usually a keyboard command once you have selected the item) and then you just have to drag the clone to the correct position in the document.

You might find it faster to create a complex rule and heading arrangement if the heading is a separate text block to the body copy. In that way, you can group the heading and the rule and any other graphic elements and duplicate them. When you have placed the duplicate in position, you can alter the heading to the new text.

In the same way, don't draw text and picture boxes each time—duplicate the first and drag the duplicates into position.

Better still, some programs will allow you to allocate a rule to a heading within the style sheets so you need only to apply the style. This is even faster.

Captions are usually unjustified even if text is justified. They are sometimes set in italics, a point size smaller than the text. However, captions can be designed in many different ways and may appear differently within the same publication to fit the various photograph or illustration formats used. There is a readability value in having them consistently fall to the bottom and/or the right of their corresponding image.

Folios and running heads

One of the key design features of a page can be the placement of the folio. It is usually at either the bottom or the top on the outer margin or fore edge, or sometimes centred at the bottom.

The reader, who has used either the contents or the index to find a particular reference and is flicking through to find the folio, must be able to find it easily. Although it is acceptable to delete the folio on full illustration or advertisement pages and chapter openings, it is well to remember that the folio helps people to locate the text they seek. Multiple pages in a sequence with folios obscured by pictures or advertising can be most frustrating.

When there is a running head, which is usually the name of the book, the chapter or a subject identifier for the page, it is usually designed to sit with the folio. Called a running head because it is placed at the top of a page, it can be a running foot (at the bottom) or even run down the outer margin. The running head might be the document title on the left-hand page and a changing subject category or chapter title on the right-hand page. In some documents such as proposals and magazines, the title and date appear on each page.

The combination of folio and running head can help to create a distinctive page layout if designed wisely. Because it will be a feature of every page of the book, it can help establish a typographic theme and may feature rules or even logos and symbols.

DOING IT FASTER
Copy and paste
Using the copy and paste functions can help you to duplicate complicated heading stylings. Remember to choose the space that precedes the heading and the space that follows it, so that the spacing of elements is consistent. Complex type treatments then need to be created only once, so that you simply select and overtype the new text.

This works for the set-up for tables and any regularly occurring text feature.

Heading hierarchy

The creative use of type contrast makes interesting layouts.

Remembering that people use headings to skim text to find the information they need, headings must jump out of the grey body copy. We tend to use bolder type or a different typeface. Just enlarging type can be enough to establish a different level of importance. Each of these techniques can be helped by the amount of space placed above and below the heading. The more space around a heading, the more important it is perceived to be, even if it is in tiny type.

Try to keep the heading linked to the text that follows it. Putting more space above the heading than below can do this. If you are using rules to separate sections, the rule should go above the heading rather than below. If there are rules above and below a heading, the rule below is often lighter (thinner or finer) than the one above.

Consider the number of times that a particular heading will be seen—if it is too prevalent, large sizes or blocks of white space may start to look clumsy (a bit like an ugly chequerboard).

You must create different levels of importance—the 'heading hierarchy'. Determine which headings are most important and least important; place all other headings between them, in order. Then create a style for each, where—by using variations in size, typeface, weight, tracking, formatting, indenting and capitalisation—you show the reader these levels of importance.

To be 'reader friendly', you need to consider levels of information within text and indicate their comparative importance to the reader correctly.

Importance is determined by differences in size, weight and capitalisation. Something can be set in a light type at a large size and it will have more emphasis than something small and extrabold on the same page.

When type is the same size, emphasis is determined (in order) by:

- capitalisation
- weight
- direction (whether it is roman or italic).

A capitalised heading at the same size as the text is more important than a heading set in bold or italics.

DOING IT FASTER

Heading hierarchy

If you have created style sheets of complex heading treatments, keep them in a style sheet that you can duplicate when you start a new document.

If you have a favourite hierarchy of headings, create it using the 'based-on' feature that many style sheets have. Then, for each document, change the 'normal' typeface that the style sheets were based on and insert the typeface for the new job. If your 'based-on' commands were worked correctly in the original style sheets, all the headings will automatically change to the new desired font, retaining the characteristics (size, capitalisation, boldening, italicising and tracking) that your style sheet had allocated to each level of heading.

The larger a design element, the more dominance in the layout it assumes. But a page is not a billboard: your reader is reading at arm's length, not across the room. So headings do not have to be enormous, just comparatively larger than the text type.

In larger headings, there need not be extra leading between lines. Tracking is tighter as size increases.

Weight in order of importance is determined by colour on the page: reversed text and extrabold text attract because, by comparison with the text block mid-grey, they are very black. Headings and titles usually rely on their size to attract attention, but often it's not the size that counts—it's what you do with it. If it's bold or extrabold, it can assume more importance than its size suggests.

Although capitals imply an extra level of importance, they should be avoided when there are very long headings.

Lower-case headings should be consistent in what is capitalised and what is not.

Hierarchy clarity

Headings and headlines should not have full stops, even if they are in sentence structure.

When deciding what should be bold or italicised, think about the level of importance to the reader.

For example, in a theatre program's actor profiles, a character's name is less important than the name of the person playing that character. However, in the cast list, the character's name helps us to identify the actor, which explains why the first column is usually the character's name. Similarly, in orchestral listings, the musician is identified according to the instrument listing. Production personnel can be listed either way, because some people may identify them by their role, but many people will be none the wiser, so you can list them much like an acknowledgments listing—with their name first.

In the profiles, you usually give prominence to the actor's name in bold, capitals or larger-than-text size, or any combination of these. This is followed by a minor reference to the character played or, in the case of production personnel who are profiled, their production role, which could be in small capitals, italics or just smaller than the name. The text then follows in a comfortable size for reading with appropriate leading. This text often includes the titles of other productions and production companies, so it is mostly in the regular weight of a font, and italics identify other production credits.

Display type

Often when you are designing a pamphlet or a book, an advertisement or a poster, an article heading in a magazine or a section title page in a manual, the information or subject matter does not lend itself to imagery, either photographic or illustrative. This is the moment when display type is seized as the design concept. But how do you start and what techniques really work with titles and headlines?

Don't let anyone tell you size doesn't matter: in design, contrast of scale (the relative size of design elements) is often the success factor. One of the main techniques is to use type confidently. Don't apologise for the lack of pictures and create a snivelling layout—be brash and loud.

Of course, you don't have to use all the type in your headline at an equal size—maybe only the first letter will be huge; maybe only the main word that defines your subject will be large; maybe a great letterform (like an optional f: f, or the ampersand: &) will be highlighted; maybe each word will be a different size.

But the argument that it's not the size but what you do with it is equally strong. For example, a well-placed rule will add that little bit of structure to your layout, but will also fill any unsightly gaps or give a sense of unity to the letterforms.

Two rules might spice up the action, particularly if they are of different widths.

Typographers also look for a pattern of letterforms that can be highlighted or structured to create an interesting pattern in the display type treatment. For example in a pamphlet on road safety, you might try to find three of the letter o in the title (or even edit the title to create this), so you could stack them in three lines and colour them red, amber and green.

The pattern could be similar letterforms or a pattern of strokes, maybe the verticals. Try to balance curves and straight strokes through the type. This means you need to consider the capital letterforms, the lower-case letterforms and any optional letterforms. You may need to use the roundness of a lower case a instead of the triangular capital A. In display type, the mixing of letterforms is a design decision that should be made to improve the look of a particular combination of letters.

DOING IT SMARTER
The squint test
Look at a page of text. Blur it by squinting (or removing your glasses). The page will be reduced to its layout elements and each will appear as a tonal block. The light grey blocks are usually body copy. A bold introductory paragraph will have a darker tone. Dark or black spots in a largely light or grey page are going to be the layout elements that attract most attention.

Your computer will save you the trouble of squinting at every page. Just reduce your page on screen and, at the lower resolution, it will often have a similar effect.

DOING IT SMARTER
Rules with type
Sometimes a good way to judge how thick a horizontal rule should be is to look at the crossbar of the capital A or the horizontal stroke of the capital L of the typeface and match the thickness. Subliminally, the horizontal rules will then look as if they belong to the typeface and create a more cohesive display.

You could also change the attributes of individual letters. So who says you can't have an italic lower case *a* in the centre of an all-roman word? You will often see this technique used to lend individuality or uniqueness to titles and logotypes. Sometimes this is done most effectively with the vowels. To create a visual liveliness, maybe the letter 'i' will be altered to italic. This can create a rhythm through a title if there are a few 'i's and the title is spread over a few lines. The italic pattern that is created runs through the roman text. If you introduce a colour change as well, the text becomes quite decorative in what is a very simple technique that doesn't hinder readability.

Double letters are particularly useful for this treatment. Double *ff* in italics should be tracked so the crossbar in the centre overlaps slightly and you create almost a new hybrid letterform. The same can be done with double capital TT.

Have a look in your specialist sets of typefaces—they will often contain a number of interesting ligatured characters. These hybrid characters lend individuality to a heading treatment and are regularly used in logotypes.

A swash character is also sometimes available in a specialist set. The swash is an extension of a character stroke (often the tails of capitals R and Q or the arm and tail of capital K are extended, for example). Often you will find you can use a swash character or a ligature from a different typeface if your selected typeface does not have that character. Alternatively, you can create the character in your font by taking the letters into an illustration program or font creation program and creating the desired character.

And what's to stop you from extraboldening every second word in the line and completely deleting the word spaces?

In fact, it is often desirable to avoid gaps in logotypes, particularly, by deleting the word space entirely and allowing the capitals to indicate the second word. Certainly, the word spacing of display type can be very narrow.

Type selection can influence your success rate with display type. There are so many faces available in so many fonts, and who says you can't mix and match them? Again, confidence and a certain panache are called for—you can combine stocky, bold young sans serifs with refined, genteel serifs past their prime.

Display type can also be a bit like a jigsaw puzzle— which piece goes where? There are so many weights and

DOING IT SMARTER
Display setting
Practise display setting by choosing a calendar quote (those one- or two-sentence quotes by famous people on desk calendars) and creating a display setting of it. This means creating an interpretive piece of typography that adds an extra dimension to the meaning or the way we read the quote because of the way in which it has been set using a combination of type characteristics. Do not use illustration; just let the type say it.

DOING IT SMARTER
Two-line and three-line headings
Regardless of the chosen alignment (centred, flush left or flush right), two-line headings should have a longer top line.

In three-line headings, the middle line should not be the shortest, so the sequence should be either:

■ short, long, short
■ short, medium, long
■ long, medium, short.

variations in most type families that you can successfully create a splendid piece of display type just by positioning the family members well.

Structuring the type, try to create a simple shape. Based on the geometric shapes of triangle, circle or square, choose line-breaks to create the most effective shape.

Chapter openings and title pages, feature article titles and logotypes are the main points for establishing the separation between you and your competition.

Altering the position of multiple headings or pieces of information in relation to each other can also add an interesting liveliness to a layout—overlap them or have them sitting on each other. If one is large enough, the other can run through it.

You might have them run-on (where the typeface changes to a new level of information in a different typeface midway through a line).

Beware of giving undue emphasis to the least important words. In book titles, see how many times the words 'and', 'is', 'with', 'the' and 'of' are enlarged to fill out a line, giving undue emphasis to the least important words for attraction to the book and definition of the target audience and content. These words are the ones that should not be in fluorescent ink or foil. They should be relegated to the background and cleverly handled within the typography to recede.

A

TOWN

LIKE ALICE

OR

Neville Shute's
A Town like
Alice

BEFORE

AFTER

**POWER
AND
GLORY**

**POWER
&
GLORY**

READ MORE ABOUT IT

Brody Neuenschwander, *Letterwork: Creative letterforms in graphic design*, Phaidon, London, 1993, ISBN 0 7148 2801 7.

Marion March, *Creative typography*, Phaidon, Oxford, 1988, ISBN 0 7148 2559 X.

Maggie Gordon and Eugenie Dodd, *Decorative typography*, Phaidon, Oxford, 1990, ISBN 0 7148 2601 4.

Rob Carter, *Working with computer type 4: Experimental typography*, RotoVision SA, Crans-Pres-Celigny, Switzerland, 1997, ISBN 2 88046 279 7.

Type Directors Club, *Typography: The annual of the Type Directors Club*, Watson-Guptill Publications, New York, 1980–, ISSN 0275 6870.

Style sheets

Whenever a magazine or book is created, the designer devises extensive style notes for the publication.

The designer incorporates all the type features into a list that defines the possible uses to which the text will be put. These are contained in a job file so that the designer can refer to them whenever similar usage surfaces, e.g. a revised edition of the book, the next issue of the magazine, a book with a similar structure.

Previously, a typesetter would load all of the necessary information into the typesetting unit and code it. When applying it to the final manuscript, the codes could be inserted at the appropriate place and the text would play out with all the correct style attributes.

This capability is built into most DTP packages and streamlines the formatting of complex text documents. But someone must load in all that information, and someone at the production end must know how to use it.

If material is designed by an outside designer and then formatted in-house, the outside designer should be commissioned to prepare and install the style sheets and master pages in the program being used.

If you are designing a newsletter, book or magazine and are responsible for its future production, create style sheets that document the entire publication.

If you're not using style sheets, you should be. Once you have set up your master pages or grid, style sheets really streamline production.

It is easiest to work out all style tags from what can be called the 'Normal' text. As the majority of text content—the body copy—falls into this category, it deserves careful attention. Define the typeface, the weight and size that will be most readable in the measure (which is the column width you have already established in creating your master pages). Determine the amount of leading most appropriate to the average number of characters across that measure.

Set the indent for the first line if you intend having one. If you intend to block the paragraphs and leave space between them, define that as 'space below' each 'Normal' paragraph. About half the leading (equivalent to a half-line space) is recommended. Save this into your style sheet as 'Normal' and, if you have the option, give it a keyboard command for easy application.

Type specification

The traditional specification of a style was: the size of type over the leading (expressed as a fraction) or the size of type followed by the word 'on' and then the leading; pt; the name of the typeface and the font weight; the capitalisation; the format ('flush left unjustified'); 'to'; the width of the text block; 'indented to'; any indention desired; the space desired expressed in points then 'space above'; the desired space expressed in points then 'space below'.

For example, '10 on 12 pt Times bold caps, flush left unjustified to 70 mm, indented to 5 mm, 9 pts space above, 3 pts space below.'

'Normal 1' would be 'based on' 'Normal' which means that it would maintain all the attributes of 'Normal' but would be, in this case, distinguished by no indent in the first line. This is used for the first paragraph following a heading, hence calling it 'Normal 1'.

If your text has dot points, you could created a style called 'Dot point' or call it 'Normal 2'. This is because it usually has all the same attributes for its type as 'Normal', so it is easy to use the 'based on' feature and then set the tab for the first line and the indent for continuation lines.

The beauty of using the 'based on' feature is that if you decide to alter the specification for normal text, that alteration will flow through, avoiding the need to respecify all your style tags. It also means you can save the style sheets and use them for another publication by simply inserting a new typeface and leading.

Three heading styles 'based on' the 'Normal' text are self-explanatory and optically keep the same size: 'Normal bold', 'Normal italic' and 'Normal caps' (this one will need looser tracking and you may specify small capitals instead). Each will usually come in handy as a heading within text or tables. Depending on your manuscript, you may wish to allocate spacing above or below each of them at this point.

Follow the same formula for captions, footnotes or endnotes.

Create a series of larger heading styles, which can be given titles such as 'A head' for most important, 'B head' for next most important, and so on; or 'Title', 'Subtitle', 'Subhead', 'Byline', 'Author', 'Continuation line', 'Intro', 'Lead para' and a set of pull-quote options (so that your pull-quotes are not all the same).

You can create as many as you like, defining as you go the size, the leading, the typeface, the weight or font of the typeface, capitalisation, the colour (black, white or any preset colours), format variations (justified, flush left, flush right or centred), the indent, the measure/text width and, if possible, any rules that are linked to the heading and the spacing between the rules and the heading as well as the space that separates the element from the surrounding text.

Test the size and weight relationships and how each level of information works with the text that surrounds it. How do the different levels of heading look if they follow each other? This often happens early in a chapter.

DOING IT SMARTER
Idea file
Keep a file of interesting type treatments and use some of the great ideas you find. Photocopy them from magazines, books and catalogues or print them off a Web site. Try to work out how it was done, and any special techniques that might be necessary to reproduce it, and maybe even identify the typefaces by using a type catalogue.

Depending on the results of these tests, refine the spacing and indenting, which are the usual attributes requiring attention, as you will have ironed out most problems with type sizes and weights before creating the style sheets.

Because complications often arise, you may need to create a series of heading options using the 'based on' feature which alter the way headings are spaced when they follow each other. Because the 'space above' one heading is added to the 'space below' the heading that precedes it, you may find you have a yawning chasm of space. So the new style tag becomes, for example, 'B head after A' which usually deletes the 'space above' the B head and will maintain the desired space below an A head when applied. Check the manuscript for the number of heading combinations you may need to consider.

Remember, as far as possible, to use the 'based on' feature for creating style sheets—it enables fast updating and alterations. You need insert only a typeface name in two of your tags and all the rest follow because they are based on those two main specifications. As shown, the easiest is the one tagged 'Normal', but you may also have a heading style (say, 'A head') that can become your other main tag.

DOING IT FASTER
Document design

Style sheets are the fastest way to produce a complex document and speed even the simplest task. Being able to allocate keyboard commands to each tag just makes the manuscript processing even faster. Understand all the options and commands you have available in each tag so you can maximise their capabilities.

If the style sheet has been created using the 'based on' feature as much as possible, you should be able to use it for future documents with just a little tweaking. Often, all you will need to do is change the typeface that is defined in the 'Normal' setting.

THE DESIGN MANUAL
Side text style sheet

A side [used for 'Read more...' and 'Doing it...' headings]
7/11 pt Transit Normal flush left unjustified, all capitals, tracked 10, 11 pt space before

B side [used for side subject headings and some captions]
9/12 pt Transit Black flush left unjustified

C side [used for internal side headings]
8/11 pt Transit Bold flush left unjustified, 5 pt space before

Side text
8/11 pt Transit Normal flush left unjustified, 5 mm first line indent

Side text 1 [used for first paragraphs]
Based on 'Side text', 0 mm first line indent

Side text 2 [used for dot points and 'Read more...' listings]
Based on 'Side text', left indent of 5 mm, first line indent of −5 mm

Side text 3 [used for dash points]
Based on 'Side text', left indent of 10 mm, first line indent of −5 mm

[**Tabs** set at 5 mm and 10 mm]

Document quick fix

When confronted with a document design task, many people feel unable to start, finding it difficult because there are too many possibilities. So is there a quick fix? There are tried and true formulas that mean you are unlikely to go too far wrong and, if nothing else, will save you from reading all the how-to books and getting confused with the conflicting advice.

Please remember: This advice is for the person who is too busy to weigh up the options and wants a quick guide. It is just a recommended series of rules that will produce safe, readable text layouts on your word-processing or page layout program.

Format

With any page size larger than B5 you should be looking at two or more columns. The columns do not have to be even: for example, in books and reports there might be one major column and a smaller side column for headings and quotes.

An A4 page should have two columns in a book or at least three columns in a newsletter.

The gutter between columns should be 5 mm.

Start with 15 mm margins all around. Margins should be larger at the foot than at the head of the page and, if your pages are facing pages, the inner margins should be smaller than the outer margins (except in the case of documents produced for ring binders).

Text should be set unjustified with minimal, if any, hyphenation.

Avoid justified setting as it relies so much on good hyphenation decisions, and hyphenation in most word-processing and page layout programs is not complex enough to make an even text block. Most people use justified setting to look neat but it often is quite the opposite due to uneven text colour because of its variable space distribution through the lines.

Use paragraph indents of 5 mm. However, preferably override the indent for opening paragraphs or first paragraphs after headings and lists.

Set two left tabs straight away: at 5 mm and 10 mm. This covers the requirement for lists. Do not indent the dot points in lists—they should be at the beginning of the line. The indent for the list entry is at 5 mm, the same point as the paragraph indent.

Avoid layers of many indents, except in tables where the tabular information dictates the type of tabs required.

Typeface selection

Select a serif typeface for the text and use at least the default recommendation of 120% leading (inter-line spacing).

Set the text size to 10 point (and the default will create 12 point leading).

Despite recommendations against it, you might still be required to set one column across an A4 page, so set the leading to 16 points at least or, if you are in a word-processing package, set your linespacing to line-and-a-half.

Using the text serif font, create the three following headings for use within text (from most important to least):

- 10 point text-weight capitals (tracked a little loose)
- 10 point bold lower case
- 10 point italic lower case.

Use them from the bottom up the list—if there is only one text heading, use the italics; if two text headings, use the bold for the most important and the italics for the least; if three, use the caps as the most important, the italics for the least.

All headings should be flush left unjustified—no centred headings with unjustified text blocks.

Sans serif headings are recommended for main headings and titles in books and headlines in newsletters. Try these options in a sans serif font:

- 18 point extrabold lower case
- 14 point bold capitals (tracked a little loose)
- 14 point capitals (tracked a little loose)
- 18 point bold lower case
- 18 point lower case

This gives you flexibility and allows eight levels of headings when combined with the text font headings above. You may want to replace the 10 point text font capitals with 9 point sans serif capitals (tracked a little loose). For an interesting heading option, create an 18 point italic lower-case heading in your text font.

When creating your style sheet, always put more space above a heading than below.

Use line returns in the 12 point setting to space the headings or create style sheets with multiples or quotients of 12 points: 6, 3, 4, 18, 24, 36 point spaces, etc.

Use italics where you are tempted to underline.

Don't use the underline, outline or shadow attributes for a font.

Pictures

Create three picture boxes (with a fine black border or frame at about 0.25 point width) and duplicate them for all picture boxes:

- The first should be one-column wide and about three-quarters as deep (for landscape—or horizontal—format photographs).
- The second should be one-column width and about one-and-a-third times as deep (for portrait—or vertical—format photographs).
- The third should be two columns wide (including the gutter width) and about three-quarters as deep.

Place captions below all photographs flush left with no indent, unjustified in 10 point lower-case italics with initial capital on first word and set to the width of the picture box.

The three recommended picture boxes, each in ratio 3:4, with a 0.25 point black border or frame

Punctuation

Use minimal punctuation:

- no full stops between initials of names
- no commas on the end of lines of an address or list
- single quotes used first; double quotes used within quotes
- lower case for all words except proper nouns and first words.

Use smart quotes to achieve open and closing quote marks.

Conventional screening
SHOWING ROSETTE

Stochastic screening
SHOWING RANDOM PIXELS

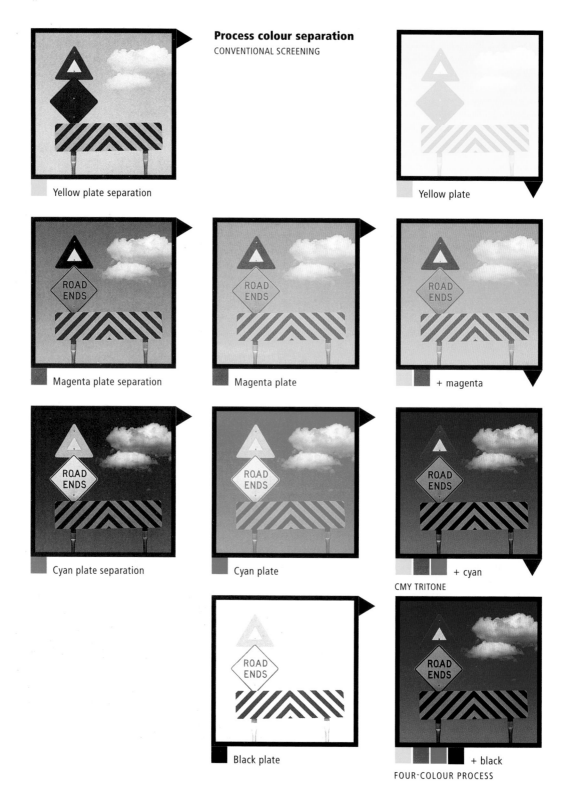

Process colour separation
CONVENTIONAL SCREENING

Yellow plate separation

Yellow plate

Magenta plate separation

Magenta plate

+ magenta

Cyan plate separation

Cyan plate

+ cyan

CMY TRITONE

Black plate

+ black

FOUR-COLOUR PROCESS

Under colour removal

CONVENTIONAL SCREENING

Yellow plate

STANDARD CMYK SEPARATION

Yellow plate

UCR

+ magenta

STANDARD

Magenta plate

UCR

+ magenta

UCR

+ cyan

STANDARD

Cyan plate

UCR

+ cyan

UCR

+ black

STANDARD

Black plate

UCR

+ black

UCR

IV

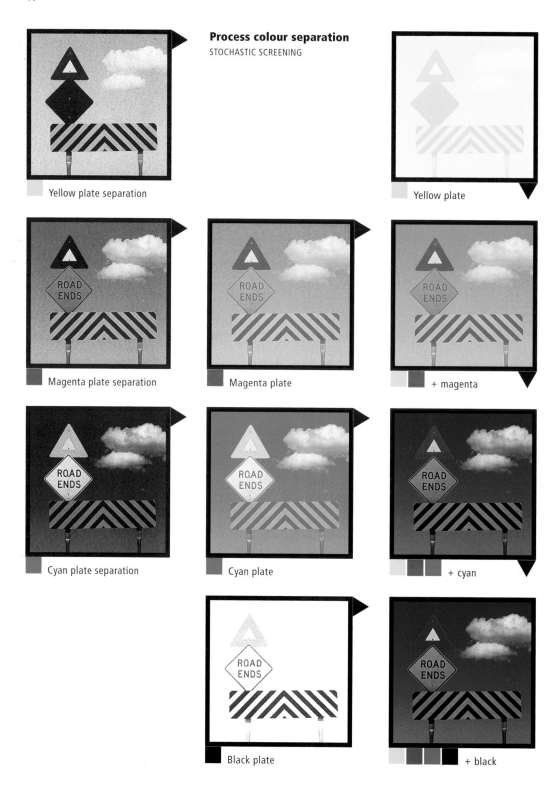

Process colour separation
STOCHASTIC SCREENING

Yellow plate separation

Yellow plate

Magenta plate separation

Magenta plate

+ magenta

Cyan plate separation

Cyan plate

+ cyan

Black plate

+ black

Duotones
CONVENTIONAL SCREENING

◼ Black halftone
ORIGINAL IMAGE

◼ Black plate
HIGH CONTRAST

▢ Yellow plate separation
LOW CONTRAST

Yellow plate

▢◼ + black
DUOTONE

◼ Black halftone
ORIGINAL IMAGE

▢ + 20% tint yellow

▢◼ Flat tint duotone
FAKE DUOTONE

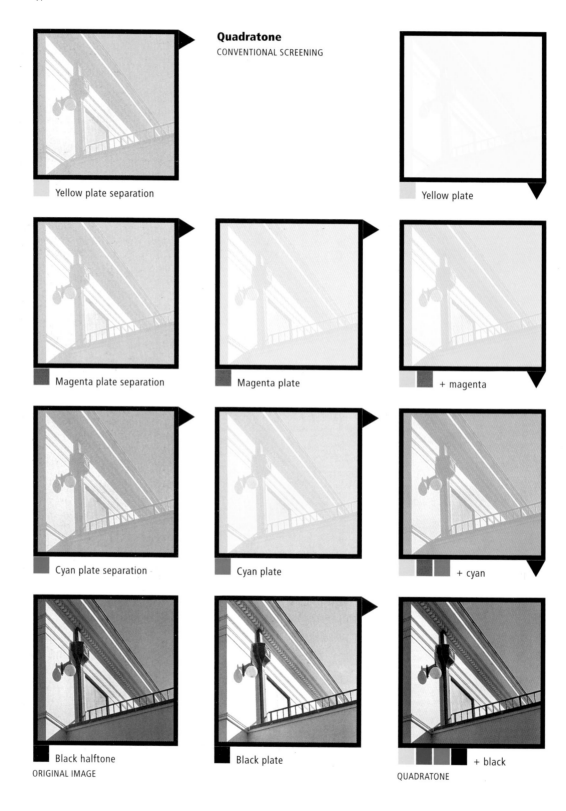

Quadratone
CONVENTIONAL SCREENING

Yellow plate separation

Yellow plate

Magenta plate separation

Magenta plate

+ magenta

Cyan plate separation

Cyan plate

+ cyan

Black halftone
ORIGINAL IMAGE

Black plate

+ black
QUADRATONE

Black halftone

ORIGINAL IMAGE

Halftone with metallic ink
CONVENTIONAL SCREENING

Black plate

SAME AS ORIGINAL HALFTONE

Metallic plate separation

REVERSE OF BLACK PLATE

Metallic plate

+ black

METALLIC HALFTONE

Black halftone

ORIGINAL IMAGE

Duotone with metallic ink
CONVENTIONAL SCREENING

Black plate

MODIFIED HALFTONE

Metallic plate separation

VERY LOW CONTRAST

Metallic plate

+ black

METALLIC DUOTONE

**Process colour separation
with fluorescent replacement**
CONVENTIONAL SCREENING

FOUR-COLOUR PROCESS (CMYK)

CMK (WITHOUT YELLOW)

Yellow plate

Fluorescent yellow replacement

CMYK WITH FLUORESCENT YELLOW

**Fluorescent yellow and
rich black**
Printing a solid colour or stipple
under solid black will intensify the
black, creating 'rich black'. This
technique is also used here to
intensify the fluorescent yellow by
printing solid yellow underneath.

Yellow plate

+ fluorescent yellow

Black plate

+ 60% cyan plate

HIFI COLOUR

Colour

Irrespective of likes or dislikes, the brighter the colour, the greater its attraction. This is a physiological response—the brightness stimulates the eye to a greater extent, which partly explains children's preference for bright colours.

Bright colours, or light colours, by definition have a high reflection value—they look closer and larger and are easier to recognise. As a general rule, they are exciting and good for the mass market. They are brash and friendly. They are good colours for accents and we consider them to be younger, less conservative, extrovert and dynamic, and they are more attractive to men. The light, bright colours are also more popular in sunny climates and seasonally in spring and summer.

Soft, dark and modified colours have an air of dignity and restraint about them and are associated with up-market audiences. They look further away and smaller than bright colours. They reflect tradition and sentiment, and are considered to be older, and they are more attractive to women. They are the colours of the establishment and sophistication. Soft, muted, dark and modified colours are more popular in cloudy climates and seasonally in autumn and winter.

Colour should be used mainly for attraction, not for communication, so use it liberally in images, display text, backgrounds and borders, but be particularly conservative in its use in text. Never compromise the contrast of foreground and background simply to create a colour effect.

Colour terminology uses *hue* to describe the pure form of a colour that enables us to distinguish a yellow from an orange. All colours have a tonal *value* as well as their hue. The tonal value of a colour describes the grey it becomes on a black-and-white monitor or in a black-and-white photo-graph. Put simply, tonal value can be dark or light.

When choosing a colour palette, select colours of similar tonal value to do a similar job, such as when colour coding a series of publications.

Tints are created when a hue is lightened. *Tones*, using colour parlance, are created when a hue is deepened by the addition of a darker colour, often black.

For a foreground to stand out from a background, the tonal value can be altered. Make the background darker and seemingly further away, hence the standard recommendation that slides in the presentation industry have dark-blue backgrounds with yellow text.

How readers view colour will depend on the lighting conditions where they are reading or their screen setting preferences for material on screen. Incandescent home lighting gives a yellow cast as distinct from the blue–white of fluorescent store lighting and the 'pure white' of daylight. Screens will often have their brightness dimmed and their contrast diminished, and sometimes even have a tinted screen over them to protect the viewer's eyes. All these choices and conditions will affect how the colours you select are seen by the audience.

DOING IT SMARTER
Spot colour
Establish a basic colour—often black in text layouts—and use another 'spot' colour only for highlights. This gives greater dynamism to the spot colour—it can be more effective in its attention-getting and interest-arousing roles.

DOING IT SMARTER
Colour photos and colour selection
If you want colours in your design to complement the photography, choose colours that appear somewhere in a photograph—the most successful choice is often not a dominant colour in the photo.

To practise this skill, choose a coloured photo and force yourself to come up with three colour variations using only background and border colour variation. Assess the results to determine which presented the photograph most successfully. This helps you to isolate the colours that drain colour from an image from the colours that may enhance it.

DOING IT SMARTER
Learning to use colour
To develop your skill in using colour, create a project where you do not allow yourself to include black or white.

To test the psychological effect of colours, try experimenting with a colour portrait using just different border and background colours, but communicate these personality attributes: strength, weakness, coolness, warmth. You can see what can be implied—why isn't this used more in, say, election advertising?

Colour coding

Colour can identify an organisation or the type of document a reader is perusing, or distinguish points of difference between one printed piece and another. Coding enables people to quickly find what they need.

Allocate a colour, or a series of colours, to each variable. The colours, when used consistently, become associated with a particular style of document or information, and effectively code material. It can be a code established for use within one publication or over a range of corporate materials.

Choose a colour to represent each arm of the organisation—the rainbow of colours represents the corporate palette for an organisation. Maybe one overriding colour links them all.

When selecting colour for a series, try to maintain a similar tonal value. For example, with a burgundy, steel blue and bottle green, you would not select a bright orange—tonally the orange would be the odd one out—but you might select a burnt orange or even a terracotta in order for the palette to have parity.

Similarly, with pastels, you would not add a charcoal. A more tonally appropriate choice would be a pearl grey. Of course, maybe the charcoal grey could become the standard instead of, for example, black text. It would be softer than black and perhaps sit more comfortably with the pastels.

Also, the charcoal grey—as the bright orange in the previous example—could become the over-arching corporate colour, because of its contrast to the established palette.

DOING IT SMARTER
Achieving colour balance
Consider the colour and tonal arrangement of your elements. Try to reduce your layout to a Mondrian-like composition. It is an effective way to analyse the interrelationship of the colours of your elements.

Colour systems

Colour reproduction is one of the most exasperating and frustrating challenges for the graphic designer who is trying to control colour through all stages of a project, from concept to rough, approval, screen and print. The computer has not made colour control any easier.

The problem

You are designing a two-colour job. You create the design on screen, selecting the colours from the palettes on screen, and it looks great on screen. You print the design to your colour printer to proof it for your client. You send the job to a printing house which prints it in the Pantone colours specified by the computer printout. The printed result is neither the colours you saw on screen, nor the colours of the computer printout.

Why is it that with 16 million colours, you still can't get the colour you want?

Let's visit the scenario again, step by step.

You created the job for the colours that looked good on screen. Your monitor uses the RGB (red, green, blue) colour system developed for television. When all the red, green and blue lights are on at full power, the screen is white. When they are all off, the screen is black. When they use varying intensities of red, blue and green light, they create all the colours you can see on screen.

Next, you proofed the design on a colour printer that uses the four-colour process similar in principle but not identical to the printing industry's four-colour process. When all the colours are printed together, they produce black. When there are none of them, the image is white (or whatever the colour of the paper you have printed the image on). When you use dots of varying size of the four colours, and overlap them, they create all the colours you can see in most magazines and catalogues.

Finally, when you printed the piece using the Pantone colours, you used colours that were mixed from chemicals different from those used in the four process colours and with an entirely different system of colour generation from the way colour is created on screen. Being transparent as most inks are, the colour surface and density of the paper on which they are printed alters them. There is room for error.

So sometimes a simple thing like matching a single corporate colour across a range of corporate material is impossible. That corporate red has a hint of burgundy in the washroom towels with corporate insignia; it's a lighter dyelot for the corporate umbrella; on that west-facing exterior awning, it has faded to almost yellow; in the annual report it looks like a ripe tomato; in the raffle tickets it looks like a jaffa orange; in the *Yellow Pages* ad, it is a murky rust; and on the Web site, it is a luminous beacon of pulsating light.

Got the picture? You do not have colour control.

READ MORE ABOUT IT

Rob Carter, *Working with computer type 3: Color and type*, RotoVision SA, Crans-Pres-Celigny, Switzerland, 1997, ISBN 2 88046 278 9.

Veruschka Götz, *Color and type for the screen*, RotoVision SA, Crans-Pres-Celigny, Switzerland, 1998, ISBN 2 88046 329 7.

Leatrice Eiseman, *Pantone guide to communicating with color*, Grafix Press, Sarasota, Florida, 2000, ISBN 0 9666383 2 8.

Shigenobu Kobayashi, *Colorist: A practical handbook for personal and professional use*, Kodansha International, Tokyo, 1998, ISBN 4 7700 2323 5.

Mattias Nyman, *Four colors/one image*, Peachpit Press, Berkeley, 1993, ISBN 1 56609 083 0.

Roger Pring, *www.colour: Effectiveness of colour for web page design*, Cassell & Co., London, 2000, ISBN 0 304 35607 7.

Halftones, stipples, screens and reverses

A *halftone* turns an image into a series of dots of varying size or pixels of varied distribution that, when far enough away, our eyes register as smooth tones of the printed colour. We perceive tone when it is actually patterns of a solid colour. In this way, we create the effect of a full tonal range in a black-and-white photograph in a newspaper by simply varying the size of the dots of black and allowing the paper to come through. Similarly, we create the effect of a complete spectrum by using only four printed process colours that are halftoned and overlapped.

Stipples are tints of a printed colour achieved in the same way, but they are made up of dots of the same size or pixels

A reverse

Stochastic screening
uses random pixels

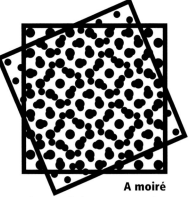

A moiré
is created when screens overlap

in a set pattern. Stipples are always expressed as percentages of a colour where 100% is the solid colour with no dots. Stipples of greater than 50% have a reverse dot within the solid colour; stipples of less than 50% are solid colour dots on the background because more of the background determines the lightness of the colour we see; 10% of a colour means that the dots take up 10% of the page area, allowing 90% of the colour you see to be the paper colour.

The pattern of dots was originally created using a series of screens, hence the term *screening*, which refers to the process of creating halftones.

There are two types of screening: AM and FM. AM (amplitude modulation) screening is conventional halftone screening with a variable-size dot. FM (frequency modulation) screening is more commonly known as stochastic screening using a random pixel.

A *reverse* is when a negative image is produced through a solid printed colour, allowing either the paper or another colour to show through.

Stochastic screening
In stochastic screening, random pixels (little square 'picture elements' that are all the same size but much smaller than the variable dots used in traditional screening) give the effect of continuous tone.

Limited colour

There are many good reasons to resist the temptation to use full colour, such as to get a cheaper print job, to produce the job faster, and to save on expensive proofing processes.

In limited colour jobs, the attraction value of colour is achieved by using tonal variation when printing colour and by using incidental colour selectively, that is, choosing paper that is coloured in the paper-making process rather than printed specially for the particular job.

To achieve a full range of tone out of one-colour production, consider using the following techniques:

- screens or halftones
- reversed blocks of text or illustrations (a reverse is a negative image usually describing white type or illustration on a black background)
- an ink colour other than black (but keep it very dark so it is still easy to read the type and still gives a good tonal range for photographs)
- a coloured and/or textured paper stock
- contrasting weights of type to give tonal contrast to the page
- some unusual cuts (even pinking shears!) or folds to add interest and create shadows.

If you have a number of items—maybe a stationery range or a media kit—use different-coloured paper for each item. This will create the effect of a wider use of colour for considerably less money. In publications such as news-letters, use a different-coloured paper for an insert or to make the outside pages look like a cover.

To add another colour without the costs of printing another colour, have a rubber stamp made and use a coloured inkpad to add an extra colour by hand.

In two-colour work, you might mix the two colours you have chosen by overlapping them to create a third colour. As a rough guide only: yellow + pink = orange; blue + yellow = green; pink + blue = purple.

Select one dark colour for type and photographs and one light and/or bright colour to add vibrance. Do not overuse the light or bright colour—save it for flashes and splashes.

Two darker colours will often create a black when overlapped which is handy for type readability but can be a production concern for a printer who will need to register the colours exactly.

CHECK LIST
One-colour design
- [ ] Print black on white paper
- [ ] Print black on coloured paper
- [ ] Print a single colour on white paper
- [ ] Print a single colour on coloured paper
- [ ] Use the ink solid, in stipple, and reverse out of it
- [ ] Add hand work (using markers, rubber stamps, stickers, pencil, paint...)

CHECK LIST
Two-colour design
- [ ] Print black and a colour on white paper
- [ ] Print black and a colour on coloured paper
- [ ] Print two colours on white paper
- [ ] Print two colours on coloured paper
- [ ] Use each ink solid, in stipple, and reverse out of them
- [ ] Overlap the solid colours and tints of the colours to mix them
- [ ] Use contrasting weights of type to give tonal contrast to the page
- [ ] Add handwork (using markers, rubber stamps, stickers, pencil, paint...)

You can use halftone screens of both colours but be very careful when overlapping screens of two different colours. You can create moiré patterns that are quite distracting. For the uninitiated, it is best to mix a solid colour with a screen of the other colour.

READ MORE ABOUT IT

Mike Zender, *Getting unlimited impact with limited color*, North Light Books, Cincinnati, 1994, ISBN 0 89134 568 X.

Gail Deibler Finke, *Fresh ideas for designing with black, white and gray*, North Light Books, Cincinnati, 1996, ISBN 0 89134 700 3.

Supon Design Group, *Great design using 1, 2, and 3 colors*, Madison Square Press, New York, 1992, ISBN 0 89134 502 7; *More great design...*, 1994, ISBN 0 942604 44 X; *Even more great design...*, 1997, ISBN 0 942604 54 7.

'Simplify, simplify: Effective two-color design' and 'Graphic alchemy: One-color design magic', two articles by Catherine Fishel in *Step-by-step graphics*, vol. 9, nos. 4 and 5, 1993.

Duotones

A duotone is an image created from two overprinted halftones. It usually has the appearance of greater depth. The same image is prepared twice and a different printing plate is generated for each colour. The darker of the two colours to be printed will be a high-contrast version created to deepen shadows and add crispness to detail areas. The lighter colour to be printed will be a low-contrast version that particularly fills in details in light areas. The dense and quite murky shadow areas in the light colour plate become good bases for the darker colour to create the deeper tones and detailing.

Duotones are often used to reproduce black-and-white photography in calendars and photography books. There is more detail in the highlight areas, more variety in the mid-tones and a deeper black in the darkest areas when you print a duotone in black and a mid-grey. The black plate is effectively a high-contrast plate to allow the grey plate, which is a low-contrast plate, to show through and fill the details.

Duotones can be made with other colours, depending on the subject matter. Buildings often look impressive with blue and black; forests and gardens are often good with green and black; for a fake sepia effect, you can even use yellow and black. Duotones of people work best in red and black. In all cases, the black plate is a high-contrast plate and the colour plate is a low-contrast plate.

DOING IT FASTER

Fake duotones

Fake duotones, or flat-tint duotones, are simply a standard black halftone reproduced with a 10–20% tint of another colour placed behind. It isn't really fooling anyone because it does not come close to the increased depth of a duotone, but its use speeds the production of presentation roughs. You need not do all the careful tonal variation to create the final duotone; you can simply indicate that it will be a duotone by using this fast process.

Tritones

Working on the same principle as duotones, tritones use three differently coloured versions of the same photograph overlapped to create an illusion of greater depth within a halftone photograph. The same principles generate a duotone but tritones use a third plate for increased detail in the lighter areas.

Process colour (CMYK)

The process colours are sometimes referred to as 'full colour' or 'four colour'. There are four process colours: cyan (a sky blue), magenta (a deep pink), yellow (a pure yellow) and black. They produce the effect of the 'full' colour spectrum by overlapping four halftones generated from the same full-colour image and printed in each of the four colours.

A separate printing plate is therefore required for each colour and the process of creating these four plates is called *colour separation*.

In abbreviation, we use K to indicate black so the standard order for specification is CMYK. When specifying a specific colour mix in CMYK, such as Australian flag red which uses 100% yellow and 100% magenta, it is cited as '100M.100Y'. Australian flag blue is '100C.80M'. There is no reference to the colour channels that are blank or 0%.

Screen angles

In the traditional separation technique, four halftones with dots of variable size have their screens placed at different angles and overprint each other to create a 'rosette' or 'flower'. Based on the same principles of colour that the Impressionist artists were exploring at the end of the 19th century, the colours both overlap and appear side by side. Your eye blends the colours and sees a representation of the full spectrum. The finer the screen, the smoother the image and the harder it is to discern the dot.

Screen angles are different when there are only two colours, like you have in a duotone, so alert your prepress house when duotones will be used.

Stochastic screening, a digital separation technique, was developed as a response to the difficulty created when computers could not match the screen angles for the traditional process exactly. As a result, the flower was

---

PRICE COMPARISON

Ink selection

$$$$$ HiFi inks*
$$$$ Process colour inks*
$$$ Metallics and fluorescents
$$ Pantone colours
$ Black ink
* Colour separation costs included

DOING IT CHEAPER

'Full-colour' tritone (CMY)

A process-colour tritone, where the black plate is removed and the cyan, magenta and yellow plates only are used, can effectively create the illusion of a complete palette of colours— the shadow areas are a dark brown rather than a black but quite effective for the cost-conscious.

DOING IT SMARTER

Sepia tone in CMYK

Copy a full-tone black-and-white scan into three of the four colour channels using black, magenta and yellow channels only. There will be no cyan plate. Alter the representation of tone in each channel: (1) remove low-end tones completely and reduce mid-tones on the black plate and (2) increase the mid-tones and deepen the low-end tones for both the yellow and magenta plates.

DOING IT FASTER

Solid colours only

Solid colours tend to make a faster and cheaper print job. As soon as you introduce a screen ruling, more care needs to be taken with the preparation and printing process.

becoming distorted and interrupting the eye's perception—there were small white 'holes' visible in the image due to the inaccurate screen angles.

Stochastic screening avoided the issue of screen angling because the random placement of its pixels achieved the same effect of mixing the colours.

HiFi colour

High fidelity (HiFi) colour is a successful but expensive attempt to increase the spectrum available in printed colour (or the colour *gamut*) by printing an extended range of colours that usually includes the four process colours but adds special colours. The extra colours enhance the ability of print to represent more of the real colour spectrum.

Some HiFi technologies are based on CMYK + RGB, making a seven-colour process, referred to as *extra trinary separation*. However, Pantone's Hexachrome process uses only six colours, made up of CMYK + orange + green.

This technology is linked to the enabling technology of stochastic screening, because the random pixels can include the extra colours, whereas traditional rosette screening has some difficulties posed by the screen angles for the extra colours.

The original image is scanned traditionally to create the four process-colour separations, but other colours are fed into the software to scan the image to separate those additional colours as well. In this way, six or seven plates are created.

For most of the 20th century, fine art reproductions used the principle of employing extra colours to increase the colour fidelity to the original work. The predominant colours in the original image determine the extended colour palette chosen. In works by Gustav Klimt, for example, gold is often used as a fifth colour.

For posters, packaging, point-of-sale and promotional materials, annual reports and collectors' editions, HiFi colour is grand, but it costs.

Mixing specific colours

When specifying mixes of process colours for background colours, blocks of colour, logos or coloured type, provide a 'recipe' to the colour separator for the colour you want to achieve. You can look to colour charts, select the printed colour you desire and create that colour in your colour menu. When your file is separated, it will use the recipe embedded in the description of the colour.

Coloured type will always be better defined if one of the colours is specified as solid (100%).

Black backgrounds in process-colour work should always have another colour placed underneath the black, usually 50% cyan or solid cyan. The black will look less washed-out. Create it as '50C.100K' or '100C.100K'. The richest black in full-colour images is equivalent to '100C.100M.100Y.100K'.

If your job will be printed in the four process colours, select the colours by looking at a printed process-colour selector. If your job will be printed with Pantone inks, look at the appropriate Pantone colour selector. If your job will be published on screen, such as a Web-site or a CD-ROM, select the colour on your computer. If your job will be produced by digital printing, run a proof on the same machine to check the colours. In this way, you will know what to expect. Remember, in all cases, your computer screen and your computer's printer can give only an approximation of the printed product.

Do not specify Pantone colours on screen when you are printing only in process colours. You should use a process-colour selector rather than a Pantone colour selector and build the colours you need. The Pantone colour equivalents that are defined in your computer will often reproduce more 'muddy' colours than you wish, because they will have small percentages of every colour in order to come close to the actual Pantone ink mix. The Pantone company has released a selector with the specifications for each Pantone colour in the nearest match available in CMYK.

Sometimes, to compensate for ink absorption on particular papers, printers will vary the mix of inks by mixing, for example, fluorescent yellow with process yellow or fluorescent magenta with process magenta to maintain or increase brightness.

Under colour removal

One of the problems for high-speed printing is the overlapping of colours in the shadow or dark areas of colour separations. This means that printing presses must be slowed down to accommodate the drying time of the numerous layers of ink. To avoid this, there are processes that have been developed to lessen the amount of cyan, magenta and yellow ink that are deposited on the paper

DOING IT SMARTER
Soy inks
Inks are traditionally made from petrochemicals, but environmental concerns have encouraged the development of vegetable-based inks. Soybeans have provided a useful base for ink production, particularly with the four CMYK inks.

DOING IT SMARTER
Coloured type
Particularly in four-colour process work, type in colour reads best when it has a clean edge, which can be achieved only with a solid colour. If the colour is made up of two or three process colours, ensuring that one of the colours is solid or 100% strength will help the type's readability. With this technique, it is best not to rely on 100% yellow as it's usually too light in tone against the paper stock.

under the black areas of a photo. They are under colour removal (UCR), grey scale conversion (GSC) and grey component replacement (GCR).

Note that although these processes are widely used for speedy production of catalogues, newspapers, magazines and other long print runs, there is a trade-off where the density of their blacks is lost. One of the great attractions of four-colour printing is the rich blacks that are created by those layers of cyan, magenta and yellow ink on which the black ink sits.

Quadratones

This is a method of producing a rich black-and-white image with the CMYK process. Scan a black-and-white photograph and reduce the resulting levels in the cyan, magenta and yellow channels, so they are contributing to the density of the print, but not colouring it. Without UCR and GSC, the blacks are richer and there is a greater range of tone through the mid-tones and more detail in the highlights.

Pantone colour system

Printed colour is mostly specified in either Pantone colour matching system numbers or mixes of the four process colours. Other colour systems are not as widely used.

Pantone is a brand name that defines a range of specific colours that are usually used in limited colour work. The colours are based on a series of standard ink colours that are combined (by a printer in amounts specified by the Pantone company) to create the Pantone range.

Pantone is a proprietary system of colour developed in the United States in the mid-20th century. More familiar as 'PMS' (Pantone Matching System) colours, the system is used by printers throughout the world as a de facto international colour standard.

Ink companies around the world are approved by the Pantone company to mix the Pantone inks and the colour selectors are available through art material shops and bookshops, and by mail or on-line order through some book companies.

The colour selectors are available on both white gloss art paper and white offset paper so you can see the way the colour will vary on different types of paper stock. With gloss art paper, the ink sits on the surface, and with the offset paper the ink is absorbed to a certain extent so the colour alters, sometimes becoming darker, sometimes becoming lighter.

Expect paper to absorb ink to some extent. Use the selector as your guide. If you know the sort of paper you are printing on, choose a colour that will look right when printed. The only safe way to do this is to look at a Pantone colour selector, not your computer screen or your printout.

The Pantone mixers (the standard set of inks from which all the others are created) are up-front in the selector and are given sensible names like Pantone Yellow, Pantone Warm Red, Pantone Reflex Blue.

The Pantone original set of colours is identified by a three-digit number, under which there is a mixing guide for the printer to create that colour. The four-digit colours extended that set at the end of the 1980s to fill some gaps in the original set.

Specifying tints

Tints are always specified as percentages of the colour. Create tints by reducing the percentage from 100% (or 'solid' colour). This was previously done in even steps of 10% as shown in Pantone Tint Selectors, but can now be finely tuned with the tint selection controls of most software. Try to avoid the extreme tints, <5% or >95%, as these have a tendency not to print or to fill-in when printed, respectively.

Metallic inks

There is a Pantone metallic colour selector that has more bronzes, silvers, coppers and party-hat colours than you could possibly ever need—over 200. They are reasonably opaque but usually print better with either a double hit of the metallic ink or with a colour printed beneath them on which the metal sits. There is also an extended drying time with their use as well as their aversion to accept overprint- ing. Any colour you wish to put 'on top' of them will usually need to be reversed out of them and then printed.

Sadly, these beautiful metals came out just when designers were becoming environmentally aware, so this set is doomed because they contain metals suspended in the ink that are environmentally unfriendly and which cannot be recycled appropriately.

There is another glitch. A computer cannot show you what a metallic colour will look like when printed. To show

Metallic inks have fine suspensions in their mix that produce their metallic sheen. Other effects are achieved in a similar manner. Microscented capsules carrying a selected fragrance can be suspended in ink, which when brushed lightly with a finger, enables you to smell them. In this example, the coffee aroma is released when you rub the surface of the coffee.
Client: Franklin Web
Publication: *Printing Matters*
Studio: Adstract Art

your client what the job will look like, get a good range of metallic nail varnishes and paint your rough!

However, some great special effects can be achieved with metallic inks and designers are trying many tricks such as replacing a colour in the four-colour process with a metallic equivalent or printing halftones in metallic ink or on metallic backgrounds.

Fluorescent inks

Although your computer screen has a different intensity from a printed piece because of the light that is being projected out of the screen dots, it cannot give an accurate effect of fluorescence.

The fluorescent colours are at the back of the standard selector and are shown twice. The second print is where they have been printed twice, which intensifies their fluorescence (this is indicated by a 2x following the colour code). Fortunately, there is a range of fluorescent highlighters available for mocking-up the effect for a client to see.

You can mix other Pantone mixers with the Pantone fluorescents but this can be a bit hit and miss and sometimes compromises the fluorescent effect too much.

Pastels

There is a Pantone pastel colour selector that extends the range of pale, gelato colours. The colours in this range were missing from the original Pantone set. Previously, when pastels were printed they were temperamental and quite uneven through a print run—sometimes heavy, sometimes light. The new mixers are said to be more reliable through a print run.

Pantone released these long-awaited pastels at the same time as the release of the extended range of metallic colours. The pastels are particularly good for fine detailed backgrounds in stationery and brochures.

Proofing systems

Never check colours on screen for printed output.

There are many proofing systems available and most will do an acceptable approximation of the printed result, but none are perfect. You will need to try a few to see the variations and to compare them with the actual output to decide which best suits your requirements.

Pastels

If you want a pale colour in a background, do not print a solid of the specific Pantone pastel; print a light tint of a more intense Pantone colour. A tint deposits less ink on the sheet and saves de-inking chemicals, which would need to be stronger to get rid of the solid colour in the recycling process.

A Chromalin or chemical proof is made up by exposing each piece of separated film onto a layer of plastic and coating the resulting image with a chemical dust that approximates the desired print colour. In process colours, the four plastic layers are sandwiched together to create a composite image. The process cannot match Pantone colours but is comparatively accurate for process-colour checking. There are often small particles of dust caught in the processing, which look like errors in the image, but are just a part of the proofing system. Always ask the film house to check the film to confirm that they are not visible.

RGB and hexadecimal colour

Computer screens, like television screens, are RGB monitors, where the colours you see are made up of varying intensities of a pattern of small red, green and blue lights. When all the lights are at full intensity, we see white. When all the lights are at lowest intensity, or off, we see black.

The standard for RGB colour description is the hexa-decimal system. It describes a colour by specifying the combination of intensity of red, green and blue lights that create that colour on screen, resulting in a six-character colour tag.

The sequence is given as two characters for each of the three colours: effectively, RRGGBB. Consequently, red is FF0000 (describing the red lights at 'full' intensity, the green and blue lights 'off'), green is 00FF00, blue is 0000FF.

So, when all lights are on full, the screen will appear white, described as FFFFFF. Equally, when all lights are off, the screen will appear black, described as 000000.

Other colours combine the lights; for example, yellow is described as FFFF00.

Hexadecimal descriptions use the numbers from 0 to 9 and the letters from A to F.

Anti-aliassing

Aliassing creates the 'jaggies' on a shape, most noticeable in curves and circles, angles and diagonals. This is because the image is made up of a series of square pixels.

All type and most graphics produced for a screen will be anti-aliassed, so they read as smooth shapes. It blurs the 'jaggies' by filling in pixels close by with colours that blur the edges of the shape.

A raster image
is bitmapped in pixels

A vector image
is mathematically described and
resolution dependent

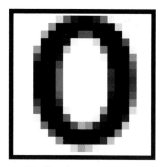

Anti-aliassing
bitmaps with intermediate tones

You will need to limit the intermediate colours used in your anti-aliassing or you will find your file size increases.

Netscape Web colour

Most Web sites are limited to the 216 colours in the Netscape colour cube (sometimes called the 'Web 216'). It features colours with the light intensities described only in this limited set of hexadecimal codes: 00, 33, 66, 99, CC, FF. Set your monitor to 256 colours to see approximately what most Web users will see.

Dithering colours

To achieve a greater range of colours than the limited 216 available, those colours are 'mixed' on screen by a process called 'dithering'. This is achieved by either interlacing stripes of two colours or by chequerboarding two colours that will create the colour you want when seen from a distance.

Dithering
by interlacing stripes of colours

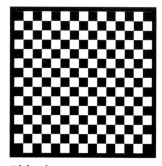

Dithering
by chequerboarding two colours

Prepress

Prepress describes the preparation process between design and printing. It is a point in the schedule where you collect all the materials that will enable accurate translation of the design into a printed document.

For example, when you are preparing your document, place low-resolution images into the document to be able to move around it faster without waiting for each large image file to download. At prepress, these are replaced with their equivalent high-resolution scans that will ensure their printed quality. So you must identify and supply both the low- and high-resolution images to your imagesetter.

Because of typefaces being supplied by many companies and each company's font description being slightly different, you will need to list and possibly supply your imagesetter with all the fonts needed in your document.

Some programs will create a list of everything that an imagesetter requires to reproduce your document, but it helps if you understand the process.

For example, when you go through the proofs noting down the font usage, you need to list not only the face but also each weight of the face you use. Also, you may sometimes forget to list the expert font sets, dingbats, symbol and picture fonts you used. They are easy to overlook, but you will not recognise your document if they are not supplied.

In Web site and multimedia development, the equivalent process to prepress falls between completion of design and uploading and is called *flight checking* and can include *alpha* and *beta testing* phases.

Finished artwork preparation

Preparation of a file in readiness for prepress is called *finished artwork*. It includes the detailed collection and checking of everything: text, typefaces, scans, layers, backgrounds, page numbers, files.

When you are supplying scans, check that the resolution is appropriate for their final reproduction, otherwise you may see jaggies in your final job. This often occurs where you made a last-minute decision to increase the size of an image to improve your layout, but forgot to rescan it at a correspondingly higher resolution for its new sizing.

Have your scans been saved as CMYK for printing, instead of RGB? Have you converted all Pantone colours into CMYK mixes for your CMYK file? Have you checked you don't have any rogue or unexpected Pantones in your Pantone file?

Have you limited the range in your black-and-white scans appropriately for reproduction? Often this requires setting the highlights at 5% and the shadows to 90% or maybe 95%.

Have your scans compensated for dot gain as advised by your printer? On some uncoated stocks, this might require reducing the 50% mid-tone dot to 45% and a 90–95% shadow dot to 85%.

If printing on a cream stock, you might also uniformly reduce the amount of yellow in order to compensate for the yellow content of the stock to maintain a more realistic colour. On other coloured stocks, consult your printer or paper company for advice on colour correction.

Check alignments and make any adjustments to kerning and other optical corrections. Also check that each text block contains the text it is supposed to and links to the correct page.

Bleed

Any image, rule, graphic, logo, background or colour—or even type—that continues off the edge of a page is said to 'bleed' and, in order for it to print correctly, it must extend beyond the page area by at least 3 mm on each side. This is then trimmed back to the page edge during the finishing processes of guillotining or die cutting.

Check that all scans have been correctly positioned for the trim. Their picture boxes now include an extra 3 mm of image. For example, you should not recentre a portrait—it should be centred on the trimmed width, not the bleed width that you see on screen.

Because bleed is so dependent on accurate trimming for its effect, it is wise not to have too fine a detail on the edge of your sheet—even just a coloured stripe parallel to the

An image that bleeds
off a page needs to print over the page area by at least 3 mm and be trimmed back to its final size.

edge can be dangerous if it is, say, 3 mm or thinner. Note that, with bleed, a 3 mm stripe would be drawn at 6 mm thick and placed over the trim edge.

Trim marks, fold marks and registration marks

Most page layout programs will automatically apply trim marks and registration marks to your file. They are required to help the printer when the job is on the press.

Trim marks need to align through the page if the pages are backed up. They will guide the guillotine operator who will trim the final job. They usually start 3 mm from the trimmed edge and are about 5–7 mm in length.

There will not automatically be *fold marks* on your job. These are similar to trim marks. They start 3 mm from the edge of the page and are fine dashed lines (rather than the fine solid line of trim marks).

Registration marks are needed whenever there are two or more colours in a print job. They are small cross hatches that are in exactly the same position on the artwork for each colour. They need to overprint exactly on press. They ensure the colours are printed in their exact placement or 'in register'. They should be placed off-centre, one to the left, one to the right, partly to be out of the way of spine fold marks, but also for alignment purposes in imposition. It can quickly be seen if a page is the wrong way up.

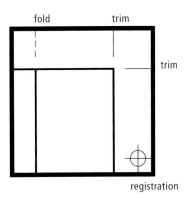

registration

Trapping

Trapping is a technique where you prepare each colour in a separated set to take account of small discrepancies in register that can occur with paper stretch or misregistration in printing. Spreading—or flooding—and choking adjacent colours achieve this.

With trapping, there will be a slight printed overlap— often as small as 0.25 point. Briefly, the principle is that the darkest colour can print tightly ('choked') and the lightest colour can bleed into it by being 'flooded' or 'spread'.

READ MORE ABOUT IT
Agfa produces a range of excellent publications including these titles:
  An introduction to digital color prepress, A guide to color separation, An introduction to computer-to-plate printing, Color bytes: Blending the art and science of color, The secrets of color management

Misregistration
where one colour accidentally overlaps another, leaving a fine white gap, could be compensated for by spreading the lighter colour and choking the darker one.

File management

Ensure you name files in a way that clearly identifies yourself, the job, the file and type of file.

For example, the files for this book were named in a series that started with 'DM01-DWD.doc', where 'DM' abbreviates the title; '01' indicates the first file; 'DWD' identifies David Whitbread Design; and '.doc' distinguishes the document from, say, the first text file.

At the end of the code most people put a full stop and an abbreviated file description: *.txt* for text files; *.pict, .tiff, .gif, .pdf, .eps* for image files as appropriate; and *.doc* for the complete document.

Always keep a back-up of your files and never give your only copy to another supplier. It is recommended that it be stored off-site (in case of fire, flood or theft).

Labelling the disk for quick retrieval is important also. You might create folders for each job to keep all picture, text and document files together. You might create a disk for each client. You might simply back-up by date.

Imposition

Printers prepare the imposition for books. Because of folding, some pages will be upside down when printed on the flat sheet and pages that will be seen together in the booklet may be far away from each other in the flat plan.

In an A6 booklet, page 8 will be to the left of page 1, page 2 to the left of page 7, etc. Notice that even-numbered pages are on the left and odd numbered pages on the right. Also note that the numbers will equal one more than the total number of pages: in this case, $8 + 1 = 9$; $2 + 7 = 9$.

For magazines and books that have coloured sections and different colour distribution throughout the book, a flat plan helps to identify where the colour falls in the imposition. The designer can then design accordingly.

Long-8s
A variation on a standard imposition is the long-8, so called because it doubles over itself to the side, with no upside-down pages. This means that alignment of pictures on a double-page spread is easier to achieve even if they are some distance apart in the imposition, because the alignment is no longer as dependent on the folding process.

8	1
6	3

2	7
4	5

Front

4	5	8	1

Back

2	7	6	3

trim short

fold
short

Foldouts

A page that folds out to accommodate a map, table, photograph or illustration needs production planning to be successful and cost-effective. The page should fold shorter than the full width, so that when the book is guillotined, the fold is not cut off; and the flap will also be anything from 1–5 mm shorter again, so it sits snugly into the spine. In the case of ring binders, it will usually be 15 mm shorter.

Sheet

1	2	3	4	5	6	7	8	A	Two colour one side
9	10	11	12	13	14	15	16	B	
17	18	19	20	21	22	23	24	C	Full colour section
25	26	27	28	29	30	31	32	D	

Flat plans

enable you to clearly see the distribution of different colour specifications according to where they will fall on the printed sheets and sections.

Quick print preparation

Much quick print is now exclusively digital or photocopied, rather than printed traditionally. In the case of digital printing, you simply supply a digital file. To save money it should be prepared with no bleed and 3–5 mm clearance on all edges.

For photocopying, provide a master that:

- uses black ink only with no screens unless you provide screened artwork to be shot dot-for-dot (or better, some other halftone technique such as a line screen—detail needs to be rugged for quick print)
- has no bleed
- has a 10 mm grip edge on at least one edge—the same edge on both sides of the sheet
- is a standard size (A4), or is bled artwork to fit on a standard size (e.g. so it will print bleeds and trim marks on an A4 sheet) and guillotine it to a smaller size
- has no registration marks—trim the artwork to actual size and do not mount it (slip it into a manilla folder, plastic sleeve or envelope).

DOING IT SMARTER

Photocopied dummies

Assemble and supply the printer with a photocopied dummy (sample) of the finished job. If they have any queries about the imposition or order of pages, they can quickly refer to the dummy.

Output resolution

There are times when paying for a bromide of your file may not necessarily increase the quality of your final print job. Sometimes on a recycled paper stock, the stock is so absorbent that it can only give a soft edge to type and graphics. A 300 dpi or 600 dpi printout will be sufficient on such a stock because the edge of the type (which in a bromide would be sharp) will print soft anyway. Don't waste money on high resolution if you do not need it.

Photocopy enlargement and reduction is cheaper than scanning and bromiding and, in the case of some very fast, very cheap jobs, is okay with regard to quality, particularly if quick-printed on recycled stock.

Many books have their text produced from laser prints of 300 dpi or 600 dpi resolution because to get bromides for each page would be too expensive. Even if you could get each bromide for $5, a 100-page, single-colour book will cost $500.

A simple way to increase the resolution is to go to your print set-up box and enlarge your printout to 133%. When you take the pages to the printer, ask the printer to reduce them back to 75% when the job is printed. It will increase the resolution to 400 dpi or 800 dpi respectively.

Direct-to-plate or computer-to-plate (CTP) digital technology avoids this costly intermediate stage.

Output resolution

There are two measurement systems used to generate output. They are both expressed similarly and are often confused. One describes the quality of digital output from an imagesetter: dpi (dots per inch). The other describes the resolution of the halftone dots for print reproduction: lpi (lines per inch).

Dpi (dots per inch)

The resolution of your imagesetter or your printer is defined in *dpi* or *dots per inch*. An inch is approximately 25 mm. Office laser printers have standard dpi settings at 300 or 600 dots per inch. Of course, with digital production, these aren't really 'dots' at all, they are *pixels*, or tiny square picture elements. So 300 dpi means 300 pixels per inch or roughly 12 pixels per millimetre.

When you look at a bromide from an imagesetter, you are looking at a resolution of 2400 or 1200 dpi. This means the pixels that make up the image are finer—at 2400 dpi there are about 96 pixels per millimetre. You get a much smoother appearance to curves, circles and, of course, the dots that make up halftone images.

Lpi (lines per inch)

Lines per inch or *lpi* refers to the resolution at which you choose to reproduce an image. It depends on the printing method and the paper chosen. For example, in newspapers, it was standard for photograph reproduction to be set at 60 lpi, which is why the halftone dot screen in old newspapers is so plainly visible.

In exclusive packaging, you might find 300 lpi, but the dot in this is barely visible with the naked eye. The difference between a 300 dpi pixel and the 300 lpi halftone dot mentioned here is that the pixel is a specific-size square but the halftone dot is a variable-size circular dot. As a result of the need for this variable-size dot, you use a machine with 2400 dpi to create a 300 lpi output.

60 lpi
300 dpi

60 lpi
2400 dpi

60 lpi
stochastic screening

100 lpi
300 dpi

100 lpi
2400 dpi

**Comparing different
output resolutions**

Conventional halftoning
an enlargement

200 lpi
2400 dpi

200 lpi
stochastic screening

Stochastic screening
an enlargement

300 lpi
2400 dpi

300 lpi
stochastic screening

Proofing

Do as much checking on screen as possible throughout the production process. This avoids unnecessary printing and paper waste. However, there are set points at which it is usual to generate a printout for proofing.

The first of these is at editorial stage, where the text document is printed for an editor to read and correct. Corrections may well be keyed directly on-screen, but the printout is useful, because screen resolution is less than printer resolution and small details like punctuation can be confusing on-screen.

The next stage is page proofs. Pages are assembled with the revised text document flowed in and pictures, typefaces and all design elements added. At this point, the editor may be brought in to recheck the document, the designer checks design details such as text and image positioning and alignment, and the indexer starts the index.

The final proofing stage should be imposed proofs from the imagesetter, which may be made up into a dummy of the final product.

Designers check that images have reproduced appropriately—that their resolution is even, their colours correct and they are correctly positioned in the picture boxes. They also check that colours for backgrounds and text are correct and that all the typefaces have translated correctly without default fonts appearing (where the imagesetter could not recognise a font, often because it was either not loaded, identified inappropriately, or not supplied). They check there are no production flaws in the film or output that may have been caused by scanned dust or lint, imperfections or scratches in the film.

Anyone involved with the job has their final check. It is signed off by the client as being 'ready for print' or 'requiring revision'. If there are many corrections, a revised proof will be needed.

Press checks

Designers often wish to see the colours on press, because it is so difficult to mock-up exactly how colours will look when printed. When the job is being printed, you might do a 'press check' so that, if there is an unforeseen problem, it can be rectified 'in-run' rather than reprinting. You will be expected to sign-off a copy when it is right. It will then become the referral copy for the printer throughout the print run. Print shops have lighting booths specifically to ensure that you are checking colour in standardised lighting conditions.

Printing

It is most important to develop a good relationship with your printer and discuss the most appropriate printing processes to achieve what you want.

There is a reason the apprenticeship and training time for prepress, printing and finishing was more extensive than the time it takes for most graphic designers to graduate—there is much technicality to cover with many nuances of application. You should not expect to know it all by simply reading about it.

In the prepress area, do not expect to be able to do it to the same level of expertise just because you have a software program that can prepare materials similar to some of those processes.

The best advice for learning about printing is to visit printers and prepress houses and ask questions. Heed the advice you receive and your product will benefit. Sound production knowledge enables you to create innovative design solutions that are founded in a production reality—your client will be able to afford to produce your design and you will be able to produce the finished artwork for its manufacture.

Here then, are just brief descriptions of the main processes you will encounter in printing and finishing. There are a few tips and hints included but the most important one is talk with your suppliers.

Preprints

If you wish to maintain your corporate colours across a range of material without having to print them each time, think about preprinting some standardised sheets on an appropriately coloured and weighted sheet of paper with one or more of your corporate inks. You can then overprint in black as required. Black is used for ease; you can print directly from your laser printer or photocopy, saving time and money. You can repeat the logo or some motif from the graphic identity.

DOING IT CHEAPER
Ganging-up
Maybe you could get together a group of people or organisations that could use their combined buying power to increase their print options, such as using process colour. All people would need to agree to use the same colours on the same paper, and have the same number of copies (remember, if everyone wants 5000 copies and you want 10 000, it just means you print two-up of yours). If you print 2, 4, 8, 16 or 32 originals at once, you start seeing printing economies and you can share the savings.

DOING IT SMARTER
Environmentally friendly trimmings
If you avoid bleeding images and bands of colour off the edges of a cover or poster, the printer's waste (the trimmings off the sheet) will be cleaner and require less de-inking, thereby avoiding use of further chemicals in the processing prior to recycling.

By preprinting, you can save printing two or three colours for every issue of your newsletter or pamphlet series—you need only overprint the information that changes each time. It is worth considering the possibility of preprinting newsletter shells or pamphlet shells—blanks that have only the standard information on them. Usually you include the corporate logo, the masthead of the newsletter (not the edition number and date), the contact addresses, phone and fax numbers, Web URLs and e-mail addresses (if they are not likely to change in the near future) and contents box (without the contents list). Then each time you come to print again, you need overprint only one colour.

If you produce 1000 newsletters every month in two colours, preprint the second colour and leave the text colour (usually black) off. Print the annual supply (12 000 sheets) at the beginning of the year as a one-off, one-colour job. The paper is purchased upfront and stored, and you will save significantly over the year. For the 12 issues, you can overprint 1000 of the preprinted sheets as a one-colour job (in this case, probably black). Your newsletter will look like you printed two colours but, because the paper was pre-purchased, you pay only for one-colour printing monthly.

Entertainment organisations and promoters regularly use this technique for theatre, concert and event posters—leaving a blank area on the poster for overprinting the details of local performances. In this way, they can afford to have full colour in all venues without the cost of individual print runs. The same savings can be made in programs, flyers and pamphlets; just leave an area or a panel for overprinting the changing details.

DOING IT CHEAPER
Production planning
Rush work is expensive—give printers, finishers and imagesetters (and even photographers, illustrators, designers and photo libraries) as much time as possible. It is not unusual to pay double rates for high-priority late work that jumps the queue.

If your job jumps the queue, other clients of your supplier will be inconvenienced as a result. You pay for the flak that will result from your lack of planning.

Even if material will be received very late for a tight production deadline, you can plan a production schedule with most suppliers that will gear up the minute they receive final materials. You can still expect to pay a premium for this sort of work, but there should not be as much disruption to other clients' schedules if you have planned appropriately.

READ MAGAZINES ABOUT IT
TEC Print
GX Report
Proprint
Australasian Printer

READ MORE ABOUT IT
Alan Pipes, *Production for graphic designers*, 2nd edn, Laurence King, London, 1997, ISBN 1 85669 110 1.
Constance J. Sidles, *Great production by design: The technical know-how you need to let your design imagination soar*, North Light Books, Cincinnati, 1998, ISBN 0 89134 838 7.
Constance Sidles, *Printing: Building great graphic design through printing technique*, Rockport, Massachusetts, 1999, ISBN 1 56496 601 1.
Michael Barnard, John Peacock and Charlotte Berrill, *The Blueprint handbook of print and production*, Blueprint (Chapman & Hall), London, 1994, ISBN 1 857130 04 9.
Trevor Wilson, *Printmate: A graphic arts reference book*, T. Wilson Publishing Company for APPM, Melbourne, 1989, ISBN 0 85828 0140.

David Bann, *The print production handbook*, Macdonald and Co., London, 1985, ISBN 0 356 10788 4.

Alastair Campbell, *The new designer's handbook*, Little, Brown and Co., London, 1993, ISBN 0 316 90658 1.

Martin Greenwald and John Luttropp, *Graphic communications: Design through production*, Delmar Publishers, New York, 1997, ISBN 0 8273 6459 8.

Australian Paper, *The printers' enemies*, Australian Paper, Melbourne [brochure].

Offset lithography

Lithography is based on the principle of oil repelling water. The inks are attracted to the image area that has been exposed on a photosensitised plate. The exposure is often produced through a photographic negative on film that exposes only the desired print area of the plate. This can also be achieved *direct to plate* through digital imaging. The water, or dampener, sits on the plate in the areas where there is no image. Lithography is therefore a planographic process, where there is no raised or sunken ink area.

The plate is often aluminium, sometimes plastic or even paper, because each of those can be wrapped around a revolving cylinder, which is the basis of a rotary printing press.

Offset lithography is based on an image being offset or transferred to a rubber cylinder as an intermediate step between the transfer from plate to paper. The paper is fed into the press either as single sheets, called *sheet-fed offset*, or from a reel, which is called a *web*, hence *web-fed offset*.

DOING IT SMARTER

Work-and-tumble

A variation on printing two-up, work-and-tumble or work-and-turn describe cheaper and faster ways to print a piece. Let's say you have a double-sided poster. The printer may ask you to prepare the artwork side by side for the front and back sides of the poster. The printer then prints them in one print run on half the sheets you need, tumbles the sheets once printed and puts them at the front of the machine again to print the other side. Then they are trimmed up and your whole print run is complete.

This process can save some costs such as making two proofs (there is only one proof to make, even though it is twice the page area). It also uses only one set of printing plates, so it saves on materials, prepress and set-up time on the press.

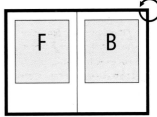

Tumbled for second pass to back up

Sheet-fed offset

Web-fed offset

Waterless printing

Without the use of dampening, waterless printing or dry lithography achieves better quality reproduction than conventional 'wet' offset printing. The image area is etched out of the silicone coating on an aluminium plate, which allows ink to sit on the aluminium substrate. This is effectively a hybrid printing style somewhere between offset lithography and engraving. The quality is evident in its ability to print finer screens that define more details in the image. Waterless printing requires different inks from conventional inks and also does not run on conventional offset printing presses without conversion.

Web offset

For catalogues, newspapers and other large print runs, web-fed offset is used where a web of paper from a reel is drawn through the printing press and continuously printed. This is often connected up for in-run collation, folding, stapling, trimming and wrapping as well. Web presses can run at high speeds, though their speed is limited by ink drying times, which is why under colour removal and grey scale conversion processes were developed.

Screenless printing/collotype

Collotype printing, like lithography, is also a planographic process but uses a light-sensitive gelatine film on a glass plate, which is exposed to create areas that will attract more or less ink. It is a slow process but can achieve almost photographic quality due to there being no halftoning process, hence the term *screenless printing*.

Laser printing, photocopying and xerography

Photocopying is based on the principles of positive and negatives charges repelling each other and attracting like. Photocopying relies on charging the paper through recognising and translating data on an original image. The information about the image is reflected through lenses to an electrostatically charged drum, breaking down the charge on the image areas. Then a fine resin dust called *toner*, which also has been charged, is attracted. This is translated to the paper sheet which runs through the heating unit, effectively toasting the toner to the page.

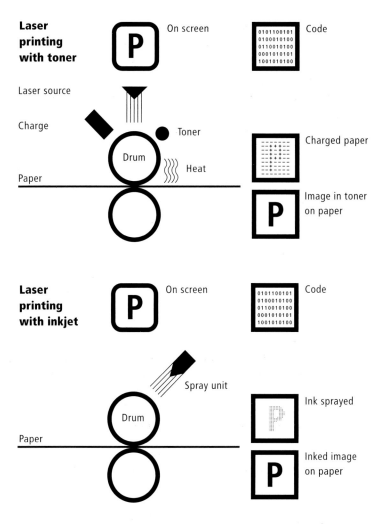

Laser printing with toner

On screen — Code

Laser source

Charge

Toner

Drum

Paper

Heat

Charged paper

Image in toner on paper

Laser printing with inkjet

On screen — Code

Spray unit

Drum

Paper

Ink sprayed

Inked image on paper

You can enlarge or reduce artwork swiftly with a photocopier and can set it to increase or decrease the amount of toner. There is also a level of distortion you can expect, making alignment uncertain from copy to copy or page to page in a multipage document, though this is a minor inconvenience for the cheap and quick quality xerography achieves. Incidentally, *xerography* comes from 'Xerox', the corporation that developed photocopying.

Using the principles of photocopying, laser printing uses laser technology to scan the original and then to charge the drum, ready for toner.

Printing two-up

It is often worth printing two or more items at once. Why not print a pamphlet series all together? You need not distribute them until they are required, but the print cost per unit should be cheaper if they are printed at the same time.

This is often a good way of being able to afford all elements of a corporate identity to be printed with the same number of colours. You might print the letterhead, the continuation sheet, the 'with compliments' slip, an invoice, and maybe even a flyer on the same large sheet of paper with the same colours and then guillotine it into the separate pieces. If each piece is produced separately, you can have significant costs in set-up each time.

The only drawback to this scheme is that you must want the same amount of each piece. But you can even resolve that. For example, by getting two of the letterhead printed which will give you double the number of letterhead to continuation sheets and, in the same way, three invoices, a single print run of 1000 sheets will cut down to give you 2000 letterheads, 1000 continuation sheets and 3000 invoices.

Printing business cards

With most organisations and businesses, there are many people who need cards. The best way to keep unit cost down is to print all the cards together in one print run. This is how printers can supply 250 cards for a very small price—if 20 people answer their ad, they print 20 cards side-by-side and trim them up.

Talk to your printer and ask how they want the card artwork supplied.

Digital printing

Digital printing translates a digital file that describes a page directly to the printing equipment. The page is recreated each time, which is why variable data handling is so easy.

There are a number of competitive technologies, based on various ink properties, usually based on particles that are fused to or sprayed on paper, having been placed with digital precision on the paper's surface. Some digital machines use 'offset' or *indirect* methods, with a blanket that transfers the image; some are direct to the sheet.

'On-demand' or 'just-in-time' printing

Printing on-demand or just-in-time means storing a document in a digital form and printing and binding it only when a customer requires a copy.

For university handbooks, corporate training and procedures manuals, Acts of Parliament and legislation—and even class textbooks—on-demand printing is an option that solves storage and warehousing issues, updating issues (because the digital file can be updated when required), distribution and inventory control. It is even environmentally sound.

In most cases, it is achieved with digital printing equipment, sometimes with variable data.

Variable data printing

Only the depth of an organisation's database of clients and prospects limits the possibilities for the personalisation of print. Direct marketing or CRM (Customer Relationship Marketing) relies on sufficient database controls and digital printing as its main printing choice.

This is more than just inserting a person's name at the top of a form letter, more even than mentioning the suburb from their address in the final paragraph. This is more like those options you have to generate a child's book for a special, personalised birthday or Christmas present—the child's name and the names of all family members, two best friends, pet, favourite colour and where they holidayed last year added to a story that has standard pictures, standard plot and gaps to fill.

'But I know you want more!' Not only this but in full colour with personal photographs, monograms and specific content choices as well!

There is no reason societies and associations—and any organisation with subscribers or members—could not gainfully use this technology. Of course, it will take database management and time, and probably a bit of extra finance, but that will be a small investment compared with the potential revenue that can be generated by providing a truly personalised service.

Consider a personalised magazine. What does it mean for content development? You will need to address articles to each of the different reader segments you identify within your target readership. You can do this by asking their preferences in a questionnaire. Match a reader's profile with a particular set of content preferences and possibly throw in a randomly selected article from another area. It means you will develop more content that will be keyed to a particular reader profile.

But how do you provide advertising space? Set the articles in groups of pages that have advertising contained within particular articles. An advertiser could then niche-market more effectively to the reader who requested that type of content. This should enable more finely tuned advertising with greater chance of translation into sales or interest in the product. So advertising is secure—though perhaps a little more expensive per piece (again, greater expense is trading off greater success through better profiling of readers).

Readers could submit photos of their own to be scanned, scaled and cropped by the magazine and worked into a set of standard cover designs. The name of the magazine could also be personalised. The trend for magazines with initials only as titles gives a clue to how this can be achieved. If *GQ* can be *Gentlemen's Quarterly* and *GH* can be *Good House-keeping*, why not *DW* for *David Whitbread*'s magazine? And if you can have *Dolly* and *George*, why not *Nicola* and *Tyler*?

When you are compiling the magazine for the reader, program the database to select articles from their prefer-ence list and work into the number of pages they have selected. The computer will generate teaser copy for the cover based on the reader's selections and a personalised contents list. It will flow the reader's name through the document with the new pagination. The ads will fall as appropriate for the reader's selected content. Pre-scanned personal photographs will be inserted. The editor's letter will be personalised with something like, 'Dear Claire,

DOING IT SMARTER
Production file

Develop a collection of data sheets on design production and planning issues, such as the following:
- Print techniques and technologies
- Artwork production techniques
- Computing hints and tips
- Design specifications for various industry standards
- Names and contact information for suppliers
- Current pricing sheets
- Printed samples
- Copies of articles from magazines and books
- Booklets and brochures
- Quotes and production schedules for previous jobs (annotated by hand if there were differences between the estimates and the actual price)

It should be practical and technical—rather than theoretical or historical—and include any potentially relevant or useful information. Organise the collection for easy access to any piece of information in the future. Use dividers and a series of contents lists in an expanding file or a ring binder with A4 plastic leaves in which to insert the material. You might include a business card file. You can use a series of magazine boxes on your bookshelf.

The collection is a living document in that, as technology changes, you can discard some pieces and replace them with current material. You will need to update the contact and price lists regularly—they might even be better on a spreadsheet on your computer.

Welcome to your third issue of *CR* magazine...' You might even have a comic strip with generic characters and commission caricatures of your readers, creating 'The Adventures of Lachlan and Danielle'. Subscriptions to this magazine could be very high indeed!

Commercially, imagine a company with a new appliance to market. It is an upgrade of an existing kitchen product that has been on the market for a number of years. The company believes that many purchasers are beginning to consider an upgrade because of the flow of calls to service centres and the average cost of fixing it.

The company can use its guarantee database to send a questionnaire to those who have purchased the appliance previously and tell them about the new product. In order to get a higher response, a kitchen refit can be offered and an extra prize of a free upgrade of the appliance to the best recipe or story about the product, asking each consumer their preferences about the product. Would it need to be operated by other members of the family? What are their names and ages? What colour from this range would best suit the kitchen decor? What textural finish would they like on the base: marble, leather or woodgrain? Customers could even send in a photo of their current appliance on their kitchen bench, stating why their kitchen needs a facelift.

Imagine their surprise when in the following week they receive a letter thanking them for their response and apologising for them missing out on the main prize, but with a special offer that shows the exact model they described in their questionnaire in a photograph on their own kitchen bench (in place of the old model), with extra attachments for Maggie and Kathleen to play with, shown and described. A full colour brochure that mentions the benefits of the new product to their family and retells their classic tale or reprints Auntie Brigid's favourite recipe could accompany this. A reply card would complete the pack—with only a single tick and payment details needing to be added.

Personalisation to this degree can be very persuasive.

READ MORE ABOUT IT

Joyce Rutter Kaye, 'Magazine 2000: Monogram', *U&lc*, vol. 19, no. 4, International Typeface Corporation, New York, Winter 1992.

Susan E. Davis, 'Designs for a custom textbook revolution', *Step-by-step graphics*, vol. 8, no. 4, Dynamic Graphics, Peoria, Illinois, July/August 1992, ISSN 0886 7682.

Letterpress

Printing from a raised image, letterpress is the printing process that Johannes Gutenberg used and is based on the principles of wood-block printing or linocut printing. A raised, backwards image is inked and transferred to paper. It is also called relief printing. Gutenberg used movable type, where individual letters were assembled into the lines of text and placed into a forme that incorporated any illustrations on wood block. You can see this process in the print shops at Old Sydney Town or Sovereign Hill.

A plate of metal or plastic is coated with a light-sensitive material, which is exposed through a photographic negative of the desired image area. The area that was exposed is sealed and the area that was not exposed is etched away by acid, leaving a raised reversed image ready for inking. The plates are then locked together in a forme and bedded in the press.

There are three types of printing presses. A *platen press* is where two flat surfaces are brought together like the action of your elbow when your hand touches your shoulder. A *rotary press* is where the forme is curved around a cylinder and paper brought to it by an impression cylinder. A *flatbed press* has a flat forme that moves under ink rollers and paper is drawn across the forme by the impression cylinder.

Gravure

Printing from a surface with variable depths of sunken image area, gravure is based on the etching process or intaglio printing. After a doctor blade has swept the excess ink off the shiny metal non-image area, the deeper cells in the plate hold more ink than the shallower cells and transfer it to the paper, making a tonal variation within each dot size variation. This gives gravure images a greater depth of tone. There is also a slight blurring around the deeper colours, which in process colour can even start to mix, creating a softer dot and almost an illusion of continuous tone.

The plate cylinder sits on an ink roller in a trough of ink. As it turns the doctor blade cleans the non-image surface of the plate and paper is drawn through the press by the impression cylinder above.

The gravure process is used in the packaging industry because it can deposit a larger amount of ink in one *pass* (run through the machine) than, say, offset printing which may take two or three passes to deposit an equivalent amount.

Engraving

Also an intaglio or sunken-image process, engraving can attain a mesmerising level of fine detail. It is very similar to gravure in principle, but the flat engraving plate is applied to the paper with considerable pressure, not only transferring the ink, but also creating a raised image on the front of the sheet and indents on the back. Engraving ink colours are also more opaque than most others, enabling light colours to be printed directly onto dark papers. In the case of metallic inks, they can be burnished (restamped) to look polished.

Screen printing

By forcing ink through a stencil image that is adhered to a screen made of fine silk or polyester, screen printing can achieve remarkable detail and also deposit a remarkable amount of ink.

This stencil printing process is used in some finishing processes, such as laminating, and is also used commercially for packaging and printing on various substrates like metal, fabric and plastic.

An image is photographically transferred to a screen by exposing a photosensitive stencil with ultraviolet light. The stencil is then washed to remove the image area. This is applied to the screen and leaves a fine mesh for the ink to penetrate. The screen is placed on top of the paper and ink is drawn across the screen by a squeegee. The screen is then lifted to reveal the printed piece. Multiple colours can be applied using separate screens. The inks are thicker and more opaque than most, although you can also print transparent inks and varnishes.

This process is also used by cost-conscious community-based printing ventures for posters and other materials because stencils cut by hand can be applied to the screen.

Stencil   Image

Squeegee squeezes ink through stencil to paper

Screen   Ink

Stencil

Paper

Flexography

Used commercially in packaging (such as Twistie packets) and to print on uneven surfaces such as containers, plastics, foil and corrugated substrates, *flexography* is based on the letterpress process. The term comes from the raised plate made of flexible rubber or polymer. It's like a huge rubber stamp. Due to the huge number of copies typically printed by this process in the foodstuff packaging area, and the flexible nature of the plate, there can be distortion through-out a print run so fine detail and small type should be avoided. Sometimes artwork will need to be distorted to accommodate the packaging requirements. You will need to work closely with the print manager to prepare material for this process.

Selecting a printer

A prospective client can expect to see samples of work produced by the printers they visit or contact. Many will have Web sites that describe the services they offer, list clients they have worked with, and show recent work, and some will have on-line quoting.

In addition to the *Yellow Pages*, there are directories and listings by other organisations, such as:

- Printing Industries Association of Australia (PIAA)
- Graphic Arts Merchants Association of Australia (GAMAA)
- Quick Printers Association of Australia (QPAA)
- Pacific Area Newspaper Publishers Association (PANPA)
- Graphic Arts Services Association of Australia (GASAA)
- Lithographic Institute of Australia (LIA)
- Packaging Council of Australia (PCA).

CHECKLIST
What you need to supply to your printer
In addition to all the material you would supply an imagesetter (see p. 251), you must supply your printer with the following:

- [ ] Number of copies required
- [ ] Number of pages
  - double-sided?
  - bleed?
  - plus cover?
  - print inside cover?
- [ ] Paper specifications
  - cover/text/specialty
  - colour, weight, brand of each
- [ ] Number of colours
  - Pantone
  - process/HiFi
- [ ] Finishing processes
  - laminates (gloss/matt)
  - varnishes (gloss/satin/matt)
  - trimming details including final size
  - folding details
- [ ] Embellishments
  - foils (metallic/patterned/clear/coloured)
  - embossing/debossing
  - thermography
  - die-cutting/scoring/perforation
  - laser cutting
  - pop-ups
- [ ] Binding processes
  - saddle stapling
  - paperback/soft back/perfect binding/burst binding
  - hardback/case binding
  - ring binding
  - spiral binding/wiro binding/half-Canadian binding
  - side stapling
  - plastic comb binding
  - thermal binding
  - post-and-eye binding
- [ ] Date required
- [ ] Delivery instructions
  - packing
  - address/es
- [ ] Any security or embargo issues

Paper

Paper selection

The qualities you are looking for when selecting paper are its:

- Colour
- Weight (particularly if mailing)
- Bulk (thickness; you may need a bulky paper to make a smaller number of pages seem more substantial)
- Show-through (opacity)
- Suitability for its task
- Brightness and whiteness (level of light reflection)
- Gloss (surface finish)
- Tactile quality (texture)
- Printability (how it will take ink; absorbency and drying time)
- Strength and flexibility (to withstand its expected handling on press and by the ultimate user; to not easily crease or tear)
- Suitability for binding and embellishment processes
- Archival quality (durability)
- Wastage from the sheet size
- Cost
- Availability
- Environmental impact

Paper can represent more than 25% of the invoice for most printing. Appropriate paper selection and awareness of paper terminology and the different qualities available can enable you to choose the right paper or *stock* for a printing task. Seek advice from your printer and paper company representative about the suitability of the chosen stock for the project.

As a design element, paper not only brings colour and visual texture to a printed piece, but also has a tactile quality that communicates subtle messages through the sense of touch. Take advantage of tactile contrasts when you are selecting paper, not necessarily contrasting papers within the same product but contrasting with the papers your audience is likely to be handling most of the time. In this way, distinctive paper selection can help to achieve separation from other paper products.

Most paper merchants are suppliers and distributors who carry a variety of papers from Australian and international paper mills. The papers fall into generic categories, which will be briefly explained. These generic categories define different qualities for different uses.

If you want to see specific papers, call the paper house reps and ask for *swatch books* (a stapled set of sample sheets labelling all the colours and weights in a particular range) and printed samples of the papers they carry. Ask for the generic category and they will let you know the full range of papers they carry in that category.

You will find that some papers are identical but called different names and charged at different prices, according to the paper company that supplies them. This is because the paper suppliers buy stocks from paper mills around the world. Sometimes a particular paper will become very fashionable, so each company will want to carry its own version. The amount of paper each purchased from the mill will be one of the reasons the price may vary from supplier to supplier.

Papers are made from *pulp*, mostly composed of plantation wood and other natural fibres such as cotton or hemp. The paper industry's environmental awareness means that there will be fibres from mill waste and printing offcuts, used papers and even fabric scraps, in most paper pulp.

As the fibre is processed, it is cooked and cleaned with water, bleaches and a chemical cocktail that eventually colours the pulp ready for paper production. Bleaching is often achieved using part oxygen substitutes—sometimes chlorine-free—rather than the chlorine gas bleaching used previously.

Gradually, paper is formed along a fine wire mesh by removing the water and moving it through presses and driers, eventually coating it with various substances to improve its print performance, and rolling or embossing it to create its specific surface quality. It is then cut into sheets or rolled onto reels for web printing.

As the fibres trundle through this process, they become aligned in the direction of the flow and this creates what is called the *grain* of the paper. Paper will roll or bow along the grain and will fold and tear easily along the grain. Books should be folded along the grain (it should run parallel to the spine). When folded against the grain, some papers might crumple or crack.

There are also some synthetic papers available.

When selecting paper, look for weight, colour, texture, strength and opacity, and its ability to perform. *Strength* is needed for papers to survive the printing, folding and binding processes and eventual use by the consumer. *Opacity* defines the paper's level of transparency. This depends on both the thickness of the paper and the composition and density of its pulp. Some low levels of opacity will allow you to see the print on the reverse of the page, or even the page behind that. You might design around this feature, but there are times when you will not want it.

When ordering paper, *ream* is the term for 500 sheets.

DOING IT ENVIRONMENTALLY SMARTER

To be kinder to the environment, reduce the size of your printed piece and print both sides of the paper. A poster can work even at A4. The back of the poster can have further details, ordering or booking information on it.

You might also choose a lighter paper rather than a heavy one. With recycled paper being a little more bulky, you can go a grade lighter in weight without sacrificing the feel or opacity of your sheet.

READ MORE ABOUT IT

Nancy Williams, *Paperwork: The potential of paper in graphic design*, Phaidon, London 1993, ISBN 0 7148 2802 5.

Catharine Fishel, *Paper graphics: The power of paper in graphic design*, Rockport, Massachusetts, 1999, ISBN 1 56496 563 5.

Paper specification

Paper is mostly defined by its weight using *gsm* ('grams per square metre') or g/m^2. This is called its *grammage*. To give a rough idea of comparative weights, photocopier papers are usually 80 gsm; letterheads and pamphlets, around 110 gsm; posters, around 170 gsm; lightweight covers, about 220 gsm; and boards are over 300 gsm.

Some heavy boards will be referred to as 3-ply or 6-sheet boards. These are boards that have been created by laminating 3 or 6 sheets together, respectively.

Paper is also defined by its thickness, which can also be termed its *caliper* or *bulk*. It is measured in *microns* (micrometres, or one-millionth of a metre) or μms by calipers. This measurement is useful for calculating the width of a spine, for example. But often a dummy is made of blank sheets of the exact paper specified, bound in the same manner as the design specifications, so you can see, feel and measure the exact width. A dummy is also useful for your client to visualise the final product. Paper houses usually provide this service.

The sequence of specification is usually colour, paper name and grammage, and it is usually best to identify the paper company in brackets at the end.

If you specify generic grades such as 'A2 matte art', or even a specific stock from a particular paper merchant, on some jobs you should include the additional specification of 'or equivalent'. You can also request that printing does not start until the stock selection is approved.

Competing paper companies will have an almost identical range of generic papers and may even carry the same specialty stock produced by the same paper mill under a different name.

Art or coated grades

Art papers are excellent smooth white surfaces for reproduction of fine details and full-colour screened images. The smooth surface is achieved by coating the paper with fine mineral clay compounds, which are then dried and *calendered*. Calendering is where the paper passes through heated rollers to polish the paper's surface. The amount and type of both coating and calendering determines its relative smoothness and shine.

Dot gain, picking and hickies

When dots are printed with ink on paper, there is often a small increase in their size due to the paper's absorption and possibly some slight distortion during the printing process. This is termed *dot gain* and it is often compensated for in prepress. During film preparation, the dots will be made slightly smaller, making the proof seem slightly lighter overall, but accommodating the expected dot gain comfortably on press.

Picking happens when the ink has been laid down and a small feathery mark is left where fibres or a coating have been lifted off the surface of the paper. This can be due to the quality of the paper or some problems with the blanket on the press.

Hickies are left where a colour area is interrupted by a small particle either in the surface of the paper or carried in the ink. The particle is often surrounded by a small halo effect where ink was not able to print.

Printers will rarely let these escape the print room and will fix them in-line during the run as much as possible.

In Australia, art papers are graded from A1—the highest quality surface and most expensive—down to A2 and A3. The grade is determined by the amount of coating on each side. An A1 sheet includes upwards of 20 gsm of coating on each side; an A2 grade, over 10 gsm of coating each side; and an A3, less than 10 gsm of coating each side.

In the United States, there are five levels from A#1 to A#5, with the grade determined by the amount of light reflected by the stock. An A#1 sheet reflects slightly more light than an A#2 sheet.

Note that these gradings have nothing to do with the international sheet sizes called A1, A2 or A3.

For most applications, a grade A2 art paper is an acceptable standard and cheaper than the A1 stocks. But for high-quality posters and publications, the A1 art sheet is recommended as a superior surface.

Gloss art or calendered paper

Gloss surfaces are created by calendering or super-calendering. Ink will take longer to dry on gloss papers, because it sits on the smooth surface. This usually gives the best reproduction of colour photographs, because the vibrancy of the colours is maintained. The categories of gloss include ultragloss and *cast coated* (the glossiest).

Matte and dull art

Matte or *dull* art papers are coated papers that do not have a gloss finish. They have been *blade coated*, where a thin metal blade smooths the surface after the coating has been applied. Matte art papers might also be called *satin*, *suede* or *velvet*.

Uncoated and specialty grades

Uncoated grades include:

- *newsprint*, which includes a large amount of mechanical pulp, where the wood fibres have not had lignin removed and therefore will yellow with age and exposure to light
- *bond papers*, weighted from 70 to 90 gsm
- *offset papers*, treated to perform well in offset presses, starting at about 90 gsm
- *laser grades*, designed to perform well in photocopiers and laser printers and to reduce curl when they pass through heating units
- *specialty grades*.

DOING IT SMARTER
Duplexes
Instead of printing a full-bleed colour on one side of a paper to contrast with the other side, you could select a duplex sheet from a paper manufacturer. *Duplex* describes any sheet that has a different surface or colour on each side. A different surface can be produced by polishing only one side of the sheet. A sheet with a different colour on each side is made from two sheets of paper that have been laminated together to create a hybrid stock. They are usually thicker and therefore used more as cover stocks where one colour is the outer cover and one is effectively the endpaper or inside cover stock. If you use a concertina fold in a pamphlet with a duplex stock, both sides of your pamphlet will show off the two stocks.

DOING IT CHEAPER
Ask your printer what stocks are 'out the back' that they want to get rid of. There might be enough of one of them for the print job you're preparing. That stock will often be cheaper, because the client it was originally ordered for may have already paid for it, due to minimum order and mill standard requirements.

Specialty grades include transparent papers and rough or antique papers, onion skin (semitranslucent) and eggshell papers, archival and permanent papers, and papers with textures embossed into them. The textures might mimic woodgrain, linen and other fabrics, stucco or leather, or they might be rippled, hammered, mottled or ridged. They might also feature inclusions such as confetti, grass clippings, petals, leaves or contrasting fibres such as silk or denim. They will often come in a suite of colours and weights that can be mixed and matched.

Some specialty papers are still handmade.

In some cases, you might choose to make a feature of a paper's *deckle edge*—the feathery edge of a sheet that is not trimmed off in some specialty grades.

Handmade

Many exotic papers are available with inserts of leaves, bark, seeds, petals, grasses, fabrics, threads, printed pieces and even sequins and glitter. These are mostly handmade but some companies are producing them in relatively commercial quantities. They will often be hand-dyed with natural dyes, herbs and spices—and some may be marbled or preprinted.

Recycled grades

Environmental concerns should have been partly solved by the 'paperless office' that the personal computer was to have heralded. But the increase in paper usage brought forth considerable pressure to at least 'reduce, reuse or recycle'.

The paper industry quite rightly noted it had always recycled post-industrial waste, but the issue was more how to recycle post-consumer waste.

The process of creating paper is tough on fibres and recycled paper keeps going through this process, each time making the fibres finer and less strong. So paper will rarely have a totally recycled content. In order for paper to have the strength it needs to survive the industrial processes and consumer use required of it, new fibres will be required. So most paper companies will now be able to tell you percentages for how much post-consumer, post-industrial and virgin fibre (wood pulp) is contained within each stock they carry.

Recycled stocks will often have an increased absorbency and greater bulk due to their softer fibres. So fine detail and spindly serifs often don't print well on them. The printer will probably run more ink to compensate for the absorption but this may cause more dot gain than usual. Solids may look mottley, due to the different absorbency levels within the recycled and virgin fibres.

When designing a product, certain decisions can limit the paper product's recyclability. The main offenders are usually finishes, such as UV and other laminates, any plastic coatings or self-adhesive glues. Try to achieve the same effect with different processes.

Post-industrial waste
Most papers have a percentage of post-industrial or pre-consumer waste in them. This includes mill broke and other mill waste—the waste paper created in the paper-making process itself, which contains trimmings and damaged paper. But post-industrial waste also includes paper trimmings that have never been printed, which are returned from printers to the paper mill for repulping. These papers will mostly have undergone some manufacturing process, but will have been discarded, largely unchanged.

Post-consumer waste
This is the content most people think of when they say 'recycled'. It is paper that has been printed, finished, bound, purchased and used by a consumer and returned to the paper mill for recycling. After cleaning and de-inking, the fibres are still a greyish colour, so they will often be bleached before being repulped to make new sheets of paper.

Stationery grades
Most paper companies produce stationery ranges of a series of papers with different surface and colour qualities but with matching weights in each range that include:
- a *writing* or *letterhead* grade with a weight of 90–100 gsm
- a *text* weight, which is designed for two-sided printing and therefore has less show-through (or greater opacity), weighing in at 100–150 gsm
- a *cover* weight suitable for business cards, starting at about 200 gsm
- matching *envelopes*.
  Your printer or paper rep can show you samples.

Laid/wove

Created by patterns in the wire mesh while the paper is pulp, laid papers are often used for stationery and have a fine pattern of horizontal or vertical lines within them. You can see it more clearly when the paper is held up to the light. Wove papers are created with a woven mesh.

Watermarks

Watermarks are created during the making of the sheet of paper. The pulp passes underneath a dandy roll, a roller of fine wire mesh that has wire artwork built onto it. Where the wire logo or type is raised, the paper will be thinner and therefore when the sheet is dried it will allow more light through so a soft image called a watermark can be seen.

This is an expensive process and economically viable only if an enormous amount of paper is being milled for an organisation. Basically, an organisation can commission a paper company to prepare a wire frame of the logo and produce the paper.

DOING IT CHEAPER

Fake watermarks

Using Pantone pastel ink, reverse a logo in pattern out of a fine stipple and print full bleed. A similar effect can also be achieved in publications with a tinted matt varnish.

Finishing processes and embellishment

Finishing processes and embellishment come at the end of a print run and put the final touches to a print job. Many can be expensive and time-consuming, so you need to plan your production schedule accordingly. They have varying degrees of impact on the environment, which are only briefly noted.

PRICE COMPARISON
Gloss/matte finishes
$$$ Celloglaze
$$ Liquid laminate
$ Varnish

Varnishes

A solvent-based coating, varnish is run like an additional ink, after all the colours have been printed. The finish can be gloss, semigloss, satin or matte. If you want to contrast matte and gloss finishes, it is best to print two varnish runs. This is often done to gloss photographs and matte the background on which they appear.

In order to create a printing plate, a separate piece of artwork is needed to define the area where each varnish is to appear.

Most varnishes contribute to air pollution.

Tinted varnish

You may want a logo, type or pattern overprinted in varnish, but sometimes a clear varnish is too subtle. So a small amount of ink is added to the varnish to alter its colour and an artwork plate is used to enable the logo, type or pattern to be seen.

Laminates

A plastic surface laminated onto a printed sheet gives the highest gloss finish. Both gloss and matte laminating plastics are available. A laminate gives a protective surface to a printed piece, but can also be applied in different areas using its liquid form.

Laminating is not kind to the environment, as the plastic cannot be effectively removed from the paper fibres. It cannot be recycled after use, and ends up in landfill.

Liquid/UV laminate

Laminating is now mostly achieved by printing a liquid laminate over a printed sheet. This is then cured by exposure to UV light, which is also an air-polluting process.

You can print from an artwork plate or just apply a solid laminate across the entire surface.

Sheet laminate

By heat-sealing the laminate from a reel of plastic sheeting to a printed sheet, the surface is sealed.

Folding

PRICE COMPARISON
Cutting/folding
$$$ Complex pop-up (includes hand assembly)
$$ Diecut/score/perforate shape
$ Guillotine/drill/fold/perforate straight

The sum total of folding technology is that paper can be folded either forwards or backwards. In diagrams, these two folds are shown with a dotted line and a dashed line (a solid line is a cut).

In various combinations, particularly with gluing and die-cutting, 3-D objects and pop-ups can be created. To help the folding process, use a score (indent) or a double score. Sometimes a form of perforation to fold sections without getting crumpled edges is used.

Guillotining/trimming/drilling

Trimming is a separate process at the end of a print run that happens on an industrial guillotine. The operator places the material under a straight blade and cuts off the unwanted extra paper.

Although the guillotine usually trims only at 90°, trimming can be done at angles by creating the appropriate chocks. For curved edges, however, you need to look at die-cutting techniques.

The holes in documents produced for ring binders are drilled at high speed.

Collating and gathering

Collators stack multiple sheets in order, ready for binding and trimming. For larger publications, collation is sometimes called *gathering*. Large publications that are produced in 16-, 32- or 64-page sections need their sections to be collated in order.

For saddle-stitched (stapled) publications, gathering is done in-line on a conveyor, where the saddle catches each section in order from the centre of the book to the cover

Paper creep
is determined in prepress and
appropriate compensation made.

Signature marks
on the spine of each section align to
show the collation sequence.

on top, and the lot is then stapled at the end of the line. The
thickness of the paper at the spine, through which the
staples are stabbed, causes the phenomenon known as
paper creep—where the text block on pages in the centre of
the book will appear closer to the outer trim edges. This is
usually counteracted at page imposition stage.

For a section-sewn book or perfect bound book, the
sections need to be piled in order. Each section will have a
section identifier (signature mark) down the spine so the
printer will know the sections have been collated in the
correct order.

Numbering

Applying numbers to invoice books and raffle tickets can be
done in-run by attaching a small letterpress automatic
numbering machine to the press. The numbering device
can be told how many times the same number must be
struck, in the case of forms being produced in triplicate,
for example.

Binding

Publications that need to be bound are usually printed not as single sheets but in signatures of 8, 16, 32 or 64 pages. These are then collated into the correct reading order and bound with their cover. There are numerous binding processes available that are briefly described and illustrated in this section. Your printer can show you examples.

Saddle stapling/saddle stitching

Pre-folded sections or sheets are collated and placed on a saddle, which is like an inverted V. The cover is added and the staples or stitching applied.

Paperback/soft cover/perfect binding

The most imperfect binding technique, perfect binding is the one that doesn't fold flat, and when you force it to open flat, the glue breaks and the pages all fall out. This is, of course, the worst case scenario, but it readily identifies the technique. Part of the problem is caused by the fact that the pages start off in sections, but the fold is trimmed off and the inside edges are roughened so the glue can adhere to each page. There are many glues that can be used and some are close to perfect.

Perfect binding also allows papers of differing weights and qualities to be collated and bound into a publication, so it has an attraction for magazine producers who want to bind in preprinted advertising sections, samples and subscription cards.

The other attraction of perfect binding is that it gives a square-backed spine, but it is best to do this with about 96 pages. It can be done with 64 pages, but is less successful.

Burst binding

A variation on perfect binding, burst binding seeks to rectify perfect binding's main problem of guillotining the fold by retaining the fold and forcing glue through notches or punctures along it. Sadly, it is still imperfect and sometimes too much glue is forced through, further limiting the ability of the book to be opened.

Hardback/casebinding/section sewn

As implied by one of its names, the book's sections are collated and sewn in order. This is then bound into a cover. Section-sewn books can have a paper cover drawn on, so not all section-sewn books are casebound.

But all casebound books are section sewn. The 'case' referred to in casebinding is the hard covers that are created to wrap around the spine of the sewn sections to protect the book's pages. The case consists of boards covered and connected by cloth, paper or leather. This is attached to the sewn sections with cloth and endpapers. It is often then decorated with head and tail bands and sometimes a ribbon for bookmarking.

Often the case will be further protected by a dustjacket, which is a wraparound paper cover with flaps that tuck inside the covers.

Ring binding

A ring binder allows material to lie flat inside a binder. The pages are drilled two, three or four times to align with standard 'rings'. The binder and its cover might be printed before assembly or they might have printed sheets bound into plastic pockets on the spine, back and front covers. There might be a set of dividers supplied or collated into the text.

Often the text is shrink-wrapped for distribution, so the pages aren't harmed in the process.

Spiral binding

A series of fine holes is drilled down the side of the guillotined and separate pages of the publication. Then a spiral of wire coated in plastic is threaded through the holes. Spiral binding allows pages to lie flat; different weights and qualities of paper can be bound together.

Wiro binding

Wiro binding is similar to spiral binding but the wire is doubled up and fed through the holes in a different pattern.

Half Canadian binding

Half Canadian binding is wiro binding with a cover that has been bound in which folds out over the wire from the back to the front, creating a square-backed spine.

Binding

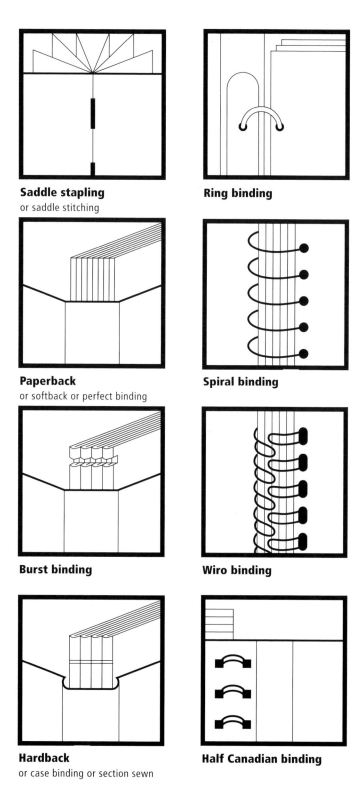

Saddle stapling
or saddle stitching

Ring binding

Paperback
or softback or perfect binding

Spiral binding

Burst binding

Wiro binding

Hardback
or case binding or section sewn

Half Canadian binding

Office binding styles

Side stapling
Separate sheets that are collated with separate back and front cover sheets are stapled two, three or four times through the left-hand side of the front cover and out the right-hand side of the back cover. The staples are some-times covered with a strip of binding cloth, which gives a relatively square back and protects the reader's hands from the staples.

Remember that side-stapled documents cannot be opened flat and material that is too close to the spine may be lost.

Plastic comb binding
Another side-binding process, using a comb binder, cuts a pattern of rectangular holes through the collated document. A plastic comb is then uncoiled, the pages inserted, and the comb recoiled to bind the document. These documents lie almost flat.

Plastic strip binding
This is another side-binding process that uses a series of punctured fine holes down the left side of the collated document. A plastic strip with protruding plastic spikes is fed through the holes and another plastic strip placed at the back. The excess length of the plastic spikes is trimmed and the back strip melted to the remaining spike. Although this is narrower than side stapling, the document still cannot be opened out flat.

Thermal binding
This is an office version of perfect binding, using heat to melt a glue strip to a document within a pre-folded cover.

Post-and-eye binding
A variation on ring binding, post-and-eye binding uses a small post with an internal thread that takes a screw on the other side of the document. The post goes through the holes drilled down the side of the document.

Craft bindings

Japanese binding
A sewn side-binding technique that has long been used commercially in Japan creates patterns with contrasting thread and secures the pages effectively. The book will not open flat.

Zigzag bindings
Zigzag bindings are a binding style from China that connects concertina-folded pages to pockets in separate front and back covers. The covers then protect and strengthen the book, often enabling it to stand.

Twigs
This is a side-binding technique that simply passes looped twine through two holes drilled through the book and its covers. A twig is then passed through the looped twine and the twine is tightened and tied at the back of the book. Many different objects can be used in lieu of twigs or twine.

READ MORE ABOUT IT

Shereen LaPlantz, *Cover to cover: Creative techniques for making beautiful books, journals and albums*, Lark Books, Asheville, North Carolina, 1995, ISBN 0 937274 81 X.

Kathy Blake, *Handmade books: A step-by-step guide to crafting your own books*, Bulfinch Press, Little, Brown and Company, New York, 1997, ISBN 0 8212 2220 1.

Angela James, *The handmade book*, New Holland, London, 2000, ISBN 1 85974 437 0.

Jean G. Kropper, *Handmade cards and books*, Lothian, Melbourne, 1995, ISBN 0 85091 708 5.

Foils

Foil stamping or foil embossing is based on the letterpress principle, but uses metallic and non-metallic 'foils' on a plastic mylar substrate or 'carrier'. When stamped onto paper by the raised image die (the metal plate), the foil is transferred from its plastic carrier to the page. This is achieved through heating the metal plate in order for the adhesive on the foil to melt to the paper. The pressure from the press usually leaves a fine indent along the edge of the image area in the softer surface of the paper.

Foiling can combine with embossing or debossing to create some impressive effects.

Office and craft bindings

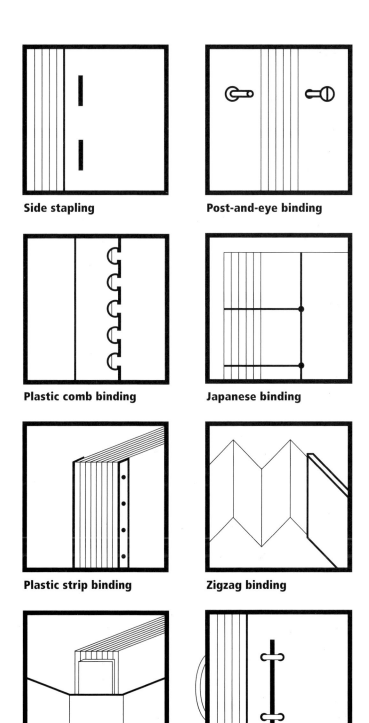

Side stapling

Post-and-eye binding

Plastic comb binding

Japanese binding

Plastic strip binding

Zigzag binding

Thermal binding

Twig binding

Metals, vinyls, clear, holograms, printed foils

Foils used to be thin metallic sheets, but the term now refers generically to any material transferred in this way. Therefore, coloured vinyl 'foils' and even clear plastic 'foils' can be stamped onto papers. White vinyl, for example, can be stamped onto a navy textured sheet of paper to provide a smooth surface on which to overprint in a process colour.

Metallic foils come in a broad range of metallic colours and finishes, from shiny and reflective to matte and low sheen, from traditional gold, silver and bronze to brushed aluminium and anodised colours. Some have holograms embedded within them or have been overprinted with patterns created by laser.

Hologram preparation is very expensive and can take a long lead-time.

There can be limitations on the area that is able to be printed in one stamp: the foil comes in reels of particular sizes and you may want to discuss wastage with your embellisher before getting too carried away.

Embossing and debossing

Embossing creates a raised image by stretching the paper itself. Conversely, *debossing* presses an image into the paper. This is achieved by a variation on the letterpress process, where male and female dies clamp and stretch the paper's fibres by a combination of heat and pressure.

Blind embossing is where the paper is raised with no printing on the image area.

Sculptural embossing is where there are many sculptured levels in the male and female dies, rather than one lift. A sculptural die is much more expensive because it is actually sculpted by an artisan—it cannot be created photographically because it is not simply one level raised or lowered like embossing and debossing.

With all embosses, there is minimal interruption to the paper sheet, making the process one of the most environmentally friendly because all it does is stretch the fibres involved. If a cover is just blind embossed, it can go straight into repulping, because there isn't even a need for the de-inking process.

PRICE COMPARISON

Raised levels

$$$$$	Hologram/sculptural emboss
$$$$	Foil stamp
$$$	Emboss/deboss
$$	Laminated stickers (hand applied)
$	Thermography

Female

Paper

Male

Embossing

Male

Paper

Female

Debossing

Thermography

At the conclusion of an offset print run, a fine resin dust can be applied to a printed piece. It sticks to the wet print area and excess dust is removed from non-image areas by vacuum. The sheet is passed through a heater where the dust pools and swells on the inked area. When cooled, the resin sets as a solid plastic raised image. This is known as thermography and is used regularly on business cards.

The technique should always be used on solid ink but does not always work on large flat areas.

Thermography should be avoided on items that might pass through the heating units in laser printers or photocopiers, as the resin will melt.

Die-cutting, scoring and perforation

A forme is created which includes a plan for scores and cuts, using dulled metal for the scores and knives or sharp blades for the cuts. This forme is called the die and it is then stamped out of a sheet, using a variation of the letterpress process.

If you want a perforation in a shape other than a straight line, it is prepared in the same way but with knife blades that have notches in them. Where the notch is, the paper is not pierced.

With die-cutting, notches are used at regular intervals so that cut pieces will not fall into the machinery of the printing press, which explains why die-cuts need to be pushed out of the paper that surrounds them.

Laser cutting

Die-cutting is limited by the flexibility of the blades used to cut the shapes and the cost of creating the die forme. If you require greater detail, you might consider laser cutting. It is capable of intricate detail and burns the paper away according to the digital file created for the cut. In this way, you can cut intricate outlines on sticker bases, where the laser only cuts the top layer, leaving the base intact.

A diecut used on a brochure cover.
Client: Rosanna Golf Links
Studio: Adstract Art

DOING IT CHEAPER
Die-cut folders and brochures
Use existing dies for folders and brochures—most printers save the formes of previous jobs 'out the back'. Ask to see your printer's collection of dies and see if any of them can be used. This will save you the cost of preparing the die.

Pop-ups

These plans show cuts with a solid line; forward folds or scores with a dashed line; and backward folds or scores with a dotted line. When cut and folded, they make the two pop-up forms below.

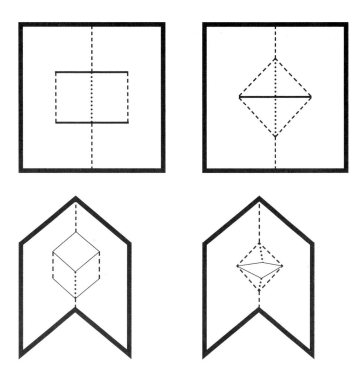

Pop-ups

The novelty of pop-ups is a method of engaging the reader with a print product. It can be so unexpected and effective. There are some simple pop-ups that you might consider using in a printed piece. Their application is limited only by your imagination. As far as stretching your budget to pop-ups, simple ones might be able to be created with just a bit of handwork, rather than expensive dies and scores.

READ MORE ABOUT IT

David A. Carter and James Diaz, *The elements of pop-up: A pop-up book for aspiring paper engineers*, Little Simon, New York, 1999, ISBN 0 689 82224 3.

Using a designer

Selecting a contractor

A prospective client can ask to see a portfolio of current work from a designer, an illustrator, a photographer, a multimedia producer, and an advertising agency (which will also have a 'reel', a video of television and radio commercials). Many will also have Web sites that describe their work processes, show recent work, and list other clients they have worked with.

In addition to the *Yellow Pages*, there are industry directories such as *The Wizards of Oz* and *OzGraphics*, and listings by other organisations, such as:

- Australian Graphic Design Association (AGDA)
- Design Institute of Australia (DIA)
- Australian Writers and Art Directors Association (AWARD)
- Advertising Federation of Australia (AFA)
- Australian Institute of Professional Photography (AIPP)
- Society of Advertising, Commercial and Magazine Photographers (ACMP)
- Illustrators Association of Australia (IAA)
- Visual Artists Guild (VAG)
- National Association of Visual Artists (NAVA).

In the *Yellow Pages*, you might look up the following categories:

- Advertising agencies
- Artists—commercial
- Designers—graphic
- Illustrators
- Internet services
- Multimedia services
- Photographers—advertising and fashion
- Photographers—commercial and industrial

Assessing a portfolio

In a portfolio, look for an appropriate production quality, a conceptual approach that shows rigorous creative thinking, and the sorts of clients the designer has previously worked for.

Discuss the audience the material was designed for to try to gauge its effectiveness. There should be some performance statistics, which may be anecdotal, as there are no hard statistics on design effectiveness usually.

References should be supplied which will help a client ascertain the work practices and professionalism of the service provider.

Presenting a design

The designer should repeat the brief, succinctly reminding clients of their requirements.

Describing where concepts have come from and how that relates to both the brief and the target audience's expected reactions—both emotive and rational responses—should set the scene for presentation.

Some silence on initial viewing allows clients to weigh the brief and to view the design, going over the introductory remarks in their head. Discuss any comments and details as they arise.

Often it is valuable for clients to take a design away without making any decisions. A contact appointment should be made so there is a clear decision period. This may be determined by the production schedule.

Design justification/rationale

Rationales should be incisive and concise, but thoroughly cover the original brief. They should explain the thinking behind the design solution.

A rationale should describe effects, not specifics. When discussing colour, it should describe feelings/effects in palettes, not descriptions of the actual colours, which can plainly be seen. Regarding text, it should not mention specific typefaces (unless they are corporate faces) but it may describe the impression that the type gives. It should describe the effect of the layout, not the dynamics—words like 'traditional' and 'strong' describe symmetry, 'dynamic' and 'modern' or 'contemporary' describe asymmetry. In regard to image selection, it should explain why the image was chosen, relating it to the content or the feel of the document/item as requested in the brief. In short, it should not be full of design jargon.

The rationale is often attached to the rough on the back or, better still, on the inside flap, opposite the rough.

READ MORE ABOUT IT

Anistatia R. Miller and Jared M. Brown, *Graphic design speak: A visual dictionary for designers and clients*, Rockport, Gloucester, Mass., 1999, ISBN 1 56496 602 X.

The design process

A design project will start with a full definition of the project and its context for the originators of the project. That is, it will outline where the project sits in relation to other activities of the originator or client. This is discussed at an initial briefing and is often followed by a period of research and analysis that further defines the project.

The next part of the process involves idea generation that will seek to cover all aspects of the project but is really a technique of gathering options. These are referred to as scribbles and thumbnails. They are often annotated with production notes. From these deliberations and ideas, roughs or visuals are developed.

The roughs are presented to the client for approval before finalising the design. In the case of publications, there might be just a cover and two pages to show how the interior pages might look. Sometimes there will be more than one rough for consideration at this stage.

On approval of the rough, there may be another stage where the design is developed further to take into account all the nuances within the project and create comprehensive visuals or finished roughs. After presentation, when these are approved, the production phase begins. Production entails the finalisation of all artwork and preparation of the job, proofing processes, and final approval before printing, embellishing, finishing and distribution (for print) or alpha and beta testing and uploading (for electronic publishing).

There should always be an evaluation of the final product and consideration of whether it met its objectives as outlined in the briefing meetings and any developments throughout the process. This may identify areas future work might need to consider.

Wim Nijhuis and Theo Boersema in *Visual Information for Everyday Use*, discuss the design process in terms of a cycle of:

- Problem identification and definition
- Analysis and observation
- Synthesis and reasoning
- Simulation and testing
- Evaluation and decision on viability and usefulness
- Acceptance of the design or iteration of the process to improve the design

Briefing

A brief is like a list of client wishes or requirements. It is not a solution—rather, it defines a problem. Some clients supply a written brief and back-up material about their organisation or product. Other clients give a verbal briefing when prompted by the questions at a briefing meeting.

A working title that will serve as a recognition title for both parties is needed, and a thorough description of the job. What is the reason for the job? Maybe it's a public relations exercise. It could be educational, instructional or advice about a public safety issue. In some cases, such as annual reports, it is a statutory requirement as well as a public document.

There may be external requirements of it. For example, if it is to be tabled in Parliament, it must be in B5 portrait format, as all Parliamentary papers. Also it will probably have a category number that describes the requirements for its production level. See the AusInfo Standards leaflet for an explanation of the classes.

It may be part of an existing series or the beginning of a new series. If the series already exists, samples of the series style should be supplied for reference at the briefing. Digital files or job files on the series should also be tabled or handed over to the designer, in order for the continuation of the series to be successful.

Discuss the audiences for the project. It helps to list the most important reader to the least important. Readers may be students, members of the media, children, the aged, businesspeople, parents, members of Parliament, industry leaders, unionists, public servants, taxpayers, and so on.

Consider ultimate distribution to gain an understanding of how the audience will receive the message. It may be available free or for purchase; on the Internet, hand-delivered or by mail; available at the newsagent or post office; by phone telesales; advertised on television or radio; subscribed to or sold over the counter; or any combination of these.

Imagine how it is likely to be used. Most people will scan or skim it, some will read cover-to-cover, some will only read summaries, and some will use it as reference.

Is there a single, most important message the audience should receive? There should also be a short description of the sort of material involved and the viewpoint that is being expressed.

CHECK LIST

A brief

Documents:

☐ Client details
- contact names, direct phone numbers, fax numbers and e-mail addresses
- full legal name of the company
- postal and street addresses
- background information about the organisation, its industry and competitors
- Web site URL (for further background information)

☐ Project description
- name, usage
- sizes, quantity
- price/budget
- any preferences/limitations: colours, images, corporate standards, existing materials
- launch date/deadlines

☐ Marketing objectives and strategy
- target market description: age, sex, social group, occupation, location
- benefit to buyer/user
- distribution method

Discuss the feel, look or tone of the communication. Should it be light or heavy? simple or complex? quality, earthy, lavish, playful or traditional? In addition to these considerations, what aspect/s of corporate personality—innovation, tradition, care, progress, high tech, friendly—need to be projected?

A corporate style manual that specifies logo usage, typefaces, colours, editorial preferences and design formats should be available for the designer.

Discuss format/s that are expected to be used and whether there is room for variation. There may be existing contracts for supply, for example, that make deviations from the format difficult.

Sample text should be available, even if only in rough draft. If not, is there an indicator of the expected amount of text and how it will be supplied? If it is supplied on disk, formats and programs should be discussed. Also, note whether the text has been or will need to be edited.

Existing images and identifiers might also be supplied or available, so it helps to discuss how they will be supplied and in what formats.

Preferences for colour, design style and type style should be discussed, and it is handy to have samples of designs that are liked and disliked.

Some individuals and organisations have a commitment to using recycled stocks and environmentally friendly processes, and these need to be discussed upfront, so that appropriate decisions can be made.

There may also be special instructions that will enable the design to work into projects in the future. For example, film poster artwork is often used for video covers and CD covers, press advertisements and wide-screen advertisements. These are all different formats—vertical, horizontal and square—so there is a production complication.

What is the deadline? In discussion, is it realistic? Maybe the desired timing requires some trimming of the expectations, or a considerable overtime budget.

Finally, what is the budget? Can the described job be completed successfully for that amount? Does it include print costs, programming, replication, distribution, design, illustration, photography and technical time, or are there other budgets for some aspects of the job?

This meeting can become quite lengthy. It may be divided into stages in order to cover all the issues. It will largely depend on the nature of the task.

Contracts

Usually a designer will prepare a contract in letter form as part of an initial proposal which at this point may or may not include any design work. The contract will cover a job description, fees, scheduling, copyright, conditions and any other agreements.

There will often be two copies, one for the client to keep, and one the client will be asked to sign and return. It is standard practice to initial each page.

It is also standard practice for a designer not to commence work until the return of that agreement.

There will often be a statement that the estimate is valid for a limited period of time, usually 90 days to a year.

Payment is usually made on invoice within 7, 14, 21 or 30 days, as agreed at the briefing or in the contract. There may be staged payments worked into the production schedule. Depending on how payment is to be made, there may be payments on completion of each stage or hourly rates plus expenses to date.

Some designers will request payment of a commissioning fee of between 10% and 50% of the total job cost before commencing the job. This is often the case when there will be many subcontractors to be paid by the designer.

Rates

A client may request that all production, including printing, finishing and distribution, be included in design fees, or may just buy the design and negotiate the production separately.

A client should expect to pay for:
- briefing and liaison meetings (except the initial contact meeting)
- design and research
- preparation of an initial proposal including competitive submissions
- preparation of roughs
- materials used
- corrections at client request
- print brokering and handling of subcontractors (often there will be a 5–10% handling fee for this)
- job recording
- any changes to the job
- any work completed even if the job is halted
- any further security requested

- any additional proofs prepared at client request
- all costs of commissioned authors, editors, photographers, calligraphers, illustrators, filmmakers, sound
  recordists and programmers, including art direction and
  briefing time
- any photography, illustration, film footage and sound file
  usage fees
- rush work or overtime requested
- any price increases for materials or suppliers that occur
  during the production period
- additional expenses arising from the assignment
  including any travel expenses.
  Production experimentation will often be cost-shared,
but this needs to be agreed at the outset.
  A client will not usually pay for:
- initial contact meeting
- coffee and hospitality
- corrections where the designer is at fault
- the first proof at each stage
- overtime or rush work due to the designer not perform-
  ing as promised
- work not performed at the halting of a project
- training sessions
- waiting time (unless caused directly by the client)
- filling in time sheets (except job record)
- cleaning up the workplace
- computer back-ups.

Rates

Rates vary and can be charged as
follows:

☐ Hourly rate + materials
☐ A flat fee
☐ Varying hourly rates for different
   types of work:
   – creative—normally charged
     at a higher rate
   – production
   – meeting time
☐ Varying hourly rates for different
   staff:
   – seniors—normally charged
     at a higher rate
   – juniors
   – technical—covers upkeep,
     upgrade and maintenance of
     technology

or a combination of any or all of the
above.

Copyright

Discuss ownership, since copyright rests with the creator
unless specifically assigned. Usually copyright is considered
to have been paid for the particular use negotiated with the
job, and any use beyond that—including reprinting—needs
to be renegotiated.

Illustrators and photographers own the originals of their
images and need only supply them in transparency or
digital form for use in the job, unless the original is
specifically purchased and reproduction rights negotiated.

In effect, a client is buying the right to reproduce an
image, not the image itself.

It is usual for designers, illustrators and photographers
to reserve the right to reproduce material produced for a
client as samples or advertising material or to enter into
competitions. They will normally credit the client as the

source of the commission and, in the case of award entries, if selected, the client will often be recognised with a certificate of achievement as well.

Any ideas, designs or illustrative material rejected by a client are considered to be the designer's property (unless rights are negotiated and purchased) and may be used by the designer freely.

Conditions

The designer has a duty of care to protect and return to the client in original condition any property or materials required in the production of the job. The designer, though, is not usually responsible for the loss, damage, destruction or unauthorised use of such materials by others.

Designers are not usually liable for the failure of other suppliers such as printers, manufacturers, reproduction houses, photographers, illustrators, authors, editors or indexers, but this will depend on the arrangements made initially and contractual agreements.

Usually, if the designer has outsourced directly to designer-chosen suppliers and is charging a brokerage/handling fee, the designer will be liable for the failure of those suppliers.

Where the client has chosen the suppliers and is dealing directly with and being billed directly by those suppliers, the client is more likely to be liable for the failure of those suppliers.

Scheduling

Normally, the timing of the various phases of the job, the production schedule and the payment schedule are agreed at acceptance of a proposal.

At any stage, if the schedule is broken, for whatever reason, the original timings will often need to be renegotiated and rescheduled.

When circumstances change and the client wants the work finished sooner, any additional costs (for overtime or queue-jumping in production) are passed on directly to the client.

READ MORE ABOUT IT

Ed Gold, *The business of graphic design: A sensible approach to marketing and managing a graphic design firm*, rev. edn, Watson-Guptill, New York, 1995, ISBN 0 8230 0546 1.

Barbara Ganim, *The designer's commonsense business book*, North Light Books, Cincinnati, 1995, ISBN 0 89134 618 X.

Jill Yelland, *The art of minding your own business*, Press for Success, Perth, 1994, ISBN 0 646 19850 5.

Cameron S. Foote, *The business side of creativity: The complete guide for running a graphic design or communications business*, WW Norton, New York, 1996, ISBN 0 393 73031 X.

Ellen Shapiro, *Clients and designers: Dialogues with CEOs and managers who have been responsible for some of the decade's most successful design and marketing communications*, Watson-Guptill, New York, 1989, ISBN 0 8230 0639 5.

Images used in *The Design Manual*
were generously provided by the
following studios:

Adstract Art
593–595 Bridge Road
Richmond VIC 3121

Done Art and Design
PO Box 375
Surry Hills NSW 2010

Louise Dews Design
13 Lamington Street
Deakin ACT 2600

Morrison Media Services
PO Box 823
Burleigh Heads QLD 4220

Msquared Research Assisted Design
Main Street
Michelago NSW 2620

Streetwize Comics
6/245 Chalmers Street
Redfern NSW 2016

Swell Design Group
31 Flinders Way
Griffith ACT 2603

Thank you,
David

David Whitbread Design
PO Box 3127
Weston Creek ACT 2611

Index

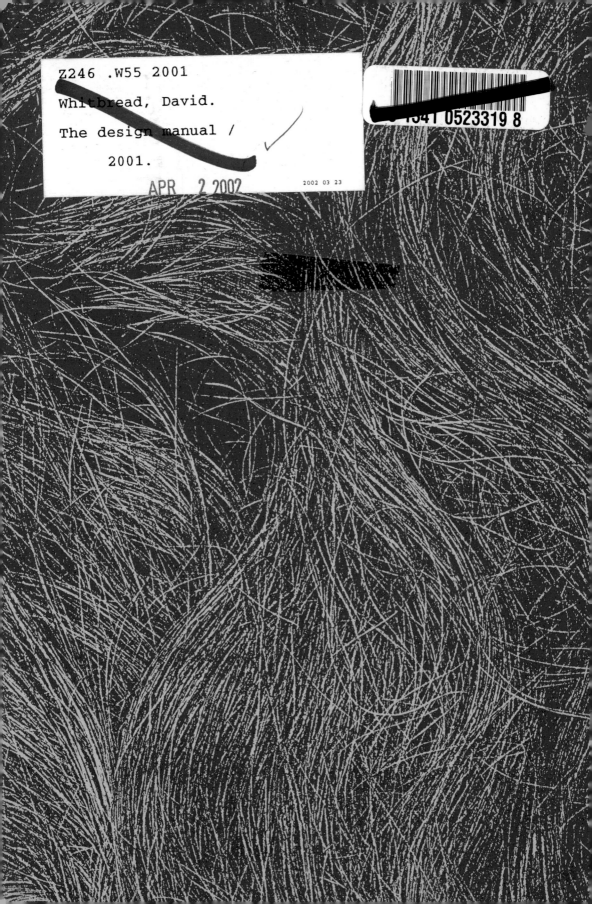